Specialist Communication Skills for Social Workers

Specialist Communication Skills for Social Workers

Focusing on Service Users' Needs

Johanna Woodcock Ross

palgrave
macmillan

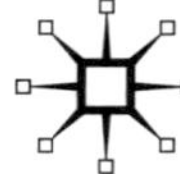

First published 2011 by
PALGRAVE MACMILLAN

Palgrave Macmillan in the UK is an imprint of Macmillan Publishers Limited, registered in England, company number 785998, of Houndmills, Basingstoke, Hampshire RG21 6XS.

Palgrave Macmillan in the US is a division of St Martin's Press LLC, 175 Fifth Avenue, New York, NY 10010.

Palgrave Macmillan is the global academic imprint of the above companies and has companies and representatives throughout the world.

Palgrave® and Macmillan® are registered trademarks in the United States, the United Kingdom, Europe and other countries.

ISBN 978–0–230–21804–8

This book is printed on paper suitable for recycling and made from fully managed and sustained forest sources. Logging, pulping and manufacturing processes are expected to conform to the environmental regulations of the country of origin.

A catalogue record for this book is available from the British Library.

A catalog record for this book is available from the Library of Congress.

10 9 8 7 6 5 4 3 2 1
20 19 18 17 16 15 14 13 12 11

Printed and bound in Great Britain by
the MPG Books Group, Bodmin and King's Lynn

For Lauren and Mark, and in memory of Hazel Brier, with love

Contents

List of Practice Examples x
Acknowledgements xii

Introduction **1**
Outline of the underpinning research 2
A practice-led focus 3
Organisation of the book 4

1. Introducing Communication Skills **6**
Summary of Communication Skills *6*
Separating basic 'universal' from 'specialist' social work communication skills 6
A 'relationship-based practice' approach 8
Reflexivity 12
The social model of disability 13
The 'social work' in social work communication skills 14
Social work communication skills do not 'come naturally' 15
Professional Standards *16*

2. Basic Universal Communication Skills **18**
Summary of Communication Skills *18*
Beginning skills to establish purposeful work 19
Empathy skills 32

Skills for gathering facts 36
Skills for ending work 37
Professional Standards *38*

3. Working with Children **39**
Summary of Specialist Communication Skills *39*
Policy and background literature 39
Practice application 43
Professional Standards *58*

4. Working with Young People with Offending Behaviour **60**
Summary of Specialist Communication Skills *60*
Policy and background literature 60
Practice application 62
Professional Standards *78*

5. Working with Parents **80**
Summary of Specialist Communication Skills *80*
Policy and background literature 80
Practice application 84
Professional Standards *100*

6. Working with People Who Use Substances **102**
Summary of Specialist Communication Skills *102*
Policy and background literature 102
Practice application 106
Professional Standards *118*

7. Working with People with Mental Health Problems **120**
Summary of Specialist Communication Skills *120*
Policy and background literature 120
Practice application 124
Professional Standards *132*

8. Working with Adults with Disabilities **134**
Summary of Specialist Communication Skills *134*
Policy and background literature 134
Practice application 137
Professional Standards *150*

9. Working with Refugees and Asylum Seekers **152**
Summary of Specialist Communication Skills *152*
Policy and background literature 152
Practice application 154
Professional Standards *165*

10. Working with Older People **167**
Summary of Specialist Communication Skills *167*
Policy and background literature 167
Practice application 170
Professional Standards *183*

Conclusion **185**

Research Appendix 192
Bibliography 195
Index 207

List of Practice Examples

Chapter 2: Basic Universal Communication Skills

2.1 Gary – preparatory stage 21
2.2 Gary – beginnings 26

Chapter 3: Working with Children

3.1 Danni – preparatory stage 45
3.2 Danni – beginnings 50
3.3 Danni – work phase 52

Chapter 4: Working with Young People with Offending Behaviour

4.1 Dean – preparatory stage 63
4.2 Dean – beginnings 65
4.3 Dean – work phase 69

Chapter 5: Working with Parents

5.1 Maxine and Ben – preparatory stage 87
5.2 Maxine and Ben – work phase 93

Chapter 6: Working with People Who Use Substances

6.1 The Collins-Evans Family – preparatory stage 106
6.2 The Collins-Evans Family – beginnings 107

Chapter 7: Working with People with Mental Health Problems

7.1 Graeme – preparatory stage 125
7.2 Graeme – beginnings 126

Chapter 8: Working with Adults with Disabilities

8.1 Sue and Steve Preston – preparatory stage 137
8.2 Sue and Steve Preston – beginnings 139
8.3 Sue and Steve Preston – work phase 146

Chapter 9: Working with Refugees and Asylum Seekers

9.1 Maria – preparatory stage 155
9.2 Maria – beginnings 158

Chapter 10: Working with Older People

10.1 Doug – preparatory stage 172
10.2 Doug – work phase 177

Acknowledgements

This book publishes the following two research projects receiving 'Innovations Funding' from the Centre for Excellence in Professional Placement Learning (University of Plymouth): J. Woodcock (2007) 'An Evaluation of Forum Theatre as a Suitable Teaching and Learning Method of Specialist Communication Skills for Social Work Practice Learning Settings' and J. Woodcock, (2007) 'Generating a Resource Containing New Knowledge of Specialist Communication Skills from Practice Learning in Different Practice Settings'.

First, I would like to thank the service users and carers, and the social work students (at the point of their qualification), who participated in this study. Special thanks go to Nick Hammond, for writing the scripts, and then directing and acting out those scripts with other actors within the forum theatre performances. Thank you for inducting me into Forum Theatre, and for showing great patience as I trialed it as a social work teaching and learning method for communication skills. My immense gratitude also to the two research assistants on the study: Dr Claire Tregaskis and Emma Whittlesea.

Finally, I would like to thank my family and friends, who, somewhat ironically, have had to put up with not being able to communicate with me as they might have liked! I am so grateful for the continued encouragement and support that my daughter, Lauren, and my husband, Mark, have given me. Sadly, at the time of writing the latter stages of the book my grandmother, Hazel, died. Memories of communicating with her are at the front of my mind. This book is dedicated to the three of them, and, in accordance with my faith, to God, whose blessing I turn back to praise.

Johanna Woodcock Ross

Introduction

Legislation and policy recognise that a basic human right is to be communicated with and consulted about decisions affecting one's life (The Children Acts 1989, 2004; *Valuing People*, 2001; *Every Child Matters*, 2003). Personalisation as a policy and practice agenda requires social workers to attend to the personal 'voice' of the service user and to encourage service-user decision-making and choice in service delivery. Despite this, social work service users frequently say their communication method is often undervalued and unrecognised (Diggins, 2004; Cree and Davis, 2007; Lishman, 2009). In view of this context, recent reviews have called for the teaching and learning of communication skills to have clearer theoretical underpinning, particularly highlighting the learning of communication skills to be applicable to differing social work practice settings with 'specialist communication skills' identified (Trevithick *et al.*, 2004). The communication skills literature itself was criticised for being a tenuous link between theory and practice in social work. Yet national occupational standards require the learning and assessment of communication skills to have a central focus within social work qualifying awards (QAA, 2000; DOH, 2002; TOPSS, 2002; NAW, 2003). The direct challenge for educators was for communication skills training to be better integrated with practice learning in order to prepare social workers for the real-life challenges of practice (Diggins, 2004). Moreover, as part of this, there needed to be more service user involvement in the design and delivery of such work.

The aim of this book is to begin to bridge the knowledge gap of relevant 'specialist social work communication skills' by recognising and applying theoretical linkages to the real-life challenges of practice actions for social workers in different practice settings. The content is drawn partly from the empirical findings from my own recently conducted research. I used a combination of an innovative teaching method and research methodology to elicit the practice learning of 'specialist communication skills' of qualifying social workers within different social work practice settings. These findings present the early mapping of theoretical linkages to the communication skills employed by social workers. As such, the findings do not stand alone within the book, but within each of the chapters I have situated and considered them within the context of policy and existing knowledge of communication issues and skills as they relate to different practice settings.

Outline of the underpinning research

The research explicitly used experiential learning (Schön, 1983), as a research methodology. I felt that undergraduate Stage 3 social work students at the very point of qualification could be supported to bridge the aforementioned knowledge gap themselves by using a 'bottom-up' method to learning, with the student actively discovering theoretical linkages to the real-life challenges and actions of their practice learning settings. This meant observing and analysing the students' communication while they were 'in action', as well as collating their critical reflections on the action immediately after it had occurred. 'Reflection-on-action' denotes learning taking place after the individual actions – such as considering why students acted as they did and unpicking what exactly took place. However, 'reflection-in-action' is described as thinking independently on the spot, engaging with feelings that are raised on a personal level and addressing the theories being used. Indeed, the second, and crucial, dimension to the study was that the knowledge sought through 'reflection-in-action' was embodied (felt) and not solely derived through abstract thought. A flexible application of Schön's concepts to practice is considered by other authors to be useful, particularly in encouraging a holistic understanding of the social, personal and political contexts of service user situations (Darragh and Taylor, 2009).

The 'reflection-in-action' was achieved through the use of the drama technique known as the Forum Theatre method within designated classroom workshops. This method facilitates conscious and embodied (felt) recognition of collective problems (in this case identifying specialist communication) and develops realistic and dialogic strategies for action (Boals, 1979; Houston *et al.*, 2001). A group of qualifying (Stage 3) undergraduate social work students (n = 55) were divided and assigned to one or more Specialist Social Work Communication Skills workshops corresponding to eight different practice settings in which they were undertaking their practice learning: children; parents; older people; adults with disabilities and their carers; people with mental health difficulties; asylum seekers and refugees; young offenders; and people who misuse substances. Each workshop involved two experienced paid actors performing a scripted role-play to the audience of students within each workshop. My role as facilitator was to invite and prompt students to interact with the actors, ensuring that: (a) interaction and discussion occurred with the role-play; and (b) that the discussion focused on communication issues, and the type and nature of communication skills relevant for particular settings. The fictional scripts were written in consultation with volunteers recruited from a Service User and Carer Consultative Group in order to reflect 'typical everyday issues' of communication between a service user and a social worker within different practice settings. These performances and on-the-spot role-play discussions were video-recorded, transcribed and analysed. The practice examples I use in this book to illustrate specialist social work communication skills are drawn from these research transcripts.

The 'reflection-on-action' was acquired through the qualifying students' responses to a semi-structured questionnaire at pre- and post-stages of the method (that is, immediately before and immediately after each of the workshops). The semi-structured questionnaire contained a combination of closed and open questions to facilitate student reflection on issues of communication and the type and nature of communication skills required by their practice setting. Students received and responded to this before the workshop, and then revisited their answers at the end of it. More details of the research methodology are supplied as an appendix on page 192 of the book.

A practice-led focus

I have sought to ground the empirical basis of the book in the reality of practice actions and practice learning. My intention is to present the content in a way that is both 'practice-led' and meaningful for social work students and practitioners to use in their practice learning. Thus it is accessible and concrete with vivid illustrations of practice but also contains a relative depth of reasoning and theorising to reach a range of different learners. With this in mind I have separated out the denser detail of my theoretical justifications for why particular communication skills are 'specialist' and 'social work' orientated in nature into a chapter of its own (Chapter 1). I address the core issue of whether it is possible to distinguish 'specialist social work communication skills' (encompassing differing skills linked to specific knowledge and policy implications of different social work practice settings) from fundamental social work communication skills that might be relevant to all service user situations across all social work practice settings in varying degrees. I have addressed this possibility by differentiating between what I have termed 'basic, universal social work communication skills' for all settings, which are integrated with and extended by 'specialist social work communication skills' for the different practice settings in which they occur.

I must emphasise that my exposition of specialist social work communication skills is introductory. These findings present an initial mapping of theoretical linkages to the communication skills employed by social workers in different practice settings. I recognise that the position is not without its problems and it is right to highlight them before proceeding. First, the complexity of some service user situations means that there will be occasions when social workers will need to refer to the specialist knowledge covered within other settings in order to complete an analysis of their practice. Human beings are complex, and their characteristics are not easily assigned to a particular 'practice setting' that constitutes an administrative category used by agencies to structure service delivery (Sapey, 2009). Rather, self-definitions of identity should be encouraged within an individualised person-centred philosophy. For the purposes of this book, this means that readers must recognise that different communication skills may be needed for different people.

Second, it should be noted that the focus of the book is on face-to-face interaction (verbal and non-verbal), rather than written or more interactive media methods. There are pragmatic reasons for this. The contextual knowledge is based almost entirely on face-to-face interaction, and the research methods used face-to-face dialogue and body language to examine the communication issues and skills.

Organisation of the book

Chapter 1 offers an introduction to theoretical ideas from within current social work that have informed my approach to the examination of social work communication skills. These provide the theoretical premises from which I have identified how these communication skills can be said to be both 'specialist' and 'social work' in nature. A key premise is that it is possible to separate basic 'universal' social work communication skills from 'specialist social work communication skills'. In Chapter 2, I describe a range of those basic 'universal' communication skills that are relevant to all social work practice settings in varying degrees. As such, they constitute a foundation for effective communication. These basic skills are drawn from the wider communication skills literature and chosen for being relevant to communication issues arising from current and dominant themes in social work practice more generally. The skills are applied to vivid social work practice examples.

In Chapters 3 to 10, I describe and discuss the specialist social work communication issues and skills relevant to the eight different social work practice settings considered in the research study. These are: Chapter 3 – Working with children; Chapter 4 – Working with young people with offending behaviour; Chapter 5 – Working with parents; Chapter 6 – Working with people who use substances; Chapter 7 – Working with people with mental health problems;

Chapter 8 – Working with adults with disabilities; Chapter 9 – Working with refugees and asylum seekers; and Chapter 10 – Working with older people. The structure and style of these chapters follow a more-or-less standard pattern, beginning with a practice example of dialogue (drawn from the research study) to illustrate some of the communication issues and skills of which social workers need to be aware and to utilise in working in each relevant practice. This is followed by a section that sets out a broad summary of the 'contextual' knowledge, which includes: (a) service user perspectives on intervention; (b) policy directives on communication issues in the specific practice setting (where it exists); and (c) what we know from the existing literature about communication issues and skills relevant to that practice setting. The final part of each chapter contains an illustration and analytical commentary of the application of specific social work communication skills to the practice example. This draws on the research findings with further reference to contextual knowledge. Thus each of these individual social work practice setting chapters stands alone in presenting specialist social work communication skills pertinent to that setting. However, before turning to an individual chapter, the reader is advised to read Chapter 2 concerning 'Basic universal social work communication skills' to achieve the full benefit of both the teaching and learning.

A concluding chapter draws out similarities, differences and patterns from the other chapters about policy requirements for practice; development of skills; and implications for education and training.

CHAPTER

Introducing Communication Skills 1

Summary of Communication Skills

- It is possible to separate basic 'universal' social work communication skills from 'specialist social work communication skills'.
- The teaching and learning of communication skills takes place within a 'relationship-based approach', which is informed by the social model of disability to locate barriers in communication.
- Effective communication requires an engagement in reflexive processes regarding the influence of 'self' on communication.
- The legislative authority role of the social worker inevitably influences communication and must be attended to; and social work communication is not instinctive but must be learnt, evaluated and rehearsed.

Separating basic 'universal' from 'specialist' social work communication skills

I draw on the definition of effective 'skilful' communication within social work as provided by Seden (2005: 2):

> Whether a communication is 'good' depends on how it is received in the situation and what is conveyed to the other person. A skilful communication enhances the other person's experience and their ability to respond and participate. What is skilful creates a sense of working together.

For Seden (2005) and other authors of core textbooks on social work communication (Koprowska, 2005; Trevithick, 2005; Lishman, 2009; Shulman, 2009), the communication between a social worker and a service user is influenced by the context in which it occurs. The context changes the assumptions and meanings underlying the words being used. To this end, these authors have sought to make these skills transferable across different contexts and service user groups. The skills are drawn from a number of counselling approaches and methods for interviewing, such as Mehrabian (1972), Egan (1990, 2007), Agazarian (1997), Hargie (1997), Kadushin and Kadushin (1997), McLoed (1998), Hargie and Dickson (2004), Nelson-Jones (2005), Ivey and Ivey (2008), De Jong and Berg (2008), and can be summarised as:

- 'active' or 'reflective' listening, attending; acceptance, often demonstrated through summarising, paraphrasing, reflecting back or 'mirroring';
- 'questioning', such as through open or closed questions, probing or prompting;
- 'demonstrating empathy', identifying feelings, using silences;
- 'challenging', recognising psychological defences and ambivalence;
- 'identifying and using non-verbal communication', such as body language;
- 'focusing', such as creating and working on a shared purpose, and keeping the communication focused, setting goals, encouraging self-efficacy and identifying service-user strengths;
- 'avoiding assumptions' and self-checking for unhelpful judgmental attitudes; and
- 'managing aggression and hostility', looking for the feeling behind the words and actions.

However, I would argue that there is justification for separating the basic communication skills that are relevant to all social work practice settings in varying degrees, from the 'specialist' communication skills, that are relevant to different social work practice settings. First, the 'transferability of skills' argument does not deal adequately with the requirement for more theoretical linkages specific to different social work contexts. If different contexts create different meanings and assumptions that affect communication practice, then those differences should be identified, and the skills for dealing with them labelled. I would argue that it is not sufficient just to hone or adapt existing skills.

Second, and related to this, the distinction builds on findings from my earlier research that sought to identify, and overcome, barriers to inclusion related to social work communication with a particular marginalised group (Woodcock and Tregaskis, 2008). This study took a combined social work and social model of disability perspective to analysing communication with parents of disabled children. Particular issues impacting on communication processes, as well as different social work strategies for communication were identified. Given these differences, it seemed important to ask the same questions in relation to other marginalised groups. Were there particular communication issues pertinent to these groups? What barriers to communication were specific to them, and what communication strategies could be utilised to overcome those barriers? Certainly, I expected differences as the policy literature identifies discrete factors relevant to different groups that can create or reinforce barriers to communication, or encourage liberation from them.

The distinction between basic universal communication skills and specialist communication skills is also made on pragmatic grounds. Social work undergraduates are taught and assessed on more basic universal communication skills during the early stages of their qualifying degree programme. In the later stages they experience practice learning in different social work settings, engaging in increasingly complex work, and requiring the learning and application of 'specialist communication skills'. The differentiation and inclusion of both types of communication skills across a range of settings meets students' learning needs as they progress through the whole programme. Moreover, the identification of specialist knowledge corresponding to specific practice settings responds to the learning needs of social workers undertaking post-qualifying academic study at specialist and advanced levels. The distinction of 'specialist communication skills' that correspond to their own practice setting, as opposed to particular types of skill, is therefore more pragmatic in facilitating the 'integrative' work of linking knowledge, policy requirements and skills.

However, as stated in the Introduction, I recognise that my position is not without its problems. It could be argued that the idea of identifying people as belonging to 'marginalised groups' or particular 'practice settings' is juxtaposed to an individualised person-centred philosophy. Certainly, human beings are more complex than merely the characteristics assigned to the administrative categories used by agencies to structure service delivery (Sapey, 2009). Service users could be offended by my categorising and labelling different groups of people in ways that potentially disrespect their own self-definitions of identity. However, I would refer readers back to the rationale of this book, which is helping social workers in the reality of their practice learning, and so have taken a practice-led perspective towards its organisation.

A 'relationship-based practice' approach

The theoretical principles underpinning the teaching and learning of communication skills in this book are situated in the contemporary framework termed 'relationship-based practice' (Bower, 2005; Ruch, 2005a, 2009; Wilson *et al.*, 2008) and informed by the social model of disability (Finkelstein, 1980; Oliver, 1990, 1996; Thomas, 1999; Oliver and Sapey, 2006; Sapey 2009). Traditional concepts surrounding the importance of achieving a relationship with a service user to enable work to occur are receiving a renewed ascendancy within social work literature, fuelled by the dominance of a developmental perspective to understanding and intervening in service users' lives. Physical and mental well-being, growth and development are predominately understood as being determined by the quality of relationships with other people within the immediate social network, but also mutually influenced by factors in the wider social environment. This dynamic inter-relationship model is also referred to as the ecological approach, with interactions understood to occur across a number of sub-systems at micro-level, meso-level, exo-level and macro-level (see Bronfenbrenner 1979; Jack, 2001, Jack and Gill, 2003). An example of the application of this approach in social work practice is its incorporation into the government policy guidance *The Framework for the Assessment of Children in Need and their Families* (Department of Health, 2000a). This provides a way of assessing children's welfare needs by investigating how wider social factors, such as structural inequality, influence children's welfare directly – or more indirectly by affecting parents' needs and their parenting capacity. However, the inter-relationship model is not just for use in children's services. Developmental trajectories, at any point in the lifecycle, can be affected adversely by difficulties experienced by one or more of these inter-relationships and create instances of developmental risk. At the same time, relationships could act as 'protective influences' to mitigate some of the developmental harm, and put people on more successful developmental pathways. As an example, social support has been seen to act as a buffer against stress for individuals, particularly in the case of maternal depression, where the provision of a confidante can reduce symptoms (Brown and Harris, 1978).

The 'relationship-based practice approach' essentially encompasses a re-conceptualisation of concepts from the psychodynamic approach, including those that relate to the 'use of self' within the professional helping relationship, alongside theoretical ideas that are social constructionist in orientation. As Ruch (2009: 350) states, '"relationship-based practice" is not an entirely new concept but rather a contemporary re-working of the psychosocial model (Hollis, 1964). A fundamental tenet of the relationship-based approach is its focus on the individual in context and on the psychological and the social, as neither the individual nor the context make sense without the other'. She cites the following as being the central features of the approach (Ruch, 2009: 350–1):

- it recognises that each inter-personal encounter is unique;
- it understands that human behaviour is complex and multi-faceted, i.e. people are not simply rational beings but have affective – conscious and unconscious – dimensions that enrich, but simultaneously complicate, human relationships;

- it focuses on the inseparable nature of the internal and external worlds of individuals and the importance of integrated – psycho-social – as opposed to polarised – individual or structural – responses to social problems; and
- It places particular emphasis on the 'use of self' and the relationship as the means through which interventions are channelled.

Thus significant emphasis is made on the working relationship being the interaction between two actors (the service user and the social worker). The two actors are socially situated with the potential to influence the dynamics of an encounter through their own characteristics, perceived status, their cultural vision and understandings, and the way they relate to other people. The psychodynamic elements of the approach emphasise the emotional dimensions of a person's developmental growth, particularly how the interactional quality of early relationship experiences affect psychological health and social functioning with others (Bower, 2005). Modern attachment theorists, in particular, have explored the importance of the parent–child attachment relationship in the way the mind processes interpersonal information to use as a psychosocial template for future relationships (Howe, 2005). People bring these relationship templates to the working relationship between a service user and social worker (Howe, 2005). Powerful feelings about these relationship experiences can be 'repressed' but then 'aroused', 'revived' and 'transferred' to the present (Salzberger-Wittenberg, 1970). Indeed, when using the relationship-based approach, social workers need to be aware of how the process of 'transference' of feelings influences their relationship with the service user. According to the classic work of Salzberger-Wittenberg (1970), 'transference' affects the way people perceive and interpret new situations with others, and then how they themselves influence those situations because people's behaviour tends to elicit responses in others that fit in with their own expectations. Counter-transference has been used to describe the reaction set off in the worker as a result of being receptive to a service user's transferred feelings. Bowlby (1962: x) neatly summarises the importance of recognising these processes of transference and counter-transference in relationships with service users:

> Transference reactions and counter-transference reactions are the stuff of which the caseworker's daily life is made. Her job is not to avoid them but to learn how best to deal with them, recognizing always that the way the [service user] and she treat each other is neither wholly a matter-of-fact coping with the present, but the result by each of an unconscious appraisal of the present in terms of more or less similar situations that each has experienced in the past.

Thus transference is inevitable and can be incredibly useful in identifying service users' feelings (Mattinson and Sinclair, 1979; Howe, 1998; Agass, 2002;

Ruch, 2005b). However, there are dangers if an uncritical approach is taken. For the social worker, there is a need to consider whether particular service user situations or problems have a tendency to trigger off unresolved problems and feelings for the social worker; these could distort perception and interfere with the interaction with the service user. Acknowledging another's pain can be unbearable as extremely intense and frightening feelings may be aroused. For example, in Rustin's (2005) analysis of how professionals could not see what was happening to privately fostered Victoria Climbie, she states that they erected various psychological defences to prevent personally witnessing and experiencing acute mental pain. The public inquiry into the circumstances leading up to and surrounding her death reported that Victoria had died following admission to hospital with malnutrician and hypothermia. There were 128 separate injuries and scars upon her body. Public welfare professionals had failed to see the serious physical abuse and neglect inflicted upon Victoria by her great aunt and her partner, despite hospital admissions and intermittent contact with housing, social worker and police officers. The inquiry prompted the largest review of child protection arrangements in the UK. Taylor (2008) similarly describes how social workers' feelings of vulnerability and anxiety about complex, emotionally challenging situations can create psychological defensive behaviours. She uses the classic study by Menzies (1960) of health organisations to identify how the psychological defences of splitting and projection seem culturally to be required to manage professional anxiety. Taylor found that social workers operated less hierarchically than nurses and projected their feelings across the organisation, criticising colleagues for carelessness and non-acceptance of responsibility, but fearing the level of their own expertise. The psychologically defensive response by some workers to this professional anxiety and responsibility was a routinised adherence to structures and procedures, to split the anxiety-provoking situation of the relationship with the service user, and promote ritualistic task performance (Buckley, 2000; Taylor, 2008).

This signifies the need for social workers to engage in reflexive processes about their 'use of self'. They must ask themselves whether the feelings they have about what a service user is trying to communicate to them is valid, or whether it is the social worker reacting to what they themselves are bringing to the situation (Salzberger-Wittenberg, 1970). Thus the need to become attuned to the ways in which feelings might be expressed is a vital component of relationship-based practice (Wilson *et al.*, 2008). As complex beings, we find that our rational thoughts are shaped by our emotions, and often express our thoughts through our feelings (Ruch, 2009). It is critical, therefore, that social workers expect feelings to be a medium of communication, and be prepared for this. Operating ritualised task performance within a problem-solving approach is not going to be sufficient to attend to service users' needs for social workers to spend time listening to their perspectives. The theoretical position I have adopted here posits that, until both thoughts and feelings are identified (and in some cases actually 'felt' in an affective sense through transference), then those perspectives will not be 'heard' or understood. Psychodynamic processes of 'containment' are considered to be crucial to achieve this attention to thoughts and feelings (Bower, 2005; Ruch 2009). Containment involves enduring, considering and understanding anxiety-provoking feelings (Bion, 1962). It is when these feelings are not sufficiently contained that defensive responses occur (Bower, 2005).

Reflexivity

The emphasis on engaging in reflexive processes about the 'use of self' corresponds to a central emphasis within contemporary social work literature on the social worker as an 'active critical thinker', examining the knowledge and assumptions underpinning their own practice (Sheppard 2000; Taylor and White, 2000; Sheppard and Ryan, 2003). The process of reflexivity specifies explicitly that social workers recognise they are social actors who actively influence the process and outcomes of a socially situated context (the social work interview) with service users who themselves are in a social context (Sheppard, 1998; Sheppard, 2000). Indeed, social constructionist ideas that inform the relationship-based approach encourage social workers to consider how they are constructing service user situations, strengths and difficulties (Ruch, 2009). These constructions are often reflected within the language or other communication methods with service users and social work colleagues. Equally, they are also evident by the methods that are not used, or have not validated that communication. Indeed, in my earlier work I identified that social workers may bring obstacles to communication within the relationship with a service user that stem not only from a privileging of formal knowledge, but also from preconceived notions and cultural stereotyping of service user situations and concerns (Sheppard, 2000; Woodcock, 2003; Woodcock and Tregaskis, 2008, Woodcock and Crow, 2010). For example, literature has documented the way in which social workers have been found to apply social prescriptions of parenting that reinforce gender categories and normative expectations of motherhood and fatherhood (Nicolson, 1993; Richardson, 1993; Smart, 1996; Sheppard, 2000). Such ideals concern the provision of warm, sensitive care which is responsive to a child's developmental needs regardless of the social circumstances in which it occurs (Woodcock, 2003). When parenting does not appear to fit with this construction of normative behaviour, it is frequently considered to be 'unreasonable' or 'deviant'.

Clearly, the operation of such cultural stereotyping as common-sense reasoning is oppressive and should be avoided. Indeed, the dangers have been well-publicised in relation to issues of cultural relativism. As long as it is consistent with their authority role and function, social workers must respect the values and beliefs of the service users with whom they work. An awareness of cultural norms and values enables social workers to be sensitive to cultural differences and variations in patterns and styles of communication. Yet it is important not to assume homogeneity in the values and practices of any family, faith, community or ethnic group. There are dangers in assuming that all values are culture specific; that they should only be appraised within the context of a particular culture; and that the values of one culture cannot be applied to another (Compton *et al.*, 2005; Laird, 2008). Such extreme presentations of cultural relativism have been argued to be evident in normative assumptions, stereotypes or generalisations being applied by professionals when seeking to disentangle 'abuse' from 'cultural practice' (Chand, 2000; Williams and Soydan, 2005; Barn, 2007). As early as the Maria Colwill Inquiry Report in the 1970s, cultural differences in relation to class and gender between the social worker and Maria's stepfather were cited as contributing to different understandings of Maria's emotional responses (Parton, 2004). Seven year old Maria was killed by her stepfather having been recently returned back to the care of her family. A number of social welfare professionals knew differing facts about Maria's circumstances, but failed to share that information with each other. The Inquiry identified the systemic opportunities for multi-disciplinary working and heralded changes to the organization and management of child protection processes in the UK.

The social model of disability

It seems that a practical application of the social model of disability approach provides greater appreciation of the impact on the communication of obstacles relating to normative expectations and required social work communication strategies than can be achieved by the relationship-based approach alone. The social model of disability approach validates insider accounts as representations of everyday reality, but also focuses on identifying structural, systemic and attitudinal barriers to disabled people's access to society, suggesting ways in which these can be overcome (Finkelstein, 1980; Oliver, 1990, 1996; Thomas, 1999). An example is evident in my earlier work (Woodcock and Tregaskis, 2008). When I applied a social model of disability analysis in addition to a social work analysis to my study of social work with parents of disabled children, I found an alternative explanation to finding that parents tended to communicate in strong terms which prioritised their child's development over other aspects of parenting. The alternative explanation was that the strong communication reflected parental attempts to overcome systemic barriers to their child receiving effective help, such as preparation for significant life stages (going to school, for example). The combined analysis highlighted how social workers need to find a communication mechanism whereby they identify and discuss systemic barriers with parents, and expect such communication in both direct and indirect ways. I also found that communication skills were needed to address attitudinal barriers within social workers themselves. Some social workers taking part in the study were either unwilling or unable to validate and recognise service users' 'private' knowledge of the individual characteristics of an impairment, and the individual way it affected family life. As a response to these findings, in this book I have proposed specific communication skills to tackle the issue of identification and the addressing of attitudinal and systemic obstacles that arise in the different practice settings. In relation to these specific theoretical concerns, I refer particularly to the work of Lawrence Shulman (1998, 2009). He illustrates communication as an interaction of coded messages that are relayed to recipients. If these are not identified and addressed successfully, they can present obstacles to communication. He also identifies particular skills that allow the worker to be ready to identify and address any obstacles. These skills are considered in the chapters that follow.

The 'social work' in social work communication skills

Both the social model of disability and the relationship-based approach espouse practice that respects the uniqueness of the individual person in his or her situation. While personalisation requires attention to the personal 'voice' of the service user, and encouragement of service-user decision-making and choice in service delivery, people who use social work services do not always do so by choice. They may be compelled to receive services through legal measures or because of material or social disadvantage. Social workers use communication skills within these legal and procedural frameworks concerning safeguarding, care and control (Seden, 2005). The authority that social workers bring through their legislative role presents a power differential that can influence dramatically any communication with service users. This context presents a critical distinction between the use of communication skills in social work and within counselling. Social work communication has to 'start where the service user is', but cannot always be 'service user-led'. Reflexive thinking requires the social worker to be mindful of the social situation that both service user and social worker are in, including the immediate social situation of the social work encounter/interview. Attention must be paid to the 'immediacy' of the communication in an encounter, where the social worker will be dealing with the service user's recurrent ambivalent, and frequently defensive and aggressive, feelings based on their fear and mistrust of social work authority (Seden, 2005). It is my contention that skills for addressing this fear should be central, and include being clear about the purpose of the intervention.

Social work communication skills do not 'come naturally'

I have found through my work that many students share a common anxiety about the quality and extent of the communication skills they bring to their work. They expect they should be able to communicate well by virtue of being 'a social work student'. Their anxiety is compounded when they begin a process of comparing their abilities to those of other students within their peer group. Questioning and self doubt occurs, raising such comments as 'She has tons of work experience with vulnerable people, so she must have excellent communication skills' or 'He has more life experience than me so he's used to communicating with people.

Other students seem to start the learning process from a completely different angle. The perspective being presented by them is that they are already effective communicators within service user settings. It is often the case that they had been working for health or social care organisations for some time and had received positive feedback about their communication abilities being appropriate to the task. Subsequent questioning and ambivalence about the relevance of the teaching occurs, with comments such as 'I know how to do this already – I've been told I communicate satisfactory' or 'This teaching is telling me different things from how I operate in practice, so it cannot be relevant.' However, on examination, the comments often mask a deeper feeling that is similar to the expectation of being able to communicate well by virtue of being 'a social work student'. There is fear in being found deficient in communication skills, particularly when they believe they should have them already.

In both cases, the anxiety seems to rest on a belief that communication skills 'come naturally' to people, particularly to the types of people who become social work students. Certainly, as Koprowska (2005) indicates, human beings have a biological drive to communicate with others to meet their physical needs. From babies, we experience and engage in verbal and non-verbal behaviour in order to survive. Koprowska describes these acquired behaviours as 'communication skills'. She encourages social workers to identify, de-construct and build on these established communication behaviours in order to communicate more effectively in the context of social work. In doing so, she identifies that social work communication skills are related but different, or extended, from those acquired through life experience and development. Lishman (2009) similarly identifies that there are ways of communicating effectively with social work service users that can and should be learnt, particularly as service users repeatedly highlight poor communication by social workers. We cannot rely on the fact that skills will be learnt in the same 'naturally acquired' manner within social work situations. Rather, an active thinking process is required.

In conclusion, it is important to note that the communication skills presented in this book start from such reflexive consideration. I have sought to examine, and make transparent, the knowledge and assumptions underpinning my interpretation of the responses of qualifying social workers taking part in the research study, and have studied the wider literature on service user perspectives and policy across the different practice settings. Thus this chapter has laid out the theoretical premises upon which I have made sense of the way that these communication skills are both 'specialist' and 'social work' orientated in nature. In summary, these premises are:

- that it is possible to separate basic 'universal' social work communication skills from 'specialist social work communication skills';
- that the teaching and learning of communication skills takes place within a 'relationship-based approach', which is informed by the social model of disability to locate barriers in communication;
- that effective communication requires an engagement in reflexive processes about the influence of 'self' on communication;
- that the legislative authority role of the social worker inevitably influences communication and must be addressed; and
- that social work communication is not instinctive but must be learnt, evaluated and rehearsed.

Within the individual chapters that follow, the reader will find that my findings have been placed in the context of existing knowledge of communication issues and skills relating to the different practice settings described.

Professional Standards

This chapter will help you to meet the following National Occupational Standards:

Key Role 1: Prepare for, and work with individuals, families, carers, groups and communities to assess their needs and circumstances

Unit 1	Prepare for social work contact and involvement
Unit 2	Work with individuals, families, carers, groups and communities to help them make informed decisions
Unit 3	Assess needs and options to recommend a course of action

Key Role 2: Plan, carry out, review and evaluate social work practice with individuals, families, carers, groups, communities and other professionals

Unit 4 Respond to crisis situations
Unit 5 Interact with individuals, families, carers, groups and communities to achieve change and development and to improve life opportunities
Unit 6 Prepare, produce, implement and evaluate plans with individuals, families, carers, groups, communities and professional colleagues
Unit 9 Address behaviour which presents a risk to individuals, families, carers, groups and communities

Key Role 3: Support individuals to represent their needs, views and circumstances. Advocate with and on behalf of people

Unit 10 Advocate with, and on behalf of, individuals, families, carers, groups and communities

Key Role 4: Manage risk to individuals, families, carers, groups, communities, self and colleagues

Unit 13 Assess, minimise and manage risk to self and colleagues

Key Role 5: Manage and be accountable, with supervision and support, for your own social work practice within your organisation

Unit 14 Manage and be accountable for your own work

CHAPTER

2 Basic Universal Communication Skills

Summary of Communication Skills

- Beginning skills to establish purposeful work
    * tuning-in
    * achieving a shared purpose
        - being clear on role
        - being clear on purpose
        - reaching for feedback
        - communicating empathy
        - using immediacy
- Empathy skills
    * reflective listening
        - observing
        - positioning
        - paraphrasing
        - summarising
    * skills to encourage the discussion of unarticulated feelings
        - reaching for feeling
        - putting feelings into words
        - using silences
- Skills for gathering facts
    * questioning to obtain factual information
        - closed questions
        - open questions
- Skills for ending work
    * summarising

This chapter describes basic 'universal' social work communication skills as found both within the research study informing this publication, as well as the existing literature concerning communication skills relating to social work. These skills are relevant, to a greater or lesser extent, to each practice setting but it is not necessary to keep repeating their definition and discussion within each ensuing specialist practice setting chapter. Illustrative examples of the various aspects of these 'universal' skills are provided throughout this chapter.

Beginning skills to establish purposeful work

The importance of working with a clear purpose, as opposed to a conversation without any aim or direction, has been emphasised by service user feedback, research and official enquiries into social work practice and current governmental practice guidance (DoH, 2006a; Lishman, 2009). Research has also identified that first meetings have a lasting emotional impact on service users and therefore are a significant stage in engaging service users in processes of help and change towards achieving that elusive state of 'partnership working' (Aldgate and Bradley, 1999; Bell, 1999; Brandon *et al.*, 1999, 2006). Put simply, beginnings are important. Given that the first meeting is such a 'critical moment' within the social work process, it is essential for the social worker to develop skills to (a) prepare for meeting the service user; and (b) achieve a shared understanding of the purpose, nature and process of the social work to follow.

'Tuning-in'

The skill of preparing oneself for communication with a service user to respond to his or her concerns is described by Lawrence Shulman (2009) as *'tuning-in'*. In much the same way as one might block out all other noise and listen intently in order to tune in a radio station, so the social worker needs to spend quiet time focusing on the concerns the service user might bring to the communication and the ways he or she might communicate those concerns. Shulman's alternative form of words for the skill is 'preparatory empathy'. It is a helpful term, neatly summarising the two actions required to implement the skill. First, the social worker needs to do the activity *before* the meeting with the service user – that is, *in preparation for* the meeting. Second, the aim of the activity is to achieve empathy with the concerns of the service user. Empathy is widely regarded as referring to the act of recognising what another person is feeling (Koprowska, 2005). Trevithick's (2005: 81) definition of empathy is that it:

> involves attempting to put ourselves in another person's place, in the hope that we can feel and understand another person's emotions, thoughts, actions and motives. Empathy involves trying to understand, as carefully and sensitively as possible, the nature of another person's experience, their unique point of view, and what meaning this conveys for the individual.

'Preparatory empathy' or 'tuning-in' therefore involves the social worker seeking to become attuned to the ways in which the service user might express his or her emotions. The need to become attuned to the ways that feelings might be expressed is a vital component of relationship-based practice. As complex beings, we find our rational thoughts are shaped by our emotions, and we often express our thoughts through our feelings (Ruch, 2009). It is critical, therefore, that social workers expect feelings to be a medium of communication, and to be prepared for it.

Shulman provides a three-stage framework to employ the skill of 'tuning-in'. This involves considering how the concerns that the service user is bringing to the communication are influenced by:

1. The way that society's norms, expectations and institutional structures (such as laws, organisational policies and so on) have been experienced by the service user.
2. The issues or difficulties this particular service user is experiencing in his or her immediate environment.
3. The immediate situation facing the service user in meeting a social worker to discuss these difficulties.

It is useful to illustrate the operation of this tripartite framework through the use of practice examples (see Examples 2.1 and 2.2). The chosen example deals with the case of Gary, a 16-year-old A-level school student who lives with his 18-year-old brother Steve. Their father is an officer in the Navy and at the time of this referral is away at sea. In operating the first stage of 'tuning-in', the social worker must consider the way that Gary experiences society's norms, expectations and institutional structures. In this case, a simple question to ask oneself is 'How does society treat teenagers?' The answer, in general terms in relation to the UK, is that the teenage years are viewed as a time of 'stress', a transitional period between being a child and becoming an adult. Teenagers are often viewed as being disruptive, moody, and seeking to assert independence from the care and control of adults. They are expected to demonstrate greater autonomy, increasing rational thought, and more social integration and concern for collective well-being, yet at the same time are considered incapable of rational decision-making by virtue of not yet being an adult (DoH, 1996). This occurs despite the fact that the cultural expectation of some families is for young people to take on caring roles for their relatives, or leadership roles within faith communities.

While the teenage years are a time of stress and strain for some, it is not the case for all young people, with many experiencing good relationships with adults and their peers. However, these largely negative societal and cultural assumptions are what Gary expects the social worker to bring to the

PRACTICE EXAMPLE 2.1

Gary

Preparatory stage

Gary, aged 16 and of white British background, lives with his brother Steve in a well-appointed home, in a well-resourced suburban area of a medium-sized city in South West England. Steve is 18 years old. He left school the previous summer and has just started a job as a salesperson for a large company. Their father is a senior officer in the Navy and is frequently away at sea. Their mother died of cancer when Steve and Gary were in primary school. They received counselling to help with their bereavement. Gary is currently taking A-levels at a local secondary school. He has a few friends whom he sees regularly. All the family would describe their ethnic origin as white British. Two weeks ago, Gary went missing. It was very unusual for him to do this, and his brother was very concerned. Gary did not arrive at school nor return home. Two days later he was found by the police being drunk and disorderly with a couple of friends and returned home. Last night, Gary ran away again. This time friends took him to the local hospital as he said he was desperately unhappy and would live on the streets. The nurse who saw Gary made a referral to the Children Services' Social Work Team. She was worried about both his emotional well-being and his physical health (if he continued to run away and live on the streets). She was concerned that he did not have a parent at home to care for him. This seemed to be a particular concern as the Christmas holidays were due to start, and support networks (such as school) might not be available. The social worker's role was to assess Gary's health and well-being, and to ensure that his care was adequate. Where it was consistent with this, the social worker would offer support in the care of Gary.

The social worker is a 30-year-old white Scottish woman, Caroline Simpson. She telephoned Steve earlier in the day to explain about the referral and to ask to meet Gary that afternoon after school. Steve said he would tell Gary of her visit.

communication. The important consideration for the social worker is 'How might Gary demonstrate these feelings?' Gary could communicate feelings of frustration and exasperation at being viewed as unable to make his own decisions, by becoming defensive through aggression or withdrawal. He might communicate mistrust of adult authority through hostility, or choose to reveal true feelings in a piecemeal fashion over time. However, he might have had positive experiences of caring communication from adults and so might be more open with his feelings, expecting to receive emotional warmth and constructive help from the social worker. It is crucial that the social worker considers as many alternatives as possible. In doing so, he or she will be more able to identify the emotion when it is demonstrated within the communication. This is not about being assumptive and deterministic about the service user's feelings. It may well be the case that other anticipated feelings are demonstrated during the communication. Yet, incongruously, the preparation helps the worker to spot those differences and attend to that unanticipated feeling, showing that he or she has understood the significance of the communication.

The second stage of 'tuning-in' requires the social worker to ponder the issues or difficulties that Gary is experiencing, as a young person, in his immediate environment. One aspect is that Gary has experienced considerable loss, both in his childhood with the death of his mother, and repeated departures of his father during his adolescence. We know that loss and other adversity affects children and young people differently, depending on age, sex, temperament, intelligence (in terms of IQ), and, most importantly, the quality of relationships with caregivers (particularly whether there is a secure attachment relationship – for a further discussion on this topic, see Howe, 2005). Children and young people go through stages of grief, but do so in a different way from adults and, depending on individual factors, may become 'stuck' at a particular stage (Jewett, 1984). Loss may remain unresolved and grief may continue to be misunderstood or unidentified by adults. Gary, for example, could be 'stuck' in feelings of guilt about the loss of his mother. It was too early in his development for him to be able to rationalise why she was suddenly unavailable to him. This causes some children in their middle years to blame themselves for the deaths of loved ones, believing that if they had acted differently there would have been a different outcome. Boys, in particular, find it difficult to demonstrate and discuss painful feelings in the face of cultural stereotypes that 'boys don't cry'. Now, in adolescence, Gary is experiencing multiple losses when his father departs for periods of service. Subsequent losses are not considered to be experienced as easier but as doubly hard, with painful feelings being brought to the surface.

Drawing on this analysis, Gary's expectation of adults might be that they are unable to identify his pain and therefore cannot help him to resolve it. As before, the important consideration for the social worker is 'How might Gary demonstrate these feelings?' Gary might communicate feelings of sadness and helplessness, withdrawing from the conversation. He might seek to mask his feelings and keep the conversation at a superficial level. He might be so surprised to find an adult openly discussing feelings that he becomes defensive and aggressive to ward off further exploration because he does not know how to deal with the situation. Alternatively, Gary might be relieved that someone is willing to listen to and understand his feelings. He might demonstrate tearful distress and let go of pent up emotion.

The third stage of 'tuning-in' requires the social worker to consider how Gary might feel meeting a social worker to discuss difficulties in his situation. The negative media portrayal of social workers is either that of 'busybodies poking their noses into private affairs', removing children or vulnerable adults from their homes without good evidence, or 'inadequate' by failing to protect children from harsh care-giving. These dominant negative media images concerning authority will influence Gary's expectations of how helpful the social worker will be to him. He might hide his feelings and concerns in an effort to convince the social worker that all is well, so that she leaves his home. He might become fearful and angry as the social worker explores the situation and his feelings. Another particular concern for Gary is that the communication with the social worker might result in his father being summoned home from his ship. Often, service personnel find this action embarrassing because their private life becomes public in their workplace; frequently, they fear repercussions on their service career. Gary would be aware of this issue and might communicate feelings of embarrassment and guilt at the situation, and demonstrate anxiety about his father's return.

Crucial to 'tuning-in' at all three stages is for the social worker to consider how her 'self' will influence and impact on the communication with the service user. Thus, at the first stage of 'tuning-in', when considering how Gary experiences society's norms, expectations and institutional structures, it is important for the social worker to ensure that she has up-to-date knowledge about teenagers-in-society. Where this is lacking, there is a moral and professional imperative to take steps to improve this knowledge prior to the communication. Indeed, research tells us that in the face of knowledge deficits, social workers' own constructions of care giving and parenting have been found to dominate their assessment work and affect their practice strategies (Howitt, 1992; Parton *et al.*, 1997; Daniel, 2000; Woodcock, 2003). Such constructions could add to the oppression already experienced by a service user by reinforcing negative cultural stereotypes.

Similarly, at the second stage of 'tuning-in', the social worker needs to reflect on 'self' in terms of whether she has sufficient knowledge of the kinds of issues or difficulties that Gary could be experiencing, as a young person, in his immediate environment. In this example, knowledge of theories of loss was required. By 'tuning-in' to 'self' at this stage, it is important that the social worker recognises that the service user's feelings of loss, grief and bereavement also have an emotional impact on the social worker him/herself. The social worker may have experienced significant loss and so be able to identify the depths of the grief being communicated by Gary. By the same token, the social worker may find it difficult to acknowledge the pain being communicated by Gary because it resonates too acutely with his or her own pain. Alternatively, the social worker may not have experienced significant loss and so may find it harder to demonstrate understanding of Gary's pain in an authentic way. What is important is that the social worker takes time to reflect on these issues before the communication takes place, so there is more chance of recognising the way that their own feelings might be communicated and take steps to deal with this.

Finally, in thinking about the influence and impact of 'self' at the third stage of 'tuning-in', the social worker needs to consider how Gary might demonstrate his feelings, not just in meeting with any social worker, but to her as a particular social worker. This requires Caroline to engage in an active consideration of the similarities and differences relating to personal characteristics between her and Gary across a range of variables, including age, sex, ethnic origin and other facets of cultural background. For example, the age difference between Gary and Caroline presents a power differential. As an adult, Caroline is considered by society to be able to make rational choices and is accustomed to having her views heard and believed. Gary, however, is not. The fact that legislation states that children's wishes and feelings should be sought and their views established as central to any decision-making (Children Act 1989; Children Act 2004) does not mean that partnership occurs as much in practice as it should. Rather, young people frequently report that their social workers do not listen to them adequately. Children are among the most oppressed members of society, who frequently experience being overpowered – whether through being told to 'shut up' or having their views devalued, or, as too often reported, being physically constrained or beaten (Kroll, 1995). Caroline needs to 'tune-in' to how she might inadvertently devalue Gary's thoughts and feelings and prepare herself to find ways to communicate the reverse. Caroline might be able to empathise with Gary's feelings of being 'unheard' or 'disempowered'. She may have experienced these feelings in her own life and so can draw on this similarity to better understand Gary's position. This is not to say that she should claim that she understands Gary's situation completely. Only he is the expert on that. Rather, the similarity gives her greater insight, which she can then look to have confirmed or refuted during their meeting when the communication takes place.

Achieving a shared purpose

'Tuning-in' prepares the way to achieve the other aim for the beginning stage of communication within social work intervention, which is to achieve a shared understanding with the service user regarding the purpose, nature and process of the social work that will occur. The beginning stage of work is often replete with examples of the service user communicating ambivalence, resistance and sometimes aggression. Often this occurs because there is no shared understanding of the purpose of the work and, crucially, how that work is beneficial to the service user in their situation.

Shulman's work on 'agendas' is helpful in understanding the interpersonal dimensions of this aspect of the communication process. Key to this understanding is an appreciation of how the authority that the social worker brings through their role and the law dominates the proceedings. Some service users seek and/or receive social work services on a voluntary basis. They bring an 'agenda' to the communication, which is about having their needs and difficulties understood, identifying their strengths and seeking to change the difficulties they experience in their situation. Frequently, however, there is a degree of compulsion or social control underpinning the reason for the social worker's meeting the service user, because the social worker has a legislative duty to safeguard and promote the well-being of individuals. The social worker brings his or her own 'agenda' of ensuring that the communication process enables the fulfilment of that authority role. In the case of our practice example, the social worker's 'agenda' was to communicate effectively with Gary in order to assess Gary's health and well-being, and to ensure that his care was adequate. Where it was consistent with this, the social worker would also offer support in the care of Gary. On meeting Gary, the social worker, Caroline, might find that the two agendas coincided. Gary might be keen, if not relieved, about having his needs and difficulties understood, and happy to work with the social worker to deal with the difficulties in his situation. In this case, the social worker and Gary could be said to be working to the same agenda.

However, Gary might be very ambivalent about meeting with the social worker, and reject her agenda. Indeed, we have just 'tuned-in' to the possibility of this occurring. His agenda might be to hide his feelings and concerns in an effort to convince the social worker that all is well so that she leaves his home. Indeed, the authority role that a social worker brings to the communication with a service user inevitability carries with it the aforementioned negative media stereotype of social workers creating fear and suspicion. Beyond this, there were other potential reasons which might mean that Gary might not want to share the same agenda as the social worker, such as being reluctant to share painful feelings about loss. In all these cases, we would describe the situation as having two conflicting agendas in operation. The consequence is that 'no work' can be said to occur as there is no shared agenda (Shulman, 2009).

Clearly, at the outset of the meeting, the social worker needs to use communication skills that create the conditions in which to achieve a shared agenda. The interpersonal processes described above indicate that this should be understood as an interactive process of introduction and negotiation. The agendas of both the social worker and the service user need to be brought out into the open. There needs to be a discussion about those agendas, and agreement on how they can be brought together to specify the purpose and processes for the ongoing work. This will involve the social worker identifying the service user's thoughts and feelings as they emerge during the discussion. The social worker's previous engagement with 'tuning-in' will have helped to prepare him or her for this work. Shulman (2009) suggests a three-part skill called 'contracting' for this process: 'being clear on role'; 'being clear on purpose'; and 'reaching for feedback'. I have chosen to extend this to include a fourth part: 'communicating empathy'. In view of this change and the practice context of emphasizing more clarity of purpose in social work intervention, I have chosen to re-name this skill 'achieving a shared purpose'.

The first part of 'achieving a shared purpose' covers paying attention to the dominating influence of the authority role. The requirement is for the social worker to be 'clear on role'. This means that, at a minimum, the social worker must tell the service user in an honest and direct way that they are a social worker. Taking into account people's capacity for understanding, they should go on within the discussion to explain the parameters of the role, such as the duties to ensure that someone is safe from harm and the limitations to ensuring confidentiality. Smale *et al.* (1993: 48), in their discussion of the skills needed to empower service users within assessment processes in care management, regard such authenticity as central and define it as

> The care manager's ability to relate to others with integrity; to be aware of their own feelings and values, as well as the significance of their agency role and the other roles they occupy dependent upon gender, race and cultural background ... there are several levels to this from the straightforward demand that workers are honest with people about themselves, their agencies and resources, to the more sophisticated demands on the worker's self-awareness and use of self in facilitating complex processes of change.

By way of illustration let us go back to our practice example.

PRACTICE EXAMPLE 2.2

Gary

Beginnings

Social worker knocks at the door several times before Gary answers it.

Gary:	Hello...
[1] Social *worker(SW)*:	Hello, are you Gary? My name's Caroline Simpson. I'm the social worker who telephoned your brother earlier to say that I wanted to visit you this afternoon. I need to see how you are doing, to check if you are all right. Is that OK? Can I come in?
Gary:	My brother said you would be coming. How long is this going to take?

▶

▶

[2] *SW*: Oh, not long. I won't take up much of your time. I expect you are very busy. I do need to talk things over with you, though.

Gary: Well, all right then, but I haven't got long. It's not like there's anything wrong or anything. It's all sorted now.

SW: Well, we'll see. Can I come in and talk to you about things then?

Gary: *Leads the way into the living room, which was untidy but comfortable and clean.*

SW: The house looks really comfortable and cosy.

Gary: Yeah. We manage fine. My dad's friend, Roy, comes round regularly to see if we need anything. He's a copper. He makes sure we've got enough money. Sometimes gets us a take-away.

[3] *SW*: It's good that you have someone keeping an eye on you. I guess you might be wondering whether I'm here to keep an eye on you too? I do have a responsibility to check that young people are safe and well, but if I'm satisfied that all is in order I won't need to bother you and your brother any more. Is that what you expected a social worker to do?

Gary: Yeah. My brother said that social workers poke their noses in when they're not wanted. You're not going to contact my dad are you? He's not supposed to come home before his leave. I get on fine with Steve usually. I'm going to be OK now.

[4] *SW*: That's what I need to check out with you – whether you are really feeling OK or whether you will feel like running away again.

A period of silence lasting about a minute; Gary slumped in the chair with his head down.

[5] *SW*: What happened to make you want to run away? It's quite a serious thing to do.

▶

▶

Another period of silence.

[6] *Gary*: I don't know why I did it. I just wanted to get my head cleared. Me and Steve keep arguing a lot lately. He keeps getting at me about my schoolwork. It's not my fault that I find the work hard. They don't teach me properly. Dad's always saying that. He says there's nothing wrong with my brain. I'm going to get on with my work now.

[7] *SW*: Have you got a lot of course work to do over the Christmas holidays?

Gary: Loads. If they didn't give me so much to do at once I wouldn't get so fed up. Mrs Smith is the worst one. She doesn't like me and keeps giving me more than everyone else. Can you talk to my form teacher about it?

SW: It doesn't sound right that you have more than anyone else does. I could talk to your teacher. Do the school know that you're living at home with your brother and that your dad is away at sea?

Gary: Probably. But I don't think they care. We get on with things all right at home.

[8] *SW*: It sounds like you don't think that anybody cares about how you are feeling, and that maybe you feel you have to get on with life because you are expected to manage. If that's right then it must be hard for you.

Gary: It is quite hard sometimes. I don't like being bossed about by Steve. He's not my dad, but he acts like he thinks he is. I don't want my dad being told about all this though. He'll be cross if he has to come back. It affects his job.

SW: Your dad needs to know how you're doing. At the end of the day, he *is* your dad and he is responsible for you, to make sure you are well and happy. What's stopping you from contacting him and telling him how you feel?

Another period of silence lasting about a minute.

Gary: I can't tell him. That's all. He'll be cross. I'll get him in trouble. I told you.

▶

SW:	Sounds like you're feeling you've let your dad down and you're disappointed with yourself. Is that right?
Gary:	I feel like I've messed everything up.
[9] *SW*:	When you say you have 'messed *everything* up', what do you mean? Perhaps I can help you with it?
[10] *Gary*:	What can you do to help? Haven't you got loads of other people to see?

We find Caroline, the social worker, stating that she is a social worker (point 1) but it is not until point 3 that she seeks to explain and discuss what the social work role involves. She says:

'I guess you might be wondering whether I'm here to keep an eye on you too? I do have a responsibility to check that young people are safe and well, but if I am satisfied that all is in order I won't need to bother you and your brother any more. Is that what you expected a social worker to do?'

Caroline's reluctance to discuss the social work role up to this point (point 3) could be understood as a concern not to upset Gary at this early stage of their relationship. She might be assuming that he would not be able to understand the parameters of her role. Unfortunately, the lack of clarity about the role only made him become more wary of her presence as an authority figure, causing an obstacle to their communication. Caroline might think she is being friendly and trying to gain rapport, such as when she says 'the house looks really comfortable and cosy', but essentially she is going around the obstacle by seeking compliance. Rather, she needs to attend to the obstacle in a direct manner and seek to remove it. Her statement at point 3 begins to do this work: 'I guess you might be wondering whether I am here to keep an eye on you too.'

The second part of 'achieving a shared purpose' requires the social worker to be 'clear on purpose'. The social worker needs to state the nature of his or her agenda, and to do so using straightforward, non-jargonistic language that is developmentally appropriate to the service user. The social worker will achieve greater success with this if they have prepared a statement in advance. In our practice example (2.2), we find Caroline, the social worker, using simple terms to explain her agenda. For example, at point 3 she says 'I do have a responsibility to check that young people are safe and well', and extends the discussion at point 4 by saying 'That's what I need to check out with you – whether you are really feeling OK or whether you will feel like running away again.' Clearly, though, Caroline should not just assume that by making these statements,

Gary has heard and understood them. She needs to check with Gary what he understood and whether he agrees with the information. This constitutes the third part of the skill – 'reaching for feedback'. It should take the form of a question that communicates a genuine desire to know the service user's viewpoint. A quick statement such as 'Is that all right by you?' will not suffice. Indeed, Shulman (2009) states that this part of the skill should actively search for the service user's stake in the work, for example, by saying 'Do you think that this is something we could work on together to make the changes you need? What's your view on this?'

Practice experience has shown me that these three parts of 'achieving a shared purpose' cannot occur unless the social worker conveys to the service user, with warmth, that they are with someone who is prepared to listen to their difficulties with care and sympathy. The service user might then be able to unfold his or her concerns without fear of blame or misunderstanding. It involves communicating acceptance of the uniqueness of each new situation with warmth, interest and concern. This is about demonstrating respect. Smale *et al.* (1993: 51) identify respect as a core skill for 'joining with people' and define it as:

'The care manager's ability to communicate their acceptance and valuation of people irrespective of their personal qualities and social or professional position.'

An intuitive understanding of another person and the difficulties in their situation is not enough, but rather involves 'the hard work of hearing, comprehending and communicating understanding of what other people say, the thoughts and feelings that they express and the way they make sense of the world' (Smale *et al.*, 1993). This describes empathic processes involved in becoming attuned to the ways in which thoughts and feelings might be expressed. As described earlier, social workers must engage with feelings as a principal form of communication if service users are to feel that their views have been heard and understood. It is especially critical to do so at this beginning stage of work, when seeking to uncover the service user's agenda and discuss how the agendas of both service user and social worker can be brought together. Indeed, there are feelings that the immediate relationship will be arousing, such as anxiety, anger or fear at either the authority role of the social worker or the creation of a new relationship. The social worker must identify and attend to these feelings or it will be impossible to achieve a shared agenda.

Seden (2005: 48) refers to this skill of commenting directly on the process happening between the social worker and service user as 'using immediacy'. It involves the worker identifying exactly what he or she observes or feels is happening to the service user in a direct manner. We can find the skill beginning to be employed in our practice example (2.2). In the dialogue between points 2 and 3, Gary shows his anxiety about the social worker's authority role by stating 'I haven't got long. It's not like there's anything wrong or anything. It's all sorted now' and 'We manage fine. My dad's friend, Roy, comes round regularly to see if we need anything. He's a copper. He makes sure we've got enough money. Sometimes gets us a take-away.' The social worker recognises that the narrative is revealing Gary's anxious feelings about her role and responds 'using immediacy': 'I guess you might be wondering whether I'm here to keep an eye on you too?' She could have taken this comment further and identified the unexpressed feelings more directly, such as 'I understand you might be nervous about trusting me because you may be worried about me being a social worker, and there are negative things said in the news about social workers, like taking children away from their families when they don't need to.' Seden (2005: 48) considers 'using immediacy' to be a skill that requires practice, and involves 'basic listening and responding skills and a willingness to be open and genuine, framing the words honestly in a calm way. It involves the practitioner in monitoring carefully their own feelings and being prepared to practice a level of self-disclosure'. These are all aspects of what I have placed under an umbrella term of 'empathy skills'. While these skills are a crucial fourth part of 'achieving a shared purpose' at the beginning stage of work, they should be employed throughout all social work intervention. As they are not limited to the beginning stage, they are discussed more fully in the following section.

Before leaving this 'Beginning skills' section, it is imperative to draw attention to one last point. This involves the situation where the meeting continues but no shared agenda has been achieved. The skill of 'achieving a shared purpose' may not have been executed successfully. In such cases, it is likely that the social worker is either completely on the service user's agenda, or is fixated on their own agenda with the service user demonstrating superficial compliance and passive involvement. The social worker may think that work is occurring but in fact it is just, as Shulman (2009) puts it, 'the illusion of work'. To avoid this, the social worker must take steps to prevent becoming so immersed in the content of the narrative that he or she fail to see the feelings that are being revealed unconsciously by attitude, gesture or tone of voice as the service user pursues his/her own line of thought. The social worker needs at the same time to adopt some objective distance as well as being attuned emotionally with the thoughts and feelings being expressed. The literature refers to this objective distancing as operating a 'third ear' (Lishman, 2009), or a 'second head', with the social worker having in mind questions such as 'What is really going on in the communication here?', 'Is the problem she or he is describing the most immediate one, or is there something more worrying?', 'What is the nature of the obstacle to our communication?' and 'What skill should I use next?' When these questions are used it is easier to recognise the illusion of work and attempt to employ the skill of 'achieving a shared purpose' once again. It would seem useful to 'use immediacy' to achieve this as it allows the social worker to comment honestly and directly on what has occurred. An example of this is: 'You know, Gary, I feel I haven't been as clear as I should have been about my job as a social worker. I think you are feeling worried about me being a social worker and whether you can trust me, and this means you are reluctant to share your concerns with me. What do you think, can we start again?'

Empathy skills

Social workers need to be able to place themselves emotionally and psychologically in the situation of the service user if they are to be able to work out that person's thoughts and feelings. The communication skills required to achieve and communicate this level of emotional attunement include 'reflective listening' (a term used by Cameron, 2008) as well as other skills, such as 'reach for feeling' (Shulman, 2009) and 'putting feelings into words' (Shulman, 2009), which I have placed under the umbrella heading of 'skills to encourage the discussion of unarticulated feelings'.

Reflective listening

Feelings may be evident by what is said, but are also revealed through tone of voice and attitude, and non-verbally through gesture and body position. In whatever way they are communicated, however, the social worker needs to receive these feelings in an open, warm and receptive manner. The skill of 'reflective listening' enables this to occur (Cameron, 2008). But because, as Cameron (2008) highlights, listening is a psychological, cognitive or mental function that focuses only on verbal expression, it needs to be carried out in tandem with 'observing' non-verbal behaviour to attend fully to the service user's total communication of feeling. Indeed, it has been cited that up to 70 per cent of the emotional content of our communication is manifested non-verbally (Stack *et al.,* 1991: 41, cited by Cameron, 2008: 24). It is essential to state that the way a person behaves non-verbally is not culturally neutral but influenced by their social and cultural background. For example, there are cultural and ethnic expectations about courteous and acceptable non-verbal behaviour, such as the amount of space and eye-contact between worker and service user. Social workers need to recognise that a wide variation of expectations exists, and as such need to have a good awareness of their own non-verbal presentation (Cameron, 2008).

The physical positioning of the social worker to encourage the discussion of feelings through their non-verbal behaviour constitutes a first stage in demonstrating the skill of 'reflective listening'. The acronym SOLER is usefully provided by Egan (2007) to describe the key elements of such positioning. 'S' refers to the position of the worker as sitting 'square on' at 90 degrees to the service user, and 'O' to the 'open' stance taken within that position, with legs and arms unfolded and hands resting, relaxed, on the thighs or in the lap. Through 'leaning forward' – the 'L' of SOLER – the worker can lessen any height difference and demonstrate interest and attention through 'eye contact', as denoted by 'E'. Indeed, a position that enables good observation for both the service user and social worker of each others' facial expressions is critical in enabling the discussion of feelings. The 'R' refers to achieving all this in a relaxed way.

Clearly, the social worker should not expect the service user to adopt the SOLER position. However, the social worker needs to try to make sense of the non-verbal behaviour that is presented by the service user. The practice example (2.2) describes Gary's body language immediately following a direct statement from the social worker about his well-being at point 4: 'There was a period of silence lasting about a minute, when Gary was slumped in the chair with his head down.' We could interpret this body language as being 'closed', with Gary withdrawing eye contact and folding his body away from the service user. Essentially, he is indicating that he is finding it difficult to communicate on the subject. In an 'open' position, he would be relaxed and sitting with his arms and legs unfolded and towards the social worker. He would be making some eye contact and other gestures to show he is participating in the conversation, such as rubbing his head when thinking. As stated earlier, there are cultural differences to these expectations. For example, some faith communities do not allow eye contact between an unmarried female and a male. In such situations it would be wrong to label the lack of eye contact as demonstrating 'closed' body language.

The second part of 'reflective listening' is for the social worker to be focused on hearing the experience of the other person. This means waiting until the other person has finished speaking, reflecting on what was said and then responding to check back that the communication was heard and understood accurately. As Seden (2005) highlights, this does not mean selecting and labelling parts of the communication that the social worker thinks are significant. Neither does it mean that it is acceptable to rush in and offer advice or offer to make a referral to a service without obtaining the full picture. The other person needs time to express his or her feelings. This means having the patience to tolerate pauses and silences that seem longer in duration than in normal conversation. Cameron (2008: 39) summarises the point well:

> 'Good listeners put the focus on the other person and on what they are offering, rather than asking for additional information, or talking about other things.'

There are two communication skills that can usefully be employed to check with the service user that you have heard and understood correctly what they were saying. The first is 'paraphrasing'. Cameron (2008: 51) views a paraphrase as 'an attempt to combine in a coherent and meaningful sentence, reflections about the client's feelings, the situations and/or their behavioural responses to it'. It encourages further exploration. This is distinct from 'summarising, which involves integrating broader themes at the end of the discussion of a particular point.

'Skills to encourage the discussion of unarticulated feelings'

Seden (2005: 26) emphasises the importance of 'listening to the base line (what is not openly said but possibly is being felt)'. As described earlier, the social worker will often perceive that some parts of the service user's descriptions are charged with feelings, which though unarticulated are revealed unconsciously through tone of voice and attitude, and non-verbally through gesture and body position. Shulman's (2009) skills of 'reach for feeling' and 'putting feelings into words' are useful for drawing out the feelings that might not be immediately at the surface or are difficult to express.

'Reaching for feeling' involves the social worker asking the service user directly about how he or she feels about a particular issue. It needs to be asked as an 'open question'; that is, a question for which a simple 'yes' or 'no' response is not sufficient. While it should be said sensitively and in a gentle tone, it nevertheless makes a demand on the service user to work on the feeling. Examples of the skill are 'How does that make you feel?' and 'What are you feeling right now?' The communication skill of 'putting feelings into words' makes the same demand, but is not framed as an open question. In using this skill, the social worker describes, tentatively but as accurately as possible, the feelings he or she perceives are being communicated and asks the service user to confirm or deny their accuracy.

The social worker must reflect on the interpersonal communication that has taken place to decide which of the skills to use to encourage the discussion of unarticulated feelings. I described earlier how the social worker needs to have in mind questions such as 'What is really going on in the communication here?', 'Is the problem she or he is describing the most immediate one, or is there something more worrying?', 'What is the nature of the obstacle to our communication?' and 'What skill should I use next?' If the social worker considers that there is an obstacle to communication based on anxiety or ambivalence relating to his or her authority role, then it makes little sense for the social worker to 'reach for feeling' and ask how the service user is feeling. The service user is unlikely to reveal feelings of ambivalence or anxiety in response. However, if the social worker uses the skill of 'putting feelings into words', then by identifying the feeling and bringing it into the discussion, the service user may be more willing to discuss its accuracy and relevance. Alternatively, the social worker might reflect that the service user may be finding it difficult to express a feeling, perhaps through fear that when the feeling is expressed they may be unable to control their reactions, or perhaps they are not yet developmentally mature enough to name and explain the feeling. The practice example (2.2) provides an example of this between points 8 and 9. The social worker uses 'putting feelings into words' by stating 'Sounds like you're feeling you've let your dad down and you're disappointed with yourself. Is that right?' This enables Gary to respond with 'I feel like I've messed everything up'.

Clearly, the social worker needs to use his or her emotional attunement to make these tentative observations, and needs to engage in reflexive processes about how they may be wrong. This involves the social worker identifying how their own preconceived notions and cultural stereotypes (based on their own experiences and biography) might cloud their judgement or indeed their behaviour in tolerating the sharing of painful feelings and allowing the service user's personality to come forward. In Chapter 1, I highlighted that social workers need to be aware of how the 'transference' and 'counter-transference' of feelings influences their relationships with service users. Counter-transference has been used to describe the reaction generated in the worker as a result of being receptive to a service user's transferred feelings. These emotions are considered a helpful guide to understanding transferred feelings that are unexpressed. As such it is pertinent to ask oneself 'What does this person make me feel?' and 'What does this tell me about the nature of their relationships, or their effect on others?' Social workers should check whether this intuition is valid according to what the service user is communicating, or whether the counter-transference is the social worker reacting to what they themselves are bringing to the situation. Particular service user situations or problems can trigger unresolved problems in the social worker which then distort perception and interfere with the interaction with the service user.

The issue of 'sharing worker's feelings' to facilitate the working relationship has been the subject of debate. Yet, according to the theoretical relationship-based framework discussed here, the development of empathy, or identification with service-user feeling, is crucial to gain an awareness of unexpressed thoughts and feelings that are conscious or are below the surface (Ferard and Hunnybun, 1962). Shulman considers the sharing of a worker's feelings to be an essential skill related to the worker's ability to present him or herself to service users as a real human being rather than a clinical, detached and objective professional. When there is a dichotomy between the 'personal' and 'professional', Shulman considers there is a loss of spontaneity, with workers appearing as guarded professionals, unwilling to allow service users access to them and their feelings. Such people will have difficulty in relating to the service user as a person who is connected to feelings.

Concerns about sharing feelings are often raised in relation to the boundaries within which personal feelings can be shared. We might ask whether the sharing of such feelings is appropriate to the professional function and task. Shulman provides an answer: if a social worker is clear about the purpose of work with the service user (through a verbal or written contract) and the particular professional function, then this offers direction, and indeed protection. As Shulman states,

> the worker's feelings about personal relationships can be shared only in ways that relate them directly to the service user's immediate concerns. For example, take a situation in which a worker feels the client is misinterpreting someone's response because of the client's feelings. The worker who has experienced that kind of miscommunication might share briefly the experience as a way of providing the client with a new way of understanding an important interaction.

He provides a contrasting example which elucidates the point well:

> If a client begins an interview by describing a problem with his mother-in-law, the worker would not respond by saying 'You think you have problems with your mother-in-law? Let me tell you about mine!' The client and worker have not come together to discuss the worker's problems, and an attempt by the worker to introduce personal concerns, even those related to the contract area, is an outright subversion of the contract. (Shulman, 1999: p.165)

A good skill for encouraging emotional attunement and the discussion of thoughts and feelings is to 'use silences'. Sitting still and in silence while maintaining an open posture and leaning forward demonstrates interest (Cameron, 2008). The silence provides thinking space. As such, the social worker should avoid breaking into it unless it has gone on for some time or the service user is communicating a feeling non-verbally and the social worker needs to verbalise empathy for this work. The silence can be used as a signal to the service user that it is his or her turn to speak and express their thoughts and feelings. As some people find silences in communication quite difficult to tolerate, this type of signal can be very powerful if used appropriately.

Skills for gathering facts

'Questioning to obtain factual information' is a critical communication skill in social work. Lishman (2009) and Koprowska (2005) emphasise the importance of suitable questioning to obtain factual information, not just the communication of feelings. If significant information is lost, then the result will be an inappropriate and less holistic assessment of the service user's situation and needs. Lishman warns social workers against subsiding into an interrogative question-and-answer stance with a lot of questions being asked at a fast rate. Service users feel disempowered by the underlying assumption of this approach that the social worker is the expert, who, in focusing on the problems, has the expertise to solve them.

Lishman suggests that the social worker reflects on the following four issues to select the right kind of question. First, the social worker should be aware that he or she is asking a question. Second, he or she should consider the purpose of that question and whether it is essential to clarify information or encourage further exploration. Third, is questioning the right skill to be used, or is an alternative, such as 'putting feelings into words' better as it encourages the service user to work on his or her feelings? Finally, having decided that questioning for facts is appropriate, what type of question should be asked?

There are two main types of questions. First, 'closed' (Lishman, 2009), also called 'narrow' questions (Koprowska, 2005), which elicit 'yes' or 'no' or some other limited factual response. This is illustrated in the practice example (2.2) at point 7, when the social worker asks: 'Have you got a lot of course work to do over the Christmas holidays?' and Gary responds 'Loads.' Koprowska (2005) notes that too many of questions like this can feel like an interrogation, and should be avoided when discussing personal issues that require exploration. Second, 'open' (Lishman, 2009) or 'broad' questions (Koprowska, 2005), which invite more extensive answers that encourage further exploration or an explanation of issues. An illustration of an open question that is asked for the purpose of clarification is at point 9, when the social worker asks: 'When you say you have 'messed *everything* up', what do you mean? Perhaps I can help you with it?'

Skills for ending work

Endings can be difficult for service users as they not only bring to mind past losses but also trepidation about the future without the assistance that has been provided (Koprowska, 2005). It is important that, wherever possible, endings are planned with service users being reminded of the meeting schedule and end time or date. The skill of 'summarising' is usefully employed to agree the main points that have been covered and the tasks that have been set to manage the next steps. If possible, it is better for the social worker to encourage the service user to do this summarising work. This enables the service user to recognise for themselves how their psychosocial situation has altered, how they will manage this period of change, and the mechanisms they have in place to achieve their psychosocial functioning in the future. Examples are: 'Tell me the main issues that we have covered today' or 'Tell me your understanding of what you have achieved over these past weeks.'

This chapter has provided an overview of the basic skills that are required for effective communication with an individual within social work situations. The following chapters present more specific social work communication skills that build on this foundation base and relate to the more specific needs of individuals.

Professional Standards

This chapter will help you to meet the following National Occupational Standards:

Key Role 1: Prepare for, and work with individuals, families, carers, groups and communities to assess their needs and circumstances

Unit 1 Prepare for social work contact and involvement
Unit 2 Work with individuals, families, carers, groups and communities to help them make informed decisions
Unit 3 Assess needs and options to recommend a course of action

Key Role 2: Plan, carry out, review and evaluate social work practice with individuals, families, carers, groups, communities and other professionals

Unit 4 Respond to crisis situations
Unit 5 Interact with individuals, families, carers, groups and communities to achieve change and development and to improve life opportunities
Unit 6 Prepare, produce, implement and evaluate plans with individuals, families, carers, groups, communities and professional colleagues
Unit 9 Address behaviour which presents a risk to individuals, families, carers, groups and communities

Key Role 3: Support individuals to represent their needs, views and circumstances. Advocate with and on behalf of people

Unit 10 Advocate with, and on behalf of, individuals, families, carers, groups and communities

Key Role 4: Manage risk to individuals, families, carers, groups, communities, self and colleagues

Unit 13: Assess, minimise and manage risk to self and colleagues

Key Role 5: Manage and be accountable, with supervision and support, for your own social work practice within your organisation

Unit 14 Manage and be accountable for your own work

CHAPTER

3 Working with Children

Summary of Specialist Communication Skills

- Avoidance of why and how questions
- Giving choice
- Child-centred contract
- Containing a child's feelings by providing and being a 'safe place' in which feelings can be explored
- Tuning-in to experience the child's world
- Identify, validate and use the child's medium of communication
- Using a storyline
- Observing
- Showing respect (using sub-skills of 'Giving choice' and 'Taking time')
- Establishing a vocabulary of feelings
- Challenging in a comfortable/non-threatening manner
- Using silences
- The use of the third object

Policy and background literature

There are clear policy requirements relevant to social workers' communication with children and young people. Social workers should give due consideration to 'the wishes and feelings' of children and ensure their perspectives are central to service planning and delivery (Section 53, The Children Act 2004). Policy and practice guidance requires social workers to safeguard and promote the welfare of children by identifying how their development is influenced by the environment in which they are parented, including an assessment of their immediate safety (DoH, 2000a; 2006a). Moreover, they have to identify how they can promote this development to meet government-specified outcomes for children in the UK as published in the Green Paper *Every Child Matters* (DfES, 2003), and given effect in The Children Act (2004). Thus policy exhorts social workers to communicate effectively with children and young people, in order to promote human rights to participation but also to ensure services are more effective by being responsive to the expressed developmental needs, including the immediate safety, of the service user. Social workers should look for 'developmental competence' in determining whether a child can make decisions about his or her own welfare (Doyle and Kennedy, 2009). Case law set a precedent with the case of *Gillick* v. *West Norfolk and Wisbech Area Health Authority and Department of Health and Social Security* [1985] 3 All ER 402. The House of Lords determined that a child under 16 years old could give consent to treatment as long as they had sufficient understanding. Arguably, though, while a child might not be deemed developmentally competent enough to have his or her wishes taken into account, any child should be encouraged to express their feelings on a matter to a social worker.

However, social workers have been criticised repeatedly for the level and quality of their communication with children and young people. Child death inquiry reports, particularly the Jasmine Beckford, Cleveland, Victoria Climbie and Peter Connolly tragedies, continually condemn social workers for their failure to communicate and observe the development of children at risk of abuse (Blom Cooper, 1985; Butler-Sloss, 1988; Laming, 2003, 2009). Young people frequently report that their social workers need to listen more adequately to them (DoH, 2000a). Arguably, these communication obstacles reflect normative assumptions concerning the relationship between children and adults in Western society. In Chapter 2 I discussed how a power differential between children and adults exists in society, with children having the frequent experience of being overpowered – whether through being told to be silent or having their views devalued, or, as too often reported, being physically restrained or beaten by parents or carers (Kroll, 1995).

The literature cites further reasons for the communication barriers, such as social workers feeling a lack of confidence and expertise, or a less conscious fear that the work might evoke strong feelings from the social worker's own childhood experiences that they wish to avoid (Daniel, 2007). Rustin (2005), for example, analysed how professionals would not see what was happening to privately fostered Victoria Climbie because they erected various psychological defences to prevent personally witnessing and experiencing acute mental pain. This may have contributed to a lack of child protection focus and a family support approach with the family. The professionals in this situation questioned whether an explanation for Victoria's deferential behaviour and marks on her skin had a cultural base by virtue of Victoria being an African child (see Garrett (2006) for a critical analysis). However, this apart, literature highlights how social workers working with people from different ethnic groups can become anxious to 'get it right' (Laird, 2008). A lack of cultural knowledge can cause normative assumptions and dominant stereotypes about the cultural practices of people from different ethnic groups to be applied. Specialist social work communication in this practice setting must demonstrate sensitivity to cultural differences and variations in patterns and styles of communication. Care must be taken not to assume homogeneity in the values and practices of any family, faith, community or ethnic group, and extreme versions of cultural relativism must be avoided.

Ironically, while the modernising policy agenda has sought to improve standards of social work practice, the impact on practice of the regulatory processes contained within it provides one possible explanation for these perceived failures in effective communication. Stepney (2006) highlights how social work practice with children and families has become so overtaken by the processes and procedures involved in demonstrating achievement of prescribed quantified outcomes that the dominant objective of intervention is 'policing'. Indeed, Doyle and Kennedy (2009: 50) describe social workers as 'having to navigate their way through a labyrinth of new rules and procedures whilst meeting deadlines and targets in new regulatory landscapes to achieve organizational performance indicators'. The context is of ever-increasing scrutiny of individual safeguarding practice, with social workers fearing their practice being reframed as 'inadequate', both by the bureaucratic performance indicators, but also by the media at having individually 'failed' a child. Consequently, they describe frustration at spending too much time in front of the computer and too little time with service users. It takes an inordinate amount of time to work through the restrictive eligibility criteria that gate-keep the limited resources available to help children and families (Doyle and Kennedy, 2009). Moreover, in the wake of the Peter Connolly case, not only has the number of child protection referrals increased but also the number of applications for care orders resulting in complex court work. This places additional strain on workers within teams that are frequently understaffed and reliant on agency workers (Pile, 2009; Unison, 2009). These systemic barriers are influencing the effectiveness of the communication strategies of social workers.

Another possible explanation for the perceived failures in effective communication lies in the existing knowledge base about social work communication skills with children and young people being complex and limited. Indeed, Luckock *et al.*'s (2006) knowledge review of empirical studies relating to communication skills with children and young people in social work found that the concept of 'communication with children' was contested across studies with no coherent body of research. Certainly, a tension seems to exist in the literature over the purposes of social work communication with children in terms of whether it is has a solely participative function or an additional therapeutic purpose. The latter is considered to emanate from notions of 'childhood' and the history of a dominance of psychoanalytic and psychodynamic approaches to working directly with children. Key concepts include a need for the social worker to:

- experience the child's world on an emotional level;
- seek to contain a child's feelings by providing and being a 'safe place' in which feelings can be explored;
- help a child understand their feelings and link these to past and present experiences;
- identify and validate the child's medium of communication and use that medium to communicate with them (for example, using symbols or play); and
- recognise the psychological effects of adversity on the child's communication strategies.

Other concepts to inform a specialist communication strategy with children and young people are apparent in the approaches already used by social work educators and social workers themselves within their practice. However, again, there is complexity and disagreement among the different approaches (Luckock *et al.*, 2006). Social work educators and practitioners make distinctions between the need for students and practitioners to:

- develop their personal capacity to communicate effectively in a more general sense;
- to do so in a way that demonstrates ethical commitment to rights of participation and 'child-centredness'; and
- to perform more micro-skills, underpinned by knowledge of child development theories which echo the psychodynamic approach:
  - keeping the child informed;
  - child-centred communication (play, symbolic, creative, expressive techniques, going at the child's pace);
  - listening to direct and indirect communication;
  - interviewing;
  - using tools such as 'ecomaps', rating scales, assessment schedules and life-story books.

Communicating with children as a response to receiving communication concerning the safety or distress of that child presents further communication issues. These relate to the need for the social worker to capture the information a child is providing, give support for any distress, but not to do so in a way that might frustrate a joint social work–police enquiry by affecting the accuracy or completeness of that evidence (Jones, 2003; Crown Prosecution Service, 2007; DoH, 2006a). Even the earliest discussions with children must uphold these principles for 'accuracy' and 'completeness' while 'minimising distress'. Within the communication the social worker must avoid the use of leading or suggestive questions (DoH, 2006a). As Jones (2003: 1–2) states:

'Accuracy is key, for without it effective decisions cannot be made and, equally, inaccurate accounts can lead to children remaining unsafe, or to the possibility of wrongful actions being taken that affect children and adults.'

The issue of whether a child has been made safe in their caregiving environment has an influence on whether that child feels able or safe enough to communicate the distress and/or fear they are feeling. Drawing again on the example of Victoria Climbie (Laming, 2003), it could be argued that a reason why she did not communicate her distressing home situation to the social worker and police officers in hospital was because she had not been made to feel safe. The chapter on 'Tracey' in Madge Bray's *Poppies in the Rubbish Heap* presents a wonderful example of responding to a child's need to be safe prior to communication about abuse.

Service user groups have identified particular communication skills needed for work with children and young people with disabilities. The need for social workers to be proactive in developing 'communication enhancing environments' for children who have or need augmentative and alternative communication has been promoted by the literature and organisations such as Scope (Potter and Whittaker, 2001; Scope, 2007). Triangle's 'Howitis' website describes some useful tools and images for communicating about feelings, rights and safety, personal care and sexuality (www.howitis.org.uk). Disabled children are particularly vulnerable in being more susceptible to abuse than their non-disabled peers, and historically many of the communication systems that disabled people use do not have a wide range of words, signs or symbols to describe feelings, parts of the body (such as genitalia) or acts of maltreatment (Wilson *et al.*, 2008).

Practice application

In operating these concepts from the background literature, and adding further concepts and discussion from the research study, it becomes evident that the preparatory stage for communicating with a child is absolutely critical if a social worker is to 'experience the child's world on an emotional level' and achieve a 'communication enhancing environment'. Within this area of specialist practice, when operating the basic communication skill of 'tuning-in' (discussed in Chapter 2) the social worker needs to engage with concepts from child development theory, as well as the psychoanalytic and psychodynamic literature. Kroll (1995) would agree, stating that such theoretical perspectives provide windows through which to glimpse the experiential world of a child and as such constitute the first stage of a meaningful 'child-centred' communication with them. I have called this early specialist communication skill 'tuning-in to experience the child's world'.

Child development theory helps social workers to understand the impact of physical and psychological adversity on a child in terms of socio-emotional and cognitive development. The specification of developmental milestones at different ages and stages of development provide important indicators from which to compare children's progress across a number of developmental domains. Social work literature and practice has paid particular attention to research about how the interactional quality of early relationship experiences affect psychological health and social functioning as well as having a biological impact on the rapidly developing brain (Zeanah *et al.*, 1997; Armstrong *et al.*, 2000; Schore, 2001). Modern attachment theorists have explored the importance of the parent–child attachment relationship in the way the mind processes interpersonal information to use as a psychosocial template for future relationships (Howe, 2005). Researchers have linked difficult early attachment relationships to children showing aggressive and disruptive behaviour, and adolescents who have anxiety disorders and/or impaired operational skills and self-regulation (Sroufe, 1983, Speltz *et al.,* 1990; Lyons-Ruth *et al.,* 1993; Jacobson *et al.,* 1994; Shaw *et al.*, 1996; Warren *et al.,* 1997). Neglected children show social and emotional difficulties as well as differences in brain size and structure (Hildyard and Wolfe, 2002; Perry, 2002).

Children bring these often insecure relationship templates to their relationships, and indeed communication, with social workers (Howe, 2005). Children with an insecure-ambivalent attachment relationship model will feel only conditionally worthwhile, uncertain of whether they will be understood and valued and therefore constantly seek to test out the emotional and physical availability of the social worker. Alternatively, they might provide responses that 'seek to please' as opposed to risking any indication of their true feelings. Children with an insecure-avoidant relationship model, however, bring to the communication their experience of having their developmental needs consistently ignored by their carers. They are mistrustful of the potential of the social worker to be helpful, preferring to rely on their own coping strategies which generally involves remaining emotionally detached to avoid inevitable rejection. Their self-esteem is often very low – feeling unlovable and without worth. A smaller proportion of children that social workers meet have internal relationship models that are disorganised. These children are in a heightened state of fear and anxiety at all times, having repeatedly experienced pain and violence from their carers instead of protection and care. As their attachment system is set on 'red alert', they are unlikely to have been able to progress on other development pathways, exhibiting severe delay both cognitively and socially.

Our practice example (3.1) shows Danni, a 12-year-old white British girl, being visited for the first time by her social worker since the social worker moved her from her family home to a foster placement. In 'tuning-in to experience the child's world', the social worker could hypothesise from her family history that Danni is likely to have developed an insecure-avoidant attachment relationship pattern and anticipate her communicating reluctance to explore her difficulties because of her mistrust of adults who are supposed to care for her. Insecure attachment relationship patterns present a developmental risk to children. Frequently they find themselves in uncertain, risky situations which cause them anxiety, such as experienced by Danni in her move to a new family, but they are unable to relate to people in a way that will reduce their anxiety. Indeed, we might hypothesise that Danni's recent behaviour in using alcohol and engaging in criminal behaviour indicates her catastrophic attempts to find a way to dissolve her anxious emotions.

PRACTICE EXAMPLE 3.1

Danni

Preparatory stage

Danni, a 12-year-old white British girl, is being visited by her social worker for the first time since he had moved her from her family home to a foster placement. Earlier that day, when the social worker telephoned Danni to confirm the appointment Danni said she did not want to stay in the foster placement.

Danni's mother has been using drugs for most of Danni's life, with Danni frequently left to care for herself. A year ago, Danni's mother resumed her relationship with Danni's father, who initially brought a stabilising influence to the family but latterly lapsed into illicit drug use. Both parents have health problems, exacerbated by the drug use, which affects their ability to work. Since starting at secondary school, Danni's school attendance has declined and recently there have been reports from neighbours and the police that she has been seen drunk and wandering the streets. Danni has never experienced a trusting, emotionally warm relationship. She has few friends among her peer group. Danni's foster placement is with Fred and Jan, a Korean couple in their mid-thirties. They have two younger children.

Yesterday, the police returned Danni to the foster carer saying that she and some friends had thrown a brick through the window of the home of an elderly woman. No charges had been brought. The social worker, Paul, is unaware of this latest incident. Paul is a 35 year old white Cornish man who has previously lived in the same part of the City as Danni and her carers.

In drawing on the basic communication skills described in Chapter 2, the social worker will need to achieve and communicate empathy for this anxiety in order to enable Danni to feel understood, and in control of her emotional and social self (Howe, 1998; Agass, 2002; Ruch, 2005b). Bion's (1962) concept of 'containment' is frequently used to describe this process, which Agass (2002: 127) summarises as

> not simply putting up with or absorbing whatever unpleasant or uncomfortable feelings the client stirs up in us. It is a much more active process of struggling to 'contain', understand and work through our own emotional responses in the hope that this will enable our clients to do the same for themselves.

It is an important communicative medium for work with children because the effect of physical and psychological adversity on their socio-emotional and cognitive development may mean that they are unable to communicate their feelings meaningfully in any other way. It is crucial for the social worker to communicate to Danni that he or she can do this containing work. To this end, I have labelled the specialist communication skill as 'containing a child's feelings by providing and being a "safe place" in which feelings can be explored'.

However, the social work will only be successful in its execution if the social worker prepares for this emotionally charged situation. As discussed in Chapter 2, an important stage of 'tuning-in' is to examine 'self'. This requires the social worker to reflect on their own childhood experiences. Questions should be brought to mind such as 'Who, where or what did I experience as a "safe place" in which to explore my most troubled, anxious experiences?' Identifying and recalling that feeling will help the social worker to absorb some of the difficult feelings that a child is likely to transfer. Similarly, the social worker will be more able to transfer the message to the child that they are 'a safe place' and are able to contain difficult feelings. Clearly, some people will find that reflection on loss and childhood a very painful process. However, it is better that this occurs during the preparation period and not during the meeting, when such feelings may emerge as counter-transference and as such be inappropriate and unhelpful to the child (see Chapter 2 for more discussion on transference and counter-transference). As Wilson *et al.* (2008: 317) state:

> draw honestly on your own personal experiences of loss and be scrupulous in reflecting on your own feelings and responses – for example, offering quick reassurance or breaking a silence may be because your own experiences/feelings make you uncomfortable, helpless, uncertain, or fearful of hearing painful emotions expressed.

Another crucial specialist communication skill to be carried out in preparation for meeting with the service user is to 'identify, validate and use the child's medium of communication'. It is important that social workers do not view speech and language as the only or preferred mode of communication. Such an attitude would undervalue and fail to recognise the variety of ways in which children make their wishes and feelings known, particularly disabled children (Morris, 2002; Marchant and Page, 2003). Child development theory indicates that children of different ages and stages of development use different media as their dominant form of communication (Piaget, 1983). Generally, children under 8 years old communicate through play or having a story read to them. Children between 8 and 12 years old will respond well to symbolic, creative, expressive techniques delivered at the child's pace. Young people in their teenage years experience adults communicating with them verbally or through text-based media such email or letters.

Some young people will be sensitive to any communication that seems overly childish or patronising. However, frequently, children and young people in contact with social workers have experienced development delay across many dimensions of their development, including their cognitive and intellectual abilities. Talking alone is unlikely to be sufficient to ensure meaningful communication with many of these children and young people. Rather, use needs to be made of tools that use visual, symbolic and culturally relevant mediums of communication alongside the dialogue, such as drawing or craft-based activities, writing poetry, using computer-based games and questionnaires or dramatic techniques such as role-play. The medium of clay, for example, has been found to be useful to adolescents unveiling harrowing experiences of sexual abuse (Wilson and Ryan, 2001). The social worker must prepare suitable materials when engaging in these communication methods according to what they know about the child and young person's cognitive ability, talents and interests, while ensuring that the methods are age-appropriate. However, I should note that some older children and young people may not always see communication aimed at younger children necessarily as patronising or inappropriate. If they are disclosing abuse as a younger child they may need to communicate at the level of the age they were when they were abused. They may need to regress and so a variety and/or a range of methods are needed. An example related by a social worker of their own practice is that they ensure soft toys are available in the room during ABE interviews. Older young people often pick them up and cuddle them as they speak about abuse.

Returning to our discussion, the social worker might be aware of particular issues from the child's situation for which the child or young person does not have the cognitive ability to completely comprehend, but which need explaining at their level of understanding. For example, events could have happened to a child at a younger age, of which they had little understanding, but which at an older age could be more fully explained and understood. Indeed, the modern attachment literature places importance on developing the 'reflective function' of young people as a significant protective factor for their development (Howe *et al.*, 1999; Howe, 2005). This refers to the way a person can alter his or her insecure internal relationship model of relationships given the opportunity to reflect on and understand how past relationships affect expectations of current relationships and the view of 'self'. Such progression towards a secure internal model of relationships, in which a child feels loved and valued through consistent responses to developmental need, is a major protective factor for their ongoing development. The issue for the social worker, at this preparatory stage, is to plan how they might communicate the issues from the children's past in a way that is appropriate to their age and stage of cognitive and social development, and uses a medium of communication that is familiar to the child. A specialist communication skill, identified by the British Agencies for Adoption and Fostering (BAAF) (1984, 1986) to achieve this purpose is that of 'using a storyline'. In the same way that a scriptwriter for a soap opera uses a storyline to explore how a particular issue manifests itself and impacts on an individual, friends and family, so the social worker uses a form of words, or even an analogy, to explain the impact of past issues to the child or young person.

By way of illustration, our practice example (3.1) indicates that the social worker could usefully prepare to explore how Danni's alcohol use is dangerous to her health and safety, and how it might be related to her feelings about present and past issues. Both of Danni's parents have health problems, exacerbated by drug use, which affects their ability to work and care for her. She may be confused and rejected by their physical and psychological unavailability to her. Her self-esteem may be very low, and she is feeling unloved and without worth. The social worker could prepare to 'use a storyline' with a suitable form of words or analogy about how Danni might be using the alcohol to dull these feelings.

At a first meeting with a child or young person, the social worker must employ the four parts of the basic communication skill listed in Chapter 2 of 'achieving a shared purpose' namely, 'being clear on role'; 'being clear on purpose'; 'reaching for feedback; and 'showing empathy'. The background literature highlighted how the authority that the social worker brings, both through his or her legislative role, and thestatus of being an adult, presents a power differential that can influence dramatically communication with a child or young person. Consequently, the social worker must ensure that he or she 'shows empathy' towards the child's feelings of ambivalence and frustration about being 'unheard' or 'disempowered' by adults generally, and apprehension at speaking to a social worker because of their legal role. Indeed, it is unfortunate, but many children are warned by parents to 'behave or you'll go into care'. Moreover, some children who have been emotionally, physically or sexually maltreated have often been threatened to keep the maltreatment a secret. This means that the social worker must use specialist communication skills to communicate clarity about their role.

First, the social worker must take into account the child's capacity to understand, and 'use the child's medium of communication', to tell the child in an honest and direct way that he or she is with a social worker. The parameters of the role should be explained, such as the duty to ensure that someone is safe from harm, and the limitations to ensuring confidentiality. Wilson *et al.* (2008: 102) describe a social worker, Sheila, who introduces her work with a new child by sharing her handmade booklet 'All About Me'. The booklet contains hand-drawn pictures about herself and her role, and she uses these to talk about how she will work with the child.

The skill of 'achieving a shared purpose' also involves 'being clear on purpose' and 'reaching for feedback' about whether the social worker and service user can work together on a shared agenda. In Chapter 2, we discussed how this involves the social worker stating the nature of his or her agenda using straightforward, non-jargon language that is developmentally appropriate to the service user. Greater success is achieved if a statement is prepared in advance. The specialist communication skill of 'using a storyline', mentioned earlier and illustrated by Sheila's use of her book 'All About Me', is helpful for communicating with children and young people. Another illustration is the use of the 'loving and caring liquid' visual analogy to show children how, having once been filled with loving and caring feelings (a cup filled with water), these can be lost ('water is spilt') or 'stirred up' and confused ('cup is shaken'), or guarded ('cup is sealed') until a time when the child will safe and be able to give and receive more loving and caring feelings ('water is poured in and out'). The social worker could describe their purpose as helping the child become less guarded ('break the seal') and finding a new family to give loving and caring feelings ('pour water from additional cups') (Wilson *et al.*, 2008).

This skill of 'using a storyline' is as useful for helping older children and teenagers to understand the purpose of the work as it is for younger children. Care must be taken to ensure that the language and analogies used are age-appropriate and sufficiently contemporary that the social worker does not appear completely out of touch with the everyday interests of young people. However, there is a corresponding danger in this of the social worker trying to be a teenager, which may cause a child's or young person's perception of the boundaries between adult and child to become blurred. A balance must be drawn. An example from the research study is of a social worker using a football team analogy to encourage Ravi, a 15-year-old avid Manchester United fan, to discuss how he could work with the social worker to plan changes in his education and relationships with his extended family. She asked him to think about his life as if it were an important European Cup football game. She asked him to name who from his social network he would want in his team as 'key players'. She explained what her role would be in the team, what his role would be, and the key positions and tactics available to all his key players. She detailed what one of her goals would be and asked what other goals might look like. To prepare for 'using this storyline' the social worker had researched the different tactics and rules of football, as well as ensuring that she knew the names and key skills of all the current Manchester United footballers. As they talked, they sketched out his ideas on a sheet of paper in order to meet Ravi's needs for a more visual and symbolic medium of communication. This sketch provided a document of agreed work.

This illustration shows how the social worker communicated 'respect' to the young person. First, she operated the specialist communication skill 'identify, validate and use the child's medium of communication' in order to communicate in a way that was appropriate to Ravi's age and stage of cognitive and social development, and which was meaningful to him. Second, she was careful to ensure that she conveyed warmth and interest in Ravi's answers, seeking to demonstrate acceptance of his perspectives. Indeed, the background literature reminds us that young people have the right, through their developmental competence, to have their views respected and accounted for in making decisions. Our practice example (3.2) similarly shows the social worker 'communicating respect' to Danni.

PRACTICE EXAMPLE 3.2

Danni

Beginnings

Social worker knocks at door of foster carer's home. Danni opens the door.

Danni: Yeah?

SW: Hello Danni. It's Paul. Can I come in, mate?

Danni: Yeah...

SW: Is it all right if I sit down?

Danni: Mmm...

SW: Oh, cool. I've come to see how you're getting on. How's things going, mate?

Danni: All right.

She looks down, pulls her baseball cap down over her face, curls her shoulders down almost into her lap.

▶

►

SW: So, tell me how things are, Danni.

Danni: All right

SW: So what sort of things are you not happy with?

Danni: Dunno.

SW: I don't want you to be worried about talking to me. See what I want to do – we're in this situation, you're in this foster placement and don't want to be here. What I want to do, and with your help, is to try and make it easy and as good as it can be for you – and I need to listen to you – but if you're not talking, I can't listen.

Social worker leans forward, opens his hands, palms up. Danni watches from under her cap.

SW: What would be the main… give me the main thing that's cheesing you off.

Danni: It's boring. (*Sits up, cap still over eyes*)

SW: OK. In terms of… it's boring because of what?

Danni: School's boring, here's boring.

SW: OK.

Danni: It's just boring.

SW: Boring, tell me more…

Danni: Umm… I just don't like it here. (*Looks at social worker from under cap for the first time*)

In the dialogue, the social worker shows appreciation of the fact that he is entering Danni's home, and that Danni has given up her time to meet him. He asks politely for permission to enter and if he can be seated. The social worker goes on to communicate acceptance of Danni's communication, even though she is indicating feelings of ambivalence and mistrust about the social worker's presence and the purpose of the work. An important aspect of this acceptance is that he calmly lets her 'take time'. He does not rush into asking a series of questions, but positively affirms and immediately acknowledges Danni's answers with a simple 'OK', as well as using paraphrasing to demonstrate 'reflective listening'. He then adapts his non-verbal communication to indicate that he would like Danni to expand on her answers ('social worker leans forward, opens his hands, palms up') and 'uses silences'. He emphasises further how he is willing to 'take time' as the dialogue proceeds in the subsequent practice example (3.3), by initiating an activity together (lunch at the cafe), and later highlights the point further by stating 'I want to spend as much time as I can with you today.'

PRACTICE EXAMPLE 3.3

Danni

Work phase

SW: Dan, anywhere you want to go? I don't know this area. Do you know anywhere we can go for a drive?

Danni: Not really.

SW: OK, let's go. How about we go to the greasy spoon café down the road? It will probably be quiet in there just now. Is that OK with you? It's better talking over a cup of tea and a bacon sandwich!

Danni: All right. (*Smiles and stands up*)

They drive to the café, order food at the counter and sit down in a quiet corner.

SW: Dan, you say that everything's boring. What's the placement like, then?

Danni: (*Shrugs*) It's all right.

SW: Is it? Is that boring as well?

Danni: S'all right.

SW: So what are Fred and Jan like?

Danni: He's all right.

SW: Fred? You see I don't know the guy, you know, he strikes me as nice enough. Is he...?

Danni: (*Interrupts in irritated tone of voice*) Bloke doesn't really want me there. Prefers *his* kids.

SW: I'm sorry to hear that. (*Pause*) Why do you say that, Danni?

►

►

Danni: (*Shrugs*) Don't know.

SW: Dan, listen mate. I want to spend as much time as I can with you today, but I need to go and see your foster parents as well. Now you're telling me that there are some things that you're not happy with – now what I'd like to do is talk to your foster parents about that, but I need to get your ideas on this. Do you understand?

Danni: Yeah.

SW: Yes? Tell me some of those things. I know you've been saying that some of the things are boring, and you've also said that you feel left out in favour of his children, but you need to give me a little bit more, because if we're going to work together on this, I need to know exactly, what and how you feel. Do you understand what I'm getting at? (*Danni nods slightly*) OK, so, if you are OK with this, can you tell me a little bit more?

Danni: I'm just a troubled kid; that's it.

Silence from both of them.

SW: You've had a hard life, but you're not a troubled kid. Your future's your own here, you can turn it which way you want, yeah? I can't do it for you and I'm not going to do it for you, but what we can do is... I could help you do it for yourself, yeah? Your life hasn't ended – you've got every way you can go at the moment, and you've got to do something for yourself.

Silence from both of them.

Danni: I want to go back with my mum and dad.

SW: OK. You know the reasons that you're with a foster carer at the moment, do you?

Danni: Yeah, but it was all right though. There I could do just what I want to do. Here, it's just... he's nagging me all the time. If one of his kids does something, it's all right, but if I do something, it's always my fault.

SW: And what needs to happen for you to go back and live with your mum and dad? It's not all down to you, is it? It's down to your mum and dad as well, yeah? And what we need to do is work to get you back home, yeah? It doesn't have to be perfect for you at home, but it's got to be better and safer than it is now. What we've got to do is make the foster care the best it can be for you, and then we can help, work to get you back home with mum and dad.

Undertaking an activity together achieves more than communicating willingness to 'take time'. Some children and young people need to be engaged in a joint activity in order to feel comfortable enough to communicate with adults. There is less need for eye contact, less pressure to talk, and the opportunity for using toys or other props or analogies to express feelings in a more indirect manner, and at the child's own pace, which may feel more comfortable for the child. Wilson *et al.* (2008) call this specialist communication strategy 'the use of the third object'.

Another aspect of 'communicating respect' is 'giving choice' to the young person. This requires explaining the rationale for the choice and the consequences that follow. In other words, it should be an 'informed choice', to which the young person can give 'informed consent'. Our practice example (3.3) illustrates the social worker giving Danni the choice to be involved in the work.

SW: Dan, listen mate. I want to spend as much time as I can with you today, but I need to go and see your foster parents as well. Now you're telling me that there are some things that you're not happy with – now what I'd like to do is talk to your foster parents about that, but I need to get your ideas on this. Do you understand?

Danni: Yeah.

SW: Yes? Tell me some of those things. I know you've been saying that some of the things are boring, and you've also said that you feel left out in favour of his children, but you need to give me a little bit more, because if we're going to work together on this, I need to know exactly, what and how you feel. Do you understand what I'm getting at? (*Danni nods slightly*) OK, so, if you are OK with this, can you tell me a little bit more?'

This dialogue communicates that the social worker genuinely wants to hear and understand Danni's point of view. He explains the benefit to Danni of her engaging in the work, and he makes clear what needs to happen – the boundaries or parameters – for the work to continue. If this verbal response was combined with specified non-verbal behaviours for helping someone to manage their angry feelings (Koprowska, 2005) then the worker would have challenged Danni successfully to work with him. I refer to this specialist communication skill as 'challenging in a comfortable or non-threatening manner'. Koprowska (2005: 149) recommends that social workers include the following non-verbal behaviours in managing aggressive situations and containing angry feelings:

- Ensure you are standing or seated at a slight angle and not 'square on', but at least a one-and-a-half arm distance away

- Look at the person's face, making frequent but not continuous eye-contact
- Show an interested and relaxed facial expression, but do not smile
- Keep your arms relaxed, away from your hair, face or around your body (as this can be interpreted as being impatient, anxious, or seductive)
- Keep your hands open and in view with palms up to indicate negotiation
- Keep the tone of your voice of low-register and calm.

Indeed, throughout the meeting the social worker must be emotionally attuned to the feelings that the immediate relationship with the child or young person will be arousing, demonstrating the specialist communication skill mentioned earlier: 'containing a child's feelings by providing and being a "safe place" in which feelings can be explored'. The combined skills of 'reflective listening' to narrative, tone of voice and attitude, and 'observing' non-verbal behaviour through gesture and body position are critical in making sense of these feelings (see Chapter 2 for more discussion). Signs of incongruence between the verbal and non-verbal behaviours show the social worker that the child may not be comfortable with the shared agenda, and is demonstrating superficial compliance and passive involvement. The issues being uncovered may be too painful or difficult for the child to discuss. The child might be afraid to disclose their experiences of maltreatment for fear of repercussions.

In this chapter, therefore, I am using the skill 'observing' to denote a specialist communication strategy. This extends its usual use as either an invaluable source of learning (Wilson *et al.,* 2008; Le Riche and Tanner, 1998), or one of the essential methods of collecting information for social work assessment of children's developmental needs (Daniel, 2007). In the case of the former, observation as a learning experience allows the social worker to stand back from intervening and interpreting behaviour ('doing') to watch and feel the experience and so become more aware of feelings that belong to the child and to 'self' ('being'). The 'art of being' and not 'doing' is considered a central process in achieving emotional engagement with a child (Kroll, 1995). In the case of the latter, observation as a method provides information about how a child functions within their social and physical world. This behaviour is appraised against stages of healthy development from child development theories. *'Observing' a*s a communication skill requires the worker to take steps to prevent becoming immersed in the content of the narrative, but at the same time adopt some objective distance to watch and feel the interaction taking place. The participants in the research study underpinning this book found that this objective distancing was achieved more easily by the social worker slowing the flow of the conversation and having in mind questions such as 'What is really going on in the communication here?', 'What is the non-verbal communication telling me about this?', 'Does what I am feeling belong to me or the child?' and 'What does this tell me about whether there is an obstacle to this communication?'

Practice example 3.2 shows the social worker using 'observing' to make sense of Danni's blunt, one-word answers ('yeah', 'alright', 'dunno', 'boring') and body language ('She looks down, pulls her baseball cap down over her face, curls her shoulders down almost into her lap'). The social worker identifies how Danni seems to be communicating feelings of ambivalence and mistrust about the social worker's presence and the purpose of the work. There is an obstacle in communication relating to the authority role, which would be resolved by the social worker 'showing empathy' for these feelings and being more 'clear on purpose'. He responds by making his body language more open and relaxed to demonstrate more warmth and receptiveness to feelings and views. He does this with his hands as he knows this is the only area that Danni can see from under her cap ('Social worker leans forward, opens his hands, palms up'). As he does this he uses the skill of 'putting feelings into words' to empathise with Danni's feelings, followed by being 'clear on purpose':

> I don't want you to be worried about talking to me. See what I want to do – we're in this situation, you're in this foster placement and don't want to be here. What I want to do, and with your help, is to try and make it easy and as good as it can be for you – and I need to listen to you – but if you're not talking, I can't listen....
>
> What would be the main...give me the main thing that's cheesing you off.

While Danni continues to respond with limited verbal narrative, her body language indicates to the social worker that she is more engaged. Immediately, we see that she 'sits up, cap still over eyes', and then a little later at the end of practice example 3.2, she 'looks at social worker from under her cap for the first time'.

Another reason for Danni's limited verbal responses is that she may only know a small number of expressions to explain her thoughts and feelings. One of the main issues that arose from the research underpinning this book was that social workers found it difficult to help some children and young people to express feelings because they had a limited vocabulary of different feelings. We know from the literature that many children in contact with social workers are frequently unused to talking about feelings, particularly children who have suffered physical and emotional neglect. As children develop, they need to have someone explain the link between their senses and their feelings, and to have those feelings labelled. Often, neglected children have not had this experience. They could be confused about feelings, and indeed may use a different word to explain a feeling to the one used by the social worker. As stated earlier, disabled children are particularly vulnerable in this respect. Thus, in order to communicate with any child about feelings and experiences, the social worker needs to 'establish a shared vocabulary of feelings'. Ideally this specialist communication strategy should occur as early in the working relationship as possible. The social worker should identify a range of feelings appropriate to the child's age and stage of cognitive and social development, and discuss what those feelings mean to the child. This might range from a simple identification of 'happy' and 'sad' feelings, perhaps using two paper plates with the two expressions drawn on, to a list or set of pictures of a hundred or more abstract feelings, such as 'overwhelmed', 'frustrated', 'excited' or 'delighted'. As before, the social worker needs to use the skill 'identify, validate and use the child's medium of communication' in discussing the different feelings with child or young person.

The background literature highlights that care should be taken in the way such exploration of feelings and gathering of facts takes place. Questions should be avoided where children do not have the cognitive ability to process and answer them. These questions tend to start with 'why' and 'how' as opposed to the easier, more factually based questions of 'what', 'where' and 'when' (Jones, 2003). Our practice example (3.3) illustrates the point well, when Danni struggles to answer the social worker's question about her relationship with one of her foster carers.

Danni: Bloke doesn't really want me there. Prefers *his* kids.

SW: I'm sorry to hear that. (*Pause*) Why do you say that, Danni?

Danni: (*Shrugs*) Don't know.

The example shows that she finds it difficult to explain why she is finding it hard to get along with her carer. Conceptually, it is a higher-order term, and too difficult for her to grasp or find the words to explain. It would have been better for the social worker to seek clarification on her point by asking her to give examples of situations in which the issue has manifested itself through using questions beginning with 'what', 'where' and 'when'. As stated earlier, it is important that these questions are not 'leading', to ensure accuracy in information gathering. Leading questions indicate to the service user the answer that the social worker is expecting to hear. The service user may feel less inclined to give an authentic answer, but instead offers the expected response (Koprowska, 2005). Particular care must be taken to avoid this in communication with children as the power differential between children and adults means that children are even more inclined to give the answer they think the speaker wants.

Finally, in Chapter 2 I described how basic good communication requires careful attention to endings. It is of particular importance in work with children and young people as they need to be sensitive to a child's understanding and feelings about separation and transition. Feelings about past separations might come to the fore and the child might seek to avoid facing those feelings. As such, it is important to prepare the child in advance for the ending of the working relationship. The child might need more than verbal communication both of the changes and achievements realised over the time period, as well as their value as a person within that relationship. A card or other token will help to convey this message.

This chapter has described and discussed the application of specialist social work communication skills that presume the capacity of children to express their thoughts and feelings on central matters that affect their developmental well-being. The onus is on the social worker to find the medium of communication that facilitates this expression. However, its success rests on the ability of the social worker to attend to the relationship dynamics in the working relationship, particularly those arising from the social worker's own experience of childhood relationships, and those that relate to the social worker's authority role.

Professional Standards

This chapter will help you to meet the following National Occupational Standards:

Key Role 1: Prepare for, and work with individuals, families, carers, groups and communities to assess their needs and circumstances

Unit 1	Prepare for social work contact and involvement
Unit 2	Work with individuals, families, carers, groups and communities to help them make informed decisions
Unit 3	Assess needs and options to recommend a course of action

Key Role 2: Plan, carry out, review and evaluate social work practice with individuals, families, carers, groups, communities and other professionals

Unit 4	Respond to crisis situations
Unit 5	Interact with individuals, families, carers, groups and communities to achieve change and development and to improve life opportunities
Unit 6	Prepare, produce, implement and evaluate plans with individuals, families, carers, groups, communities and professional colleagues
Unit 9	Address behaviour which presents a risk to individuals, families, carers, groups and communities

Key Role 3: Support individuals to represent their needs, views and circumstances. Advocate with and on behalf of people

Unit 10	Advocate with, and on behalf of, individuals, families, carers, groups and communities
Unit 11	Prepare for, and participate in decision-making forums

Key Role 4: Manage risk to individuals, families, carers, groups, communities, self and colleagues

Unit 13	Assess, minimise and manage risk to self and colleagues

Key Role 5: Manage and be accountable, with supervision and support, for your own social work practice within your organisation

Unit 14	Manage and be accountable for your own work

Key Role 6: Demonstrate professional competence in social work practice

Unit 18	Research, analyse, evaluate and use current knowledge of best social work practice
Unit 19	Work within agreed standards of social work practice and ensure own professional development
Unit 20	Manage complex ethical issues, dilemmas and conflicts
Unit 21	Contribute to the promotion of best social work practice

CHAPTER

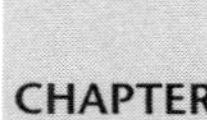

Working with Young People with Offending Behaviour

Summary of Specialist Communication Skills

- Developing early rapport
- Defending the rights of the service user
- Communicating consequences in a non-threatening manner
- Listening for clues
- Focused questioning
- Assessing for truthfulness
- Assessing for remorse and willingness to reform
- The avoidance of 'why' and 'how' questions
- Expressing empathy and understanding without necessarily signifying agreement
- Giving choice
- Reflective listening

Policy and background literature

The measures introduced by the Crime and Disorder Act (1998) require that social workers work alongside representatives from the police, probation, health and education within local multi-agency Youth Offending Teams (YOTs). The statutory aim of this work is the targeted prevention of offending and re-offending by children and young people (Audit Commission, 2004). Literature highlights particular communication issues relevant to this setting in addition to those covered within the previous chapter on 'Working with Children'.

For young people who have offended, workers use an assessment called ASSET. ASSET must be completed with all young people subject to a 'Final Warning' or due to be sentenced to a custodial or community order. The purpose of ASSET is to identify the risk factors known to be associated with offending, drawing on a wide variety of sources of evidence, in order to:

- make a recommendation to the court on a suitable sentence;
- identify the activities that the young person will be required to complete as part of their sentence;
- identify whether work needs to be done with their parents/carers; and
- identify how to protect the public.

The areas the assessment covers give an idea of some of the communication issues for the social worker. These include issues around offences and criminal history, living arrangements, family and personal relationships, employment, training, education, neighbourhood, lifestyle, substance use, physical health, and emotional/mental health. However, ASSET requires the additional examination of the perception of others, thinking and behaviour, attitude to offending, motivation to change, risk of harm and a self-assessment, called 'What Do You Think?'. Moreover, many interventions are designed to help young people think about the consequences of their behaviour, for the victim as well as for themselves (Crawford and Newburn, 2003). Indeed, the overriding concern of determining future 'risk of offending' is one that dominates practice in this setting, and as such I assume it will influence communication strategies. However, I should note that it is one that has come under heavy criticism from theorists, who emphasise that a welfare rather than a punitive 'criminal justice' perspective should be taken (Armstrong, 2004; Case, 2007).

Indeed, a tenet underpinning the most recent joint inspection of YOTs in the UK (HMI Probation, 2009) was that a person who is in contact with a YOT has to be seen as a child or young person as well as someone who has offended or who might be about to offend. As children or young people, they should have access to services in the same way as other children in the locality. Yet children and young people in contact with YOTs have been found to experience a number of difficulties that should be taken into account within communication, such as physical health needs, emotional/mental health needs, schooling difficulties or learning difficulties, with the statutory entitlement of 25 hours of education a week rarely being achieved (HMI Probation, 2009). Problems often co-exist, such as declining school achievement, poor attendance and substance misuse. The social worker needs to take these emotional issues and learning disabilities into account as part of their communication strategy. In particular, they need to respond to literature that has highlighted how autism and learning difficulties may affect the service user's communication of remorse or willingness to reform (Bishop, 2008; Batten, 2009).

Youth offending is often related to other familial problems, such as parental substance misuse and conflict. Indeed, in relation to identifying communication issues, the literature highlights the need to recognise the frequency of the young person having experienced stressful confrontations in their home, and often in school. The meeting with a social worker – as an adult with authority – is likely to produce further feelings of stress and uncertainty in a situation that is already stressful. Social work in YOTs can focus on improving parenting behaviour and the parenting environment, with the possibility of applying to the courts to obtain parenting orders to enforce the work on a compulsory basis.

Communication around issues of compulsion and control is also required when working with the high numbers of young people subject to remands in custody or sentenced to custody. Bail supervision and support are points of contact between a young person, the court and the YOT. These circumstances may raise particular communication issues relating to the social situation of the young person as being already involved in the wheels of the justice system and feeling disaffected from society. He or she may be feeling very fearful and alone (Sanford *et al.,* 1981).

Finally, YOTs work increasingly with children and young people who have not yet offended but have been identified as being at risk of doing so. The work seeks to help prevent them being drawn into the youth justice system. For these young people, the YOT uses an assessment called ONSET. ONSET is used to identify whether a young person would benefit from participating in a prevention programme, as well as to identify and address his or her needs in an attempt to reduce the likelihood of the young person engaging in offending behaviour. Clearly, the need to communicate about 'offending' to children and young people who have not yet offended, or been known to offend, presents more communication challenges for a worker.

Practice application

The breaking down of communication barriers between the service user and 'the system' – specifically social workers – by building rapport, is of paramount importance in this practice setting. As young offenders, service users are already disaffected from society (particularly authority) and there is a danger that communication between service user and social worker will be mediated by the young person feeling that they are communicating with the social worker under duress or threat of punitive action. In fact, we might understand the major themes in specialist communication skills in this practice setting as falling largely into an umbrella category of building rapport and breaking down barriers.

Practice example 4.1 shows how social workers need to utilise specialist communication skills to develop rapport between the social worker and service user from the outset to ensure productive and meaningful communication. Dean is meeting a social worker from the local Youth Offending Team to begin work on an ASSET assessment as part of the process involved in receiving a Final Warning for an offence in which it was alleged he had hit someone. Previously, both Dean and his parents had received social work services aimed at preventing his offending behaviour. However, currently, Dean is estranged from his parents and is 'sofa-surfing', spending nights on sofas in friends' homes. His representation of the world is in terms of 'them' (authority figures) and 'us' (young people). His disaffection and disengagement from society is palpable. Using a specialist communication skill of 'developing early rapport' at the earliest stage of the interview is critical in seeking to overcome his previous negative experiences of social work.

PRACTICE EXAMPLE 4.1

Dean

Preparatory stage

Dean is a 15-year-old youth living in an overcrowded city area. He describes his ethnicity as black – his mother is white British and father is Black British, of African-Caribbean descent. Both are employed. Over the past year Dean has rarely attended school. Previously, both Dean and his parents received social work services alongside two Youth Offending Team intervention programmes (a mentoring programme and a parenting programme) aimed at preventing offending behaviour. Dean has committed four minor offences and one serious offence, for which he received a reprimand and a warning. He has been involved with the police for three years now. Currently, Dean is estranged from his parents, and is 'sofa-surfing' – spending nights on sofas in friends' homes. At this point, he has been to a Police Station and received a Final Warning. A member of the Youth Offending Team was present for that Final Warning and offered Dean the opportunity to work with the team, using the ASSET assessment procedure, to design a programme to help prevent Dean from re-offending. Dean is now to meet a different social worker from the Youth Offending Team to begin the work.

'Phatic communication' has also been used within the communication literature as a term to describe the purpose and form of communication strategy I am outlining here (Burnard, 2003; Koprowska, 2008). As a form of everyday communication, its purpose is to promote and maintain friendly relationships through demonstrating sociability as opposed to giving or seeking information.

The use of this communication in professional relationships is considered to reduce anxiety in service users. As Burnard (2003: 680) states:

> When we chat in this way, we are, perhaps, saying 'I am friendly, unhostile and I want to know you and acknowledge you!'

The communication the social worker needs to transmit is that she is interested in Dean as a person, and that she, too, is a person and not an automated authority figure. At point 2, in Practice Example 4.2 we find the social worker achieving this through using the empathy skill of 'putting feelings into words' to show understanding of Dean's ambivalence. She extends this skill by identifying how, as a human being, she may make errors but that she is genuinely seeking to be helpful. She emphasises this by stating her desire to receive his feedback on her usefulness. Most importantly, she seeks to demonstrate how she is drawing a line between this, her own approach and that of previous social workers. In doing this, she is not inviting criticism of those previous working practices, but looking ahead to how they might work together in a way that is more useful to Dean. I summarise this part of the social work communication approach at the earliest stage of the interview as operating a specialist communication skill of 'expressing empathy and understanding without necessarily signifying agreement'. This skill is used later in the interview:

> I'm sure a lot of young people in your situation have felt that people don't care. But what I want to say is, can we start afresh? You've not worked with me before, I've not worked with you, so ... if you don't think I'm doing something right, then please tell me, yeah? If you don't think it's working or don't think I care, tell me, because I value your opinion.
>
> *Dean shrugs, moves around in his seat, picks at something on his jacket.*

There is a second reason for building rapport at this early stage in the interview. This concerns the need to establish rapport to prepare for later exploratory questioning of potentially anxiety-provoking issues. These concern the factual circumstances of the offence, but also personal information surrounding attitudes, beliefs, psycho-social functioning, and in particular, the quality of familial relationships. Indeed, the requirements of the ASSET assessment in identifying the degree of victim empathy, extent of remorsefulness, motivation for change and potential to engage in treatment and/or support programmes means that the level of personal information to be acquired increases as the interview proceeds. A social worker is more likely to be able to explore these increasingly personal issues if there is a development of rapport throughout the interview which is there from the outset. Moreover, there is a view that early rapport improves the validity of the information being provided (Jones, 2003).

Further techniques for achieving this specialist communication skill of 'developing early rapport' to prepare for later exploratory questioning include using the specialist communication skills identified in the previous chapter on working with children and young people in relation to 'achieving a shared purpose'. In this practice setting it is not only important to be clear on the role of the social worker and the purpose of the youth offending work, but also to ensure that the communication of this information is actually being understood by the young person and agreed upon. In Practice Example 4.2, points 3 to 5, the social worker seeks to explain the reasons for the meeting and the completion of the ASSET assessment. She is wholly transparent about the processes involved. Critically, she reminds Dean of the voluntary nature of his engagement in the work, while at the same time identifying that he will benefit from the work being done ('the final warning is voluntary – no one is gonna make you sit here and take part in the process...'). In specifying the outcomes of the assessment she communicates to him that the work will have a use – not just empty words – and that she believes in his potential to complete the work with her. In the previous chapter we used the term 'giving choice' to describe this kind of communication activity. In our practice example, the social worker does not continue with the interview until Dean actually states his agreement to engage with the work and achieve the outcomes (Example 4.2, point 5).

PRACTICE EXAMPLE 4.2

Dean

Beginnings

SW: *knocks on the door.*

[1] *Dean*: Yeah. Here.

SW: Hi, I'm Lorraine from the Youth Offending Team. Are you all right? (*She shakes Dean's hand*) Nice to see you. (*SW sits down*)

SW: How's it going?

Dean: Yeah.

SW: I understand you were at the Police Station last week and received a Final Warning – how did you find that?

Dean: Well, it's one of those things, ain't it?

►

►

SW: I understand you met one of my colleagues when you were there who probably handed you some leaflets and told you about the Youth Offending Team. What I want to do, first of all, is explain to you why we are getting together, if you like. And hopefully from there, to plan work we can do in the future. We need to do an assessment today, aspects of your life and things that might affect your offending behaviour that we can work on together. Do you know anything about the Youth Offending Team?

Dean: Stuff like a social worker, ain't it?

SW: We ll, kind of. There are social workers in the Youth Offending Team. There are also police officers, probation officers, people from health, people from education. Basically, we work as a team to try and to prevent you from re-offending and to stay out of trouble. Yeah? Does that make sense?

Dean: You gonna try to do what? I just wanna be left to do what I wanna do, you know what I mean?

SW: Well, we can talk about that.

Dean: You don't wanna talk about that though.

SW: Well, unfortunately once you've had a Final Warning we have to talk about it.....

Dean: I tried to talk about it before, but no one ever listened, did they? Now it's you lot. Social Services before – none of 'em are any better.

[2] *SW*: I'm sure a lot of young people in your situation have felt that people don't care. But what I want to say is, can we start afresh? You've not worked with me before, I've not worked with you, so ... if you don't think I'm doing something right, then please tell me, yeah? If you don't think it's working or don't think I care, tell me, because I value your opinion.

Dean shrugs, moves around in his seat, picks at something on his jacket.

[3] *SW*: Perhaps it'll help if I explain a bit more about this work around the Final Warning? (*Looks at Dean and allows a little silence*) I know that at the Police Station you said you would be prepared to

►

▶ do this work, but in my experience there's often so much going on that people agree to things they're not sure about, or forget what they've agreed to! Understandable, yeah? So, tell me, do you know about Final Warnings, then?

Dean: Get locked up.

SW: Not exactly, not unless you do something really serious. Basically, a final warning is kind of a second stage in the process of the Youth Justice system. I understand you've had a reprimand up to now, yeah? The final warning stage is voluntary – no one is gonna make you sit here and take part in the process – but I'm kinda hoping you will because, at the end of the day, if you do and we work successfully together, then ideally it's gonna help stop you re-offending, yeah? If you don't, or you choose not to get involved in the process, then I have to write down that this is where you have got to in the system. After that, if you did go on to re-offend and appeared in Court, then the Magistrate would actually be told you didn't take part in this process, yeah? Does that make sense?

Dean: Yeah.

SW: In that case, if you were to re-offend, then you'd go to Court and the Police wouldn't be able to let you off with another warning; and the Courts have a choice of what to do about you. So that's why it's better to focus more on not re-offending again, yeah? We need to do a thing called an ASSET assessment – I will ask you some questions, to decide what should go into a programme to help stop you re-offending.

Dean: So what kind of things are you gonna ask me?

[5] *SW*: I'm going to be honest with you. Some of the questions are going to be very personal. They need to be if we are going to come up with a programme that's going to be as real and meaningful to you as possible. You need to be as honest as you can about those things. What you tell me is put on our database and we share that with other people in the Youth Offending organisation. If you tell me something that shows you might be harmed in some way, I will need to make sure you are protected, so I'll tell people who can protect you, yeah? So, shall we complete this ASSET assessment together?

Dean: Yeah.

SW: Yeah? Good.

In relation to the skill of 'giving choice', a key finding from the research study underpinning this book was that 'defending the rights of the service user' was an important theme of specialist communication skills in working with young offenders. In this specific practice setting, where the young person is faced with a punitive system, they felt it was their role as social worker to communicate the right of voluntary engagement as the service user might not necessarily have been notified about this. This involved not just communicating to the service user that engagement was voluntary, but also defending the right of the service user to refuse to participate. Clearly, the theme of defending the rights of the service user contributes to 'develop early rapport' by building the trustworthiness of the social worker in the service user's eyes.

This all sounds rather 'heavy', but a key technique in achieving rapport, and indeed 'achieving a shared purpose', mentioned above is to use humour and the service user's language. The use of humorous banter and slang is embedded in youth culture; therefore use of banter and humour by social workers in their own discourse with the young offender helps to break down the view of the social worker as an authoritarian figure, by putting the social worker and service user on a more equal footing, through the medium of language. There is a danger of the social worker trying to be a teenager and, as stated in Chapter 3, this may create a distortion in the child's or young person's perception of the boundaries between adult and child. A balance must be drawn. Examples from Practice Example 4.3 (pp. 69–72) include:

- *SW*: Probably what you call 'a bit' and what I call 'a bit' are different .... (*Laughs*). *Dean*: You a light touch? Only one can? (*Smiles*). *SW*: Yeah, that's true... (*Laughs*) (point 8)

- *SW*: So how were you feeling? 'Cos I think I'd be drunk and wiped – some people, like me, get drunk on anything. So how did you feel? (point 10)

- *SW*: 'Any history there of aggro between you guys?' (point 14)

- *SW*: 'And had this bloke given you lip before?' (point 15)

- *SW*: 'So the police came along, they all did a runner, but you got picked up? So what happened then?' (point 16)

In ethical terms, when 'giving choices' to a young person about whether to engage in youth offending work this should not only involve giving information about the processes involved once they have engaged in the work, but also, importantly, the consequences for that young person if they do not engage in the work. It is about obtaining 'fully informed consent' or 'fully informed dissent'. The challenge for the social worker is to communicate the consequences of the situation to the service user in a manner that is non-threatening in order to continue to build rapport and maintain the quality of interaction achieved thus far.

There seem to be two aspects to this specialist communication skill of 'communicating consequences in a non-threatening manner'. First, the social worker should avoid threat and judgement when communicating consequences. Using Practice Example 4.2 as an illustration, from points 3 to 5 the social worker explained to Dean the consequences of what would happen if he did not complete the ASSET assessment, but in a way that wasn't judging him: it simply gave him information. A key to this success was in the social worker not making the information too 'personal' by explaining that the process itself existed as something separate from him – that is, it was not created by his actions as a punitive response to him personally. Significantly, it was crucial to frame the consequences as information-giving rather than a reprimand. Second, the social worker identified the trade-off for compliance. This involved providing a balance to the information provided – identifying the positive consequences and belief in the potential for change and a different future. The social worker could have added 'If you do engage maybe I'll never have to see you again and you can put this behind you. If you do re-offend then the next step of the process is that you will go to court and the court can sentence you to any number of different punishments.'

It must be emphasised that the operation of this communication skill is not as simple or obvious as it seems. The policy context to this practice setting is that of criminal (youth) justice, propounding a punitive system as opposed to a welfare system. This context places pressure on the social worker to stop the offending behaviour, which in turn has the potential to reinforce a zealous discourse with the service user about the consequences of re-offending. Indeed, the social work participants of the research study underpinning this book stated that this emphasis on showing the service user the consequences of their offending behaviour was 'drummed into us'.

PRACTICE EXAMPLE 4.3

Dean

Work phase

[6] *SW*: To begin with, I'd like you to tell me a little bit about exactly what happened?

Dean: Hanging with a few mates, smoking and…

SW: When you say a few mates, how many?

▶

Dean: Four.

SW: Four, yeah, and what time of day was this?

Dean: About six in the evening.

[7] *SW*: So, had you been drinking? You say you'd been smoking.

Dean: Yeah, a bit, but not loads.

[8] *SW*: Probably what you call 'a bit' and what I call 'a bit' are different …. (*Laughs*)

Dean: You a light touch? Only one can? (*Smiles*)

[9] *SW*: Yeah, that's true… (*Laughs*)… So, you're there with four of your mates; early evening; couple of drinks – what classes as a couple of drinks?

Dean: Cans of cider, about two and a bit; then some vodka.

[10] *SW*: So how were you feeling? 'Cos I think I'd be drunk and wiped out – some people, like me, get drunk on anything. So, how did you feel?

[11] *Dean*: Alright, just a bit happy. But I was chilled out – we'd been smoking as well.

SW: So what were you smoking?

Dean: Weed. Just weed, innit? My mate gets some good stuff.

[12] *SW*: Had you been smoking all day?

Dean: Just a couple of hours before.

[13] *SW*: OK, so you're feeling merry. What happened then?

Dean: We got into a fight with these other lads – bit of shoving.

SW: What actually started the fight? I mean, where were you?

Dean: The park, innit? (*Looks in a frustrated manner at social worker*)

SW: Yeah, whereabouts were you at the time, you know... Just thinking of the location and where you were actually stood, or sat?

►

Dean: Well you got to the park and then there's the road next to it – then parked cars – and we was just by the park entrance and they was giving us some lip.

SW: So are you saying it was them that started it?

Dean: They were just making fun and it ended up… a fight.

SW: OK. Did you know any of the young people in the other group?

Dean: Yeah.

[14] *SW*: Any history there of aggro between you guys?

Dean: Yeah, aggro (*shrugs, hands up, smiles*). Know what I mean?

SW: Explain to me what you did.

Dean: They started it!

SW: OK. Where were you when this happened?

Dean: There was only a few of us. We all had a go… but it was unfortunate… they all kind of run off and I tripped and hurt my leg. One bloke had his nose broken.

SW: One of your group?

Dean: No, one of theirs.

SW: How did that happen?

Dean: They reckon it was my fault. That's why I'm here, ain't it?

SW: Well, I'm interested in your views, really.

Dean: They said if they get any of the others, they'd grass up our friends – I wouldn't do that. That's why I'm here.

SW: Had anything else been going on that day that had put you in a bad mood, a bad frame of mind?

Dean: No, I was chilled out until they started being lippy like. Like, whatever, knock 'em out (*Indicates fist on hand*).

►

▶

[15] *SW*: And had this bloke given you lip before?

Dean: Yeah, always giving us grief. Like one of 'em was seeing my mate's girlfriend.

[16] *SW*: So there's history there then? So the Police came along, they all did a runner, but you got picked up? So what happened then?

Dean: Got took to the Police Station, they started chatting... then 'the Social' turned up and gave me grief.

SW: What, do you mean me?!

Dean: No, not you.

SW: So we've talked through what happened. Now we need to talk through some personal questions. Is that all right with you?

Dean nods his head.

SW: You don't mind? Right. (*Speaks in a quieter and gentler tone*) Where are you living at the moment?

Dean: Staying at a friend's house.

SW: Staying at a friend's house, and how long have you been there?

Dean: A few weeks.

SW: A few weeks – is that someone you know well?

Dean: Yeah, I've been at school with 'em.

SW: You've been to school with them – a close friend. Do they know your family life? Do your parents know them as well?

Dean: Yeah. I asked if I could stay there.

SW: Is it quite busy at home? Have you got lots of brothers and sisters?

Dean: A couple.

SW: Do you know if any of them are involved in any criminal activity? (*Dean is quiet and shrugs. Short silence*) So you're living with these friends now. Do you mind me asking where you were living before that?

▶

Dean: At home.

SW: At home, with your mum and dad, yeah? So what made you… what happened when you left home?

Dean: Just didn't get on.

SW: And do you still stay in contact with your family?

Dean: Every now and then.

SW: Every now and then. So was it their choice or yours that you move out?

Dean: They don't like the stuff I do. They can't deal with it.

Practice Example 4.3 further illustrates how the communication skills for the assessment process are influenced by the youth justice context to the work. The model used for gathering information for the assessment is procedural. The social worker takes the role of expert asking the questions he or she needs to complete the work. Criminal justice terms and jargon are evident throughout the Practice Example and all over the research transcripts. Communicating with a young person within the youth justice system appears to have some qualitative differences from that of communicating with a young person within the welfare system. This raises a significant ethical dilemma for social workers, as the welfare needs of young people in contact with youth offending teams are significant. For example, our practice illustration (4.1) identifies Dean as a young person who is homeless and adrift. This entitles him to receive an assessment as a 'child in need', with resultant support services including accommodation under councils' section 20 (1) duty of The Children Act 1989 to look after children whose parents or carers cannot accommodate them. The entitlement of welfare support for homeless youths has come under the spotlight with the House of Lords Judgment (2009) on the case *R(G)* v. *London Borough of Southwark*, which gave legal clarification concerning the way 16/17-year-olds in need of housing and support are managed. However, for the purposes of the discussion here about communication, the criminal justice orientated context creates pressure for the social worker because the neglect, or separating out, of the welfare issue might inhibit 'tuning-in' and thus the development of emotional attunement for effective communication.

The first of these main differences in communicating with young people in the youth justice context appears to be that of 'listening for clues'. This involved actively listening for information emerging during the interview that might shed light on the determining or intervening factors giving rise to the offending behaviour. In most cases the social worker would mentally note that information, and return to it later in the interview or at a subsequent date. In our Practice Example 4.3, we see that the social worker is 'listening for clues' about whether Dean was drunk, and therefore hypothesising whether the drinking of alcohol was a contributing factor to the offence taking place. The questions seek to ascertain how much alcohol Dean had consumed at the time (to establish Dean's perspective of the circumstances of the offence) but also how much alcohol Dean regularly consumed (to establish whether alcohol consumption exists as a risk factor to Dean re-offending). The skill of 'listening for clues' uses 'open questions' (for example, Practice Example 4.3, point 9: '... what classes as a couple of drinks?') and 'closed questions' (for example, 4.3, point 10: 'So how were you feeling? 'Cos I think I'd be drunk and wiped out'). These skills were outlined in Chapter 2 as skills for gathering and exploring facts. It is not enough for the social worker to accept the information at face value but to explore its relevance to offending. As such, in this practice setting contextual information (either theoretical, or empirical research, or through victim statements) was being used to introduce an issue that is likely to be difficult to uncover, such as where the information is embarrassing, or potentially incriminating. In Practice Example 4.3, the social worker uses her knowledge of how alcohol is a frequent antecedent contributory factor to violent offences to explore the circumstances of this alleged offence. She does not use an 'open question' in an indirect manner, such as 'What were you doing at the time?' Rather, she is more focused in the conversation by seeking to ascertain whether the young person had consumed alcohol: 'So, had you been drinking? You say you'd been smoking'(4.3, point 7). Thus, we might understand this use of 'open questions' and 'closed questions' as 'focused questioning'.

Another specialist communication skill for this practice setting that is different from that in Chapter 3 in working with children and young people, is that of 'assessing for truthfulness'. The social worker checks information provided by the victim statements and witnesses against what the service user is saying. The social worker also checks for quantity of detail in recalling the events (time, place, persons involved, objects, smells and other sensory information) and consistency of the dialogue taking place at this time. These are some of the common elements of the memory-based approach entitled 'Statement Validity Analysis' to evaluate accuracy of accounts (or uncover deceit) in a structured format during interviews with children (Wilson and Powell, 2001). Other elements include whether the child or young person shows motivation to be deceitful, and whether he or she express empathy or understanding of the motivation or behaviour of another person. Skills from Chapters 3 and 4 are also important in terms of checking that the non-verbal behaviour is congruent with the verbal assertions. It is important to note that some social workers in the research study stated that they felt uncomfortable in assessing for truthfulness themselves. They stated that they preferred to present a report that states the service user's perspectives. In such instances, the judgement of truthfulness would take place at a subsequent date or event, when all the different sources of information would be compared. A quote from the research transcript illustrates this point:

Social worker 1: I don't think it's my place to find out the truth. I don't think it's my place to record the discrepancy between the disclosures and what the young person's saying. I wouldn't say which is true. So whoever the report then goes to – the panel or the court – if they want to explore that, then they can explore it.

Johanna: Ah, so you are looking for facts – getting the meat on the bones rather than digging around?

Social worker 2: Rather than questioning the truth of it.

Johanna: So you are saying that questioning the truth doesn't happen in this situation – it happens with someone else, another time, outside the court?

Social worker 3: Sometimes.

It seems to go without saying that it is important for social workers to have good basic communication skills for gathering facts and 'showing empathy' (Chapter 2) in order to apply these specialist communication skills in this practice setting. The degree of mistrust of authority and disbelief in the potential of the social worker to be helpful means that the social worker must continually attend to the building of rapport and the development of the working relationship throughout the interview. The ability to use non-verbal as well as verbal techniques to demonstrate 'reflective listening' is central to this success. Body language needs to be 'open' and encourage the gathering of more information through nodding, sitting in a relaxed way (preferably without paper, pen and clipboard) and opening the arms as a way of indicating 'tell me more'. To achieve this it is important to convey 'respect', discussed in Chapter 3 and as relevant here in demonstrating acceptance of the young person. This uses the values of unconditional regard and identifying the service user as a person and not merely as 'an object of concern'. Indeed, as the young person relates his or her account, information may emerge that is potentially distressing or anxiety-provoking for the social worker. Here, it is useful to use, again, the skill of 'expressing empathy and understanding without necessarily signifying agreement'. Another quote from the research transcript illustrates the operation of these skills:

Social worker 3: The social worker is establishing a rapport and getting a relationship and he's gathering information, he's getting information from him [the service user] by using humour.

Johanna: He [*the social worker*] was moving his head and body side-to-side. Was there non-verbal communication?

Social worker 4: Yeah, he's using his hands quite a lot.

Johanna: How is he using his hands?

Social worker 4: He's using his hands like this (*Lifts arms up, opens them out wide and shakes them about*) He's quite animated, he's not just sitting, writing. He's talking like to a person, not just a clipboard getting information, he's actually having a conversation. And by having a conversation, he's gathering information. It doesn't feel like he's interviewing. He's actually having a chat.

Social worker 5: When the service user was talking more freely about the offence, at the park, he was giving more eye contact; then he opened his legs; then he went like that (*Opens arms wide*). Then, later, when he started talking about the Police, he went like that (*Opens arms wide again…laughs*)

Johanna: I guess that is communicating that you are listening… The service user is saying some really quite contentious and dangerous things, and you're accepting what he's saying. Would other people struggle with that complete acceptance and maybe want to express a judgement like 'well you know that's dangerous' to them?

Social workers murmur disagreement.

The specialist communication skills for working with children and young people from Chapter 3 identify the importance of using a medium of communication that is familiar to the child and is appropriate to their age and stage of cognitive and social development in order to promote understanding of the issues under exploration. As suggested in that chapter, certain types of questions are to be avoided because children do not have the cognitive ability to process and answer them. These questions tend to start with 'why' and 'how' as opposed to 'what', 'where' and 'when' (Jones, 2003). Young people in contact with youth offending teams tend to be in their teenage years, and are sensitive to any communication that seems childish or patronising. Yet this specialist communication skill of 'avoiding the why and how questions' is equally relevant to them. Indeed, the background literature indicates that young people in contact with youth offending teams often have developmental delay across all dimensions, but particularly experience difficulties in relation to physical health, emotional/mental health, schooling and learning (HMI Probation, 2009). It is unlikely, then, that talking alone is going to be sufficient to ensure meaningful communication with many of these young people. Rather, use needs to be made of tools that employ visual, symbolic and culturally relevant media of communication alongside the dialogue, such as drawing, or computer-based questionnaires.

The need for social workers to communicate with young people in this practice setting using language and other media of communication that they can understand and utilise themselves as not just a matter of professional skill but also a moral enterprise. Social workers are not only 'assessing for truthfulness' in relation to the young person's version of events concerning the alleged offence, but also using that skill to explore the young person's attitudes and behaviour in relation to victim empathy and the extent of the desire to change behaviour in response to his or her remorse. We might refer to this specialist skill as 'assessing for remorse and willingness to reform'. Misunderstandings in the communication of this skill can have severe consequences for the young person, such as an increase in the severity of sanctions or a limit on the number and type of interventions made available to them. Yet, worryingly, the potential for misunderstandings to occur seems to be high. These issues of 'victim empathy', 'willingness to reform' and 'communicating truthfulness' are 'high order' concepts that young people, particularly those with cognitive and psycho-social development delay, may find difficult to understand. Often, their own experience of relationships with parents, other family and peers is replete with instances of being rejected, neglected and devalued as a person. They might still be developing their ability to empathise with the emotional pain of another person, particularly if they have developed psychological defences to experiencing emotional pain themselves (Howe, 2005). Indeed, as stated earlier, literature highlights how social workers need to show awareness of the way autism and learning difficulties may affect the presentation of remorse or willingness to reform.

This chapter has described and discussed how the specialist social work communication skills for youth offending work have some similarities to but also differences from those used more widely with children and young people with significant welfare needs. The differences arise from the priority given within the social work role to preventing young people from offending or re-offending, and the procedural context of the work with many technical concepts applied. Key specialist communication skills involve gaining a quick rapport with young people, who are often disaffected from society, to communicate and elicit understanding of the consequences of offending behaviour, and the degree of remorsefulness and willingness to reform.

Professional Standards

This chapter will help you to meet the following National Occupational Standards:

Key Role 1: Prepare for, and work with individuals, families, carers, groups and communities to assess their needs and circumstances

Unit 1 Prepare for social work contact and involvement
Unit 2 Work with individuals, families, carers, groups and communities to help them make informed decisions
Unit 3 Assess needs and options to recommend a course of action

Key Role 2: Plan, carry out, review and evaluate social work practice with individuals, families, carers, groups, communities and other professionals

Unit 5 Interact with individuals, families, carers, groups and communities to achieve change and development and to improve life opportunities
Unit 6 Prepare, produce, implement and evaluate plans with individuals, families, carers, groups, communities and professional colleagues
Unit 9 Address behaviour which presents a risk to individuals, families, carers, groups and communities

Key Role 3: Support individuals to represent their needs, views and circumstances. Advocate with and on behalf of people

Unit 10 Advocate with, and on behalf of, individuals, families, carers, groups and communities

Key Role 4: Manage risk to individuals, families, carers, groups, communities, self and colleagues

Unit 12 Assess and manage risks to individuals, families, carers, groups and communities

Key Role 5: Manage and be accountable, with supervision and support, for your own social work practice within your organisation

Unit 16 Manage and be accountable, with supervision and support, for your own social work practice within your organisation

Unit 17 Work within multi-disciplinary and multi-organisational teams, networks and systems

Key Role 6: Demonstrate professional competence in social work practice

Unit 18 Research, analyse, evaluate and use current knowledge of best social work practice
Unit 19 Work within agreed standards of social work practice and ensure own professional development
Unit 20 Manage complex ethical issues, dilemmas and conflicts
Unit 21 Contribute to the promotion of best social work practice

CHAPTER

Working with Parents 5

Summary of Specialist Communication Skills

- Identifying a practical response of seeking to overcome the systemic barriers
- Identifying the social worker's personal attitudes and preconceptions of parenting
- Positive framing of development rather than using negative deficit notions
- Demonstrating knowledge of the individual child
- Identifying, discussing and empathising with systemic barriers with parents

Policy and background literature

Government policy (*Every Child Matters*, 2003: 6–7) states that all children should have the opportunity to fulfil their potential and grow up in secure, loving families, and sets out five key outcomes that matter for the state with respect to this:

- Being Healthy
- Staying Safe
- Enjoyment and Achievement
- Making a Positive Contribution
- Economic Well-being

Legislation requires social workers to provide services to support parents to enable them to deliver these outcomes for their children, and thereby safeguard and promote their welfare (The Children Acts 1989 and 2004). This is supported by Article 8 of the European Convention on Human Rights – the right to respect for family life.

This suggests that, in communicating with parents, social workers should recognise how the legislation confirms that parents should have responsibility for, and a meaningful relationship with, their children, with the important proviso that this is safe and in the child's best interests. Indeed, the core overriding principle, set out in The Children Act 1989, is that the child's welfare must be the paramount consideration in decisions concerning the child's upbringing. While the concept of welfare is not defined in the Children Act 1989, the factors mentioned above within the Every Child Matters Outcomes Framework provides a guide, as well as those constituting the 'welfare checklist', which are used to assist Courts in their determination of 'welfare':

- The ascertainable wishes and feelings of the child – in light of his or her age and understanding;
- The physical, emotional and educational needs of the child;
- The likely effect of any change on the child's circumstances;
- The age, sex, background and any other characteristics which the Court considers to be relevant;
- Any harm which the child has suffered or is at risk of suffering;
- How capable the child's parents (and/or any other relevant person) are of meeting the child's needs; and
- The range of powers available to the Court.

Within policy and the current literature, parenting is considered to be a relationship that is multiply determined by a constellation of factors which impact and interact on and with one another (Belsky and Vondra, 1989; Reder and Lucey, 1995; DoH, 2000a; Woodcock, 2003). Importantly, with the introduction of the government policy *The Framework for the Assessment of Children in Need and their Families*, there has been more attention given to both safeguarding *and promoting* the developmental welfare of children, where previously attention had centred exclusively on establishing whether abusive behaviour had occurred, or was likely to occur (DoH, 1995, 2000a, 2006a). The role for the social worker in using the Framework is to establish and/or support the viability of the family, and indeed the capacity of the parent (in the context of the familial and wider social environment), to meet the needs of a child whose health and development may be impaired, or who is unable to meet a reasonable standard of health and development, or who is disabled (DoH 2000a). Given this, we should expect communication to focus on improving the parenting relationship, diminishing developmental risk to children and the vulnerability of the family, and seeking to establish protective factors (Rutter, 1985; Cleaver *et al*, 1999). Crucially, such protection might involve taking immediate safeguarding action by arranging the care of children within other families. Indeed, legislation confers upon social workers the duty to investigate and assess whether a child is at risk of significant harm, or likely to be at risk of significant harm (The Children Act 1989).

Considerable attention has been given to the influence and impact of 'self' upon parenting assessment. One aspect of this, concerns the influence of the constructions of parenting held by the social worker themselves. Such constructions can act as attitudinal barriers to the communication between a social worker and a parent. Feminist analysts have found social workers operating cultural stereotypes of the role of 'mothers' and 'caring', such as prescriptions to provide sensitive and responsive care regardless of social circumstances (Sheppard, 2000; Turney 2000). Other research has emphasised how beliefs were influenced by workers experiences of their own parenting and their own child's development pathways (Daniel, 2000; Holland, 2000; Woodcock, 2003).

Additional dynamics concerning the impact of 'self' can occur between the worker and service user causing attitudinal communication barriers in parenting assessment. The first relates to the social worker looking for only confirmatory evidence of one, perhaps a favoured, hypothesis to describe the quality of the safeguarding behaviour of the parenting relationship under assessment. Dingwall (1986) first described this as the 'rule of optimism' and located it within practice which can be 'professionally dangerous'. Parton (1991, p.55, cited in Kroll and Taylor, 2003) describes it as an approach which 'meant that the most favourable interpretation was put upon the behaviour of the parents and that anything that may question this was discounted or redefined'.

He further linked the concept to the two dynamics of 'cultural relativism' and 'natural love'. Cultural relativism in its extreme form refers to professional assumptions that all values and behaviour are culture specific and that they should only be appraised within the context of a particular culture. There are dangers in adopting this perspective that the values of another culture cannot be applied to another, particularly as regards human rights and the protection of children. One cannot appraise or allow parenting practices in terms of it being 'culturally relevant' to a particular culture, without simulaneously appraising it in the light of whether it is abusive or casues harm to all parties. Laird (2008) highlights the dangers of engaging in processes of cultural relativism when lacking knowledge or expertise in working with families of different ethnic and cultural backgrounds to one's own. Dominant stereotypes and normative assumptions about the cultural practices of people from different ethnic groups might be applied that do not account for individual differences in family forms, religious beliefs, lifestyle choices and outlooks.

In addition, the Peter Connolly tragedy (Laming, 2009) illustrates the relevance of Parton's dynamic called 'natural love'. 'Natural love' refers to the belief that all parents love their children because it is a natural or instinctive phenomenon. Parton says that when this belief is held, it is very difficult for practitioners to challenge it because it represents the origin of human behaviour. In Peter's case, the emphasis of the work was on family support than child protection. Workers had more evidence of Peter being a child receiving care from a loving mother, than a child whose injuries could potentially have been covered up. Social workers need to remember that not all parents love their children as an instinctual response. Children can hold all kinds of meanings to their parents on conscious and unconscious levels (Reder *et al.*, 1993). For those interested, Kroll and Taylor (2003: 247–50) provide useful application of Parton's three concepts to social work practice with substance using parents.

Howitt (1992) similarly suggests that social workers assess parental behaviour against societal and attitudinal templates, for example 'reasonable parenting'. He argues that this is a significant element in social work reasoning that can result in 'error making' in social work decisions. Parton *et al.* (1997) also identify how social workers use common-sense reasoning devices to make decisions, usually in situations of uncertainty, such as in assessing risk of harm. This would involve clarifying the expected features of parenting in a situation and using the presence or absence of these features to judge the possibility of abuse occurring. In my earlier research on parenting assessment (Woodcock, 2003) I encouraged practitioners to move beyond their 'surface-static' perceptions of parenting behaviour as task-orientated and unchangeable, towards regarding parenting as fluid and variable over time and context due to the influences of social as well as individual factors. This all points to specialist communication skills of recognising how, as a social worker, you influence the processes and outcome of any parenting assessment.

The literature highlights how social workers can find themselves caught in an aggressive and defensive communication pattern with a parent. Parents express a common concern when they come into contact with services – fear that their children will be 'taken away' (Buchanan and Young, 2002; Taylor and Kroll, 2004). The fear of initiation of child protection procedures can cause some parents to display erratic behaviour such as avoiding contact with social workers. Theorists from an attachment theory perspective (Howe, 2005) and systemic perspective (Reder and colleagues, 1993; 1995; 2001) have proposed that parental difficulties in engagement can reflect long-standing interpersonal difficulties that can be traced back to severe adverse experiences in childhood. Reder, Duncan and colleagues (1993; 2001) have explored how internal conflicts about care and control persist from childhood and are re-enacted in relationships as adults, including those with social workers. These may take the form of excessive or ambivalent dependence on other people and sensitivity to feelings of loss even if this is threatened and not real. Another form is sensitivity to feeling controlled, manifested as 'fight or flight'. Indeed, a systems perspective is applied to describe how families operate boundaries along a continuum of 'openness and closedness' depending on the degree to which people within the system are allowed to share information, or enter or leave the system. Parents in contact with social workers were often found to find the required changes and adaptations threatening and so closed off contact, whether in a direct way through unavailability, or a less direct way through passive resistence. In contrast, an open system has greater contact with other systems and is more flexible and capable of adapting to change.

The findings of my earlier research concerning the parental assessment and provision of family support services to parents with children with developmental disabilities identified social workers as one of a number of professionals within a complex interagency network of services that tended to operate a negative deficit approach to their child's needs (Woodcock and Tregaskis, 2008). The parents identified frustration at the continual repetition of the child and family's history of problems. The lack of interaction between professionals was a constant theme, causing a multitude of practical obstacles. This highlights the perceived challenge of the well-informed service-user, identifying again how social workers can find themselves caught in an aggressive and defensive communication pattern with a parent. When communicating with parents, social workers need to recognise how these parental feelings and behaviours are coping mechanisms – the result of experiencing structural barriers to their child receiving services, as well as dealing with the personal pain and trauma of their child's disability.

Practice application

Practice Example 5.1 begins with a new social worker (Makemba) meeting Ben and his mother, Maxine, to review whether the services being provided to Ben are promoting and safeguarding his developmental welfare needs. The social worker is seeking to support Maxine and her husband in their parenting of Ben, and where appropriate, offer services to facilitate this further.

The background literature highlighted that a number of societal barriers are likely to impact on the communication processes between the social worker and Maxine (Woodcock and Tregaskis, 2008). Of concern, at the outset, is that these barriers are likely to be located within the social worker himself as attitudes and behaviour (Marchant and Page, 2003). Indeed, in my earlier research among families with disabled children I identified how social workers need to recognise the ways in which their own preconceived notions and cultural experiences shape their view of children's needs, particularly when the child has an impairment (Woodcock and Tregaskis, 2008). Some of the social workers described in the study were unprepared or unable to discuss the nature of the impairment, particularly individual differences specific to a child, preferring instead to adopt a generalised application from formal knowledge of the impairment. The social workers were reluctant to open themselves up to hearing parental 'private' (and therefore 'new') knowledge about the individual characteristics of the impairment, and the individual way it affects family life. The fact that some professionals were either unable or unwilling to do this suggested that the problem lay with them, and that particular communication skills were required to overcome this. A key suggestion was for social workers to engage purposefully in a preparatory process of self-reflection to consider ways that they bring such obstacles to the situation.

This suggests that Shulman's (2009) communication skill of 'tuning-in', as described in Chapter 2, is crucial for the worker to employ before he goes to meet Maxine. As a process of 'preparatory empathy' it will enable Makemba to identify and address the obstacles to work and be ready to listen and respond to Maxine's expression of feelings and thoughts, however direct or indirectly they are expressed. This preparatory empathy will be important, because the background literature has highlighted a high emotional content to communication with parents, particularly in relation to feelings of fear and apprehension at the authority role of the social worker in making decisions about parenting. The social worker has legislative duties to safeguard and promote the well-being of individuals, bringing an inevitable underpinning of compulsion or social control to the reason for the meeting. The fear and apprehension at this authority is exacerbated by the negative stereotype of social workers, mentioned earlier, as either 'busybodies poking their noses into private affairs', removing children or vulnerable adults from their homes without good evidence, or 'inadequate', through failing to protect children from harsh care-giving. In addition to these feelings of fear, my research study of parents of disabled children identified that parents of such children often presented strong feelings of pain and frustration that frequently were related to the influence of systemic barriers in their lives (Woodcock and Tregaskis, 2008).

In applying these findings to Practice Example 5.1, the social worker needs to prepare himself to discuss and contain such strong feelings, whether of pain and frustration and/or apprehension or fear during their meeting. The important consideration for the social worker is 'How might Maxine demonstrate these feelings?' He needs to consider as many alternatives as possible while ensuring that he is not completely assumptive or deterministic about those feelings when he meets Maxine. The level of fear, apprehension, frustration and pain indicates that he might expect these feelings to be expressed verbally and non-verbally as ambivalence, resistance and aggression regarding the work taking place. Certainly, the background literature highlights how these feelings emerge when parents are worried and ambivalent about the purpose of the involvement with a social worker. This reiterates the point made in Chapter 2, that the social worker must engage in a communication strategy that seeks a shared understanding of the purpose of the work and, crucially, how that work is beneficial to the child and parent within their situation. There needs to be an interactive process of introduction and negotiation to achieve a shared agenda to enable the work to take place. The social worker will need to encourage discussion about the parent's and child's agendas and his own agenda, and achieve agreement on how these agendas can be brought together to specify the purpose and processes for the ongoing work. This communication skill was described in Chapter 2 as 'achieving a shared purpose'.

Perhaps for this practice setting ('working with parents'), over all others, it cannot be emphasised enough how important, yet difficult, it is to use the communication skill required to 'achieve a shared purpose'. First, the background literature highlights the myriad of issues for social workers in seeking a relationship-based approach with parents who may themselves have 'unresolved care and control conflicts', or an internal working model of relationships that is an 'insecure attachment style'. Not least, these relationship dynamics can cause a family to operate as a 'closed system', displaying overt avoidance towards the social worker's interaction, or covert, passive compliance.

Second, the quality of social worker communication is almost certainly influenced by the current social, political and organisational context following the Inquiry Reports of the recent deaths of Victoria Climbie and Peter Connolly discussed in earlier chapters (Laming, 2003; Laming, 2009). Media and management scrutiny of individual practice against prescribed performance targets has resulted in increased workloads, increased applications for care orders, greater demand for resources, more time spent on administrative processes in front of a computer than spent interacting with service users, and low staff morale among front-line social work staff. The emotional resources required of a social worker to analyse interpersonal communication dynamics and 'show empathy' to 'hard to reach' parents are arguably more difficult to access within this context.

Yet the social worker must recognise the degree to which communication is played out at the level of feeling and engage with it, if a service user is to feel he or she is really being listened to and understood. As explored in Chapter 1, rational thoughts are shaped by our emotions, and we often express our thoughts through our feelings (Ruch, 2009). The beginning of Practice Example 5.1 illustrates this well.

PRACTICE EXAMPLE 5.1

Maxine and Ben

Preparatory stage

Ben is approaching his fourth birthday. A new social worker (Makemba) is meeting Ben and his mother, Maxine, to review whether the services being provided to Ben are promoting and safeguarding his developmental welfare needs. Ben has Down's Syndrome, and suffers with related heart problems. The extent of his learning disability is under review by the educational psychologist. The social worker is seeking to support Maxine and her husband in their parenting of Ben, and where appropriate, offer services to facilitate this further. The family are of white British ethnicity. Makemba is a Black Zimbabwean man of 40 years who qualified as a social worker in Zimbabwe and has been a social worker in the Joint Agency Team (JAT) for this local authority in the UK for the past 3 years.

Beginnings

The social worker rings the doorbell. Maxine slides the door open.

[1] *Maxine*: You've come to do Ben's review, right?

SW: Yes. We haven't met before – My name's Makemba. I've taken over from Janet. I've been a social worker for a few years in JAT, but not had the chance to meet you. Is your husband here too?

Maxine: No, he's at work. There are so many meetings for Ben. He can't get to all of them. Come in. Do you want some coffee? Ben, be careful with that! Careful! Good boy. (*Ben crawls over to the doorway and bangs a toy against the door frame*)

SW: No, I'm OK thank you. Hello Ben. (*Crouches down to Ben's height and looks in his face. Smiles*) Ben, I'm Makemba. What's that toy?

Ben ignores him, turns around and returns to where he was sitting with his toys on the floor. He has a selection of brightly coloured trucks and pre-school educational toys which light up and make sounds. He moves the toys around, picking them up and banging them down. Maxine and Makemba follow Ben into the room and sit down on the sofa and accompanying armchair.

Maxine: Quietly, Ben. Quiet. Shush. (*Said in a quiet voice with a finger to her lips*)

[2] *SW*: He is happy with his toys there, isn't he? (*Pause*) I expect it doesn't seem long since Ben's last review? What would you say has changed, or needs to happen in this review of his needs?

►

▶

[3] *Maxine:* I just want to make sure that I can get the best for Ben. Of course I'm worried, but I want him to go into mainstream school. It's getting a bit frustrating

Silence for five seconds.

[4] *SW:* Can you tell me a bit more about your frustrations and your worries?

Maxine: Well, you know, I'm concerned about making sure Ben's, you know, developing OK, but there's so many different services ... and they don't explain things fully ... and a lot of things go over my head and nothing seems to be getting done and it just seems to be getting delayed and delayed.

SW: What do you really want to happen?

Maxine: Nothing's happening.

SW: I mean, what do *you* want to see happen?

Maxine: You know, I can't help worrying because I want to get Ben into mainstream school, and at the moment there's all these services but nothing seems to be happening. You have to put their name down at the school at this age but obviously, I can't...

SW: And what exactly isn't happening?

Maxine: Well the fact that we're almost in July and there's nothing set in stone, there's no structure. It's as though the services aren't following the same structure. I don't mean exactly the same structure because I know they have different reasons, but I still haven't been told whether, you know, the possibility of Ben getting into mainstream school. This has been going on for four or five months now and it just keeps getting delayed and delayed, so at the moment I think what's the point of the meetings because we're going round and round... it's a vicious circle!

SW: So what would you like to happen from here? Where would you like it to go?

Maxine: I'd like you to communicate more with each other.

[5] *SW*: It's natural to be really concerned about your child's development and it would be really helpful if I spoke to some of the professionals that you've spoken to and see if I can co-ordinate some of the information that they have got. And then I'll get back to you with it.

▶

▶

Maxine: Well, that's been tried before. That's what I'm saying, you don't seem to communicate. They are not treated as individual cases, you know, my son is always talked about on the negative side, you know. I know he has certain needs. All children have certain needs. But I'm not getting told anything at all!

[6] *SW*: So how about if I give you an actual timescale when I would come back and talk to you? You know, next week, we'll actually make another date for a week's time and I'll get as much of that information together. Would that be helpful to you?

Maxine: Yeah, I want to get this sorted.

[7] *SW*: Then, if there's any gaps then, we can discuss those. We won't leave it for a long time because you're obviously concerned.

Maxine: I don't want it to be left a long time.

[8] *SW*: Well, I'll book a meeting with you today and I'll come back next Friday. I'll have gathered up as much information as I can and I'll bring it back to you. (*Writes down the agreement in his diary in view of Maxine*)

The social worker shows that he has previously 'tuned-in' to the need to hear and respect parental 'private' knowledge about the individual characteristics of an impairment and the individual way it affects family life. He asks an 'open question' to ascertain Maxine's perspectives (point 2): 'What would you say has changed, or needs to happen in this review of his needs?' Maxine responds by expressing feelings about her concerns for schooling and starts to hint at her negative experience of systemic barriers operating between agencies in respect of this (point 3): 'I just want to make sure that I can get the best for Ben. Of course I'm worried, but I want him to go into mainstream school. It's getting a bit frustrating...' The social worker demonstrates empathy for these feelings, perhaps showing that, again, he had previously 'tuned-in' to the possibility of these feelings emerging during their meeting. The empathy is demonstrated by using the communication skill described in Chapter 2 of 'putting feelings into words' in the form of an 'open question': (point 4): 'Can you tell me a bit more about your frustrations and your worries?' He demonstrates, in doing so, that he has 'listened reflectively' to Maxine's communication. Indeed, from this point onwards, until point 8, Maxine unfolds more feelings of frustration at the systemic barriers she is experiencing in obtaining information about Ben's developmental progress and any decision about his schooling.

This section of the dialogue raised two interesting issues for the social workers in the research study who were participating in the enactment of this role-play as forum theatre. First, they stated that they felt Maxine's projection of frustration and anger within themselves. Processes of transference are considered to be useful and inevitable within social work communication with service users, as the relationship exposes past experiences of relationships, particularly those relating to receiving help and care. 'Counter-transference' has been used as a concept to describe the reaction triggered in the worker as a result of being receptive to a service user's transferred feelings (Salzberger-Wittenberg, 1970). The social workers in our study seemed to be describing such processes of 'counter-transference', but interestingly, their communication response was to seek to contain the feelings generated – those of the service user, but also those of themselves. Indeed, their own feelings were about feeling helpless in the face of knowledge deficit, and a desire to reassure and calm Maxine. 'Containment' is described as an 'active process of struggling to "contain", understand and work through our own emotional responses in the hope that this will enable our clients to do the same for themselves' (Agass, 2002: 127). It is a communicative medium that enables people to feel understood, and in control of their emotional and social selves (Howe, 1998; Agass, 2002; Ruch 2005b). The following extract from the research transcript describes how the social workers discussed using a practical response of 'getting the missing information' as a way of providing containment for the feelings of frustration being expressed by Maxine and the helplessness experienced by themselves:

Social worker 1: The overriding thing is frustration. That's the thing that comes across. So you need to get at, to address that frustration right from the word 'go' and establish what that is.

Social worker 2: And establish an agenda. Obviously, if she's got a different agenda from the social worker, who is there for a different reason, then you need to somehow deal with that.

Social worker 3: You could say, 'That's something I can help you with. I could make some enquiries about that possibility', couldn't you?

Johanna: Why would you want to do that? I'm not saying you're wrong. I just want to understand why you felt that was needed?

Social worker 3: She's so just kind of ... she's getting herself upset ... she's saying nothing is happening and, you know, you haven't got anything to give her, but there is a possibility that I may be able to make enquiries about that situation.

Social worker 4: I understand that this parent needs more information, but aren't we missing the point? This boy has such a special need that he might need to go to a special school and we're not actually addressing her fears around that.

Social worker 3: Well, when the information has been gathered next week and identifies that, then that's the discussion to have. But, I don't know, maybe she's not willing to offer up that [information] because she doesn't see her child as having a learning disability. She may not have dealt with that obstacle yet. That's my thinking. I've got to do some research on what's been said so far.

Thus, this decision to seek to show containment through operating a specialist communication strategy of 'identifying a practical response of seeking to overcome the systemic barriers' through obtaining the missing information, essentially provides containment for the social workers' feelings of helplessness as much as the frustration expressed by Maxine. This poses a dilemma. If this skill is based as much on the social worker's felt responses as on the service user's expressed feelings then should it be given validity as a specialist communication skill? On the one hand the skill can be criticised for reinforcing attitudinal barriers of a privileging of formal knowledge and 'professional explanations' over parental 'private' knowledge. Yet, on the other hand, service users told us they felt more reassured by social workers who sought to overcome systemic barriers, who 'did what they said they would do', and who wrote down their agreed action. The important issue was that the social worker believed the service user, or even identified for themselves that there was a systemic issue causing difficulties in the first place.

The second issue raised by the social workers as part of the research study was that Maxine seemed to be emphasising schooling and social skills development rather than her relationship with her child. The parents of children with disabilities in my earlier research study were similarly perceived by social work analysts as prioritising their child's acquisition of social skills with peers in order to promote integration and reduce social isolation for their child over and above their relationship with the child (Woodcock and Tregaskis, 2008). The reason for the observation was that social workers, within their parenting assessments, are required to look for indications of prescribed social work dimensions of parenting, particularly those within the national policy guidance, *Framework for the Assessment of Children in Need and their Families*

(DoH, 2000a). One key dimension is to ascertain the warmth and reciprocity of the parenting relationship as a way of determining whether and how parents are responding to the developmental needs of their child. In the earlier study I sought to understand why these parents communicated so strongly about aspects of child development. I found that, while social workers sought to understand parenting behaviour in social terms, it was not sufficient, as it required the *social model of disability analysis* to recognise the reasons that this was about parental attempts to overcome systemic barriers to their child receiving effective help, such as preparation for significant life stages (like going to school).

This discussion reiterates the need for social workers 'to identify, discuss and empathise with systemic barriers with parents' as a specialist communication skill. An example of one such systemic barrier, which is cited in Practice Example 5.1 is the service failure to take the needs of Ben, Maxine and her husband, as an individual child and family, into account, in favour of a 'one size fits all' model. Another barrier alluded to by Maxine concerned a failure to provide 'joined-up services' to meet individual needs. These barriers are considered to arise when services are developed primarily to meet the normative needs of the provider, and take insufficient account of the diverse needs of client groups (Barnes, 1991).

The dialogue demonstrates the social worker applying these skills through seeking to 'show empathy' for the developmental concerns by 'putting feelings into words', and then using the skill of 'identifying a practical response of seeking to overcome the systemic barriers' by offering to obtain the missing information (point 5).

Maxine responds with disbelief that this practical response will make any difference – perhaps understandably, given the degree of difficulties she has faced with systemic barriers. The social worker then repeats the skill at points 6, 7 and 8 to deal with her disbelief and reinforce that he *will* do this information-gathering work. However, it is the non-verbal communication of actually writing down the agreement and a future date in the diary that finally provides the containment for the feelings being expressed (Practice Example 5.1, point 8).

In Practice Example 5.2, the dialogue proceeds with the social worker seeking simultaneously to attend to the two agendas required for this practice setting:

(i) the need to hear and respect parental 'private' knowledge about the individual characteristics of an impairment and the individual way it affects family life;

(ii) looking for indications of prescribed social work dimensions of parenting, particularly those within the national policy guidance, *Framework for the Assessment of Children in Need and their Families* (DoH, 2000a).

PRACTICE EXAMPLE 5.2

Maxine and Ben

Work phase

[9] *SW*: You say you are concerned about Ben and different kinds of schools. What are your concerns? I'd like to understand your views on this situation.

[10] *Maxine*: Well, because all I ever hear from services such as yourself, education, psychology, health, is that I don't know the difference between, you know, an ordinary child, whatever that is, and I'm constantly being told that my child has learning difficulties, you know, disabilities. Now, that's all well and good but I don't understand the difference from an ordinary child. Why is it being pinned on Ben so much? Is that the reason that nothing is happening, because services are going to actually presume that he won't go into mainstream school because 'oh no, he has a learning difficulty'? That is one thing me and my husband are livid about. I've asked that before. I don't see the need to pinpoint and pigeonhole people, particularly children. That's something I'm beyond frustrated about!

[11] *SW:* You're fed up with how professionals see Ben, as if he has deficits in different areas... and you don't like this label of disability used about him. (*Maxine looks at Makemba, sits still for about ten seconds and nods*) So, how do you think Ben is developing at the moment? Is he doing the kinds of things you would expect? Have you got other children...?

Maxine: No.

[12] *SW*: So you haven't got another child to compare... what about at playschool, does he play with other children? Is he talking?

[13] *Maxine*: Yes, the reports we received... the doctor said that development-wise Ben would be better off in a special educational needs school. But other services said that mainstream school would be OK for one or two times a week. That's what us as a family would really like to do because he is developing... I see him developing.... He's probably going to be in a special education school, but I would like him to be in a mainstream school so he interacts. I don't want there to be such a distinction when he gets older, there's no life experience that way.

►

►

[14] *SW*: That's a really good way of doing it. A compromise....

Silence for five seconds.

[15] *SW*: You've told me what the professionals think. It's really important for me to hear what it's like for you and your son, you know, your family. What's a day in your life like for you and Ben?

Maxine: Right, OK. Well, my husband goes to work at 8.30 – he goes to work in the City. Then obviously breakfast with Ben, and then he goes to playgroup from 10.30 to 2.45pm.

SW: Do you stay with him, or do you leave him?

Maxine: No, I've stayed in the past but I do stuff at home as well... prepare for when he comes home... if that makes sense.

[16] *SW*: Gives you a bit of time.

Maxine: Yeah, not in a horrible way....

SW: But a bit of time.

Maxine: Yeah, it's demanding with children anyway.

[17] *SW*: So, how is he when you leave him at playgroup – does he like it?

Maxine: Yeah, he seems to enjoy it. He interacts well. It's a playgroup with a variety of children anyway – in the developmental process. So, I've stayed there, and I've watched him and played, just me and him, and other children have joined in as well.

[18] *SW*: Does he like the other children?

Maxine: Yeah, he's very funny. But it's nice because he interacts with children from all walks of life and problems and I think that's lovely... you know, that's probably why I want Ben to have both... not the best of both worlds, but....

SW: Opportunities? (*Maxine nods at this*) What happens at 2.45pm?

Maxine: Well, 2.45pm I go and pick him up and there's a park so we come back and go there; or just come straight home and he does lots of ... pasting and things like that – nothing too obviously advanced, just... just lots of things....

►

▶
[19] *SW*:	Things that he enjoys?
Maxine:	Yeah, yeah, yeah.
SW:	Do you have a good relationship with him?
Maxine:	Yeah, we laugh a lot.
SW:	I'm really interested about where you're getting your support from. Do you have family or friends?
Maxine:	Don't have many friends, but yeah, family.
SW:	Are they supportive?
Maxine:	Yeah. I would say so. Also, my husband's very supportive.
SW:	What time does your husband get home? I'd like to arrange a time when we can all meet.
[20] *Maxine*:	He gets home about seven.

Communicating in a way that attends to this 'shared agenda' seems difficult and highly skilled. The degree of fear and apprehension surrounding the authority role of the social worker means that parents are likely to be alert and vigilant to the possibility of their child's developmental progress being misunderstood. As noted above, my earlier research identified parents describing the fear that they were in some way inadvertently caring for their child inappropriately and fearing protective action might be taken (Woodcock and Tregaskis, 2008). In view of this, care needs to be taken to ensure that communication is focused on the individual developmental characteristics and progress of a child as opposed to identifying the general developmental milestones a child is not achieving. Parental resentment and upset at their child not being viewed as a child first, with individual needs, but rather as a child with stereotypical features of a medical impairment is exemplified by Maxine's statement in Practice Example 5.2, point 10:

> Well, because all I ever hear from services such as yourself, education, psychology, health, is that I don't know the difference between, you know, an ordinary child, whatever that is, and I'm constantly being told that my child has learning difficulties, you know, disabilities. Now, that's all well and good but I don't understand the difference from an ordinary child. Why is it being pinned on Ben so much? Is that the reason that nothing is

happening, because services are going to actually presume that he won't go into mainstream school because 'oh no, he has a learning difficulty'? That is one thing me and my husband are livid about. I've asked that before. I don't see the need to pinpoint and pigeonhole people, particularly children. That's something I'm beyond frustrated about!

The social worker demonstrates 'reflective listening' in responding empathically to this statement by Maxine. In doing so, he uses the basic communication skill described in Chapter 2 of 'summarising'. (Practice Exercise 5.2, point 11: 'You're fed up with how professionals see Ben, as if he has deficits in different areas... and you don't like this label of disability used about him.'). Maxine's non-verbal communication, observed via her body language (sitting still and having eye contact with the social worker) and the resultant silence (possibly thinking and 'working' on the social worker's statement), seems to indicate that her feelings about this have been contained. Unfortunately, the social worker ends the silence with a set of statements that do the opposite – he seeks to compare Ben's developmental progress with that of other children. This comparison approach presents a danger of describing Ben's development in negative terms – that is, looking for deficits or differences across generalised developmental standards. Maxine's response to this is to return to being defensive. She repeats her desire for Ben's developmental progress to be regarded in individual terms by emphasising the fact that she notices small achievements in Ben's developmental progress, regardless of expert opinion (Practice Exercise 5.2, point 13). These statements from Practice Example 5.2, points 11 and 14 are reproduced here:

[11] *SW*: So, how do you think Ben is developing at the moment? Is he doing the kinds of things you would expect? Have you got other children...?

Maxine: No.

[12] *SW*: So you haven't got another child to compare... what about at playschool, does he play with other children? Is he talking?

[13] *Maxine*: Yes, the reports we received... the doctor said that development-wise Ben would be better off in a special educational needs school. But other services said that mainstream school would be OK for one or two times a week. That's what us as a family would really like to do because he is developing... I see him developing... He's probably going to be in a special education school, but I would like him to be in a mainstream school so he interacts. I don't want there to be such a distinction when he gets older, there's no life experience that way.

[14] *SW*: That's a really good way of doing it. A compromise... (*Silence for five seconds*)

Thus the dialogue from the practice example and findings from the background literature illustrate how specialist communication skills of 'positive framing of development rather than using negative deficits notions' and 'demonstrating knowledge of the individual child' are clearly of paramount importance here. If these skills are not employed, then social workers are more likely to face strong emotions and opposition from parents.

So why does the social worker seek to engage Maxine in a comparison of Ben's development with other children at this point? One answer lies in the background literature, which tells us that, in the face of knowledge deficits, social workers often rely on common-sense reasoning devices (Howitt ,1992; Parton *et al.*, 1997; Woodcock, 2003). For example, the studies of Daniel (2000), Holland (2000) and Woodcock (2003) emphasised how social work constructions of parenting were influenced by workers' experiences of their own parenting and their own children's development pathways. There are dangers with this. Indeed, Howitt (1992) identifies how, in assessing parental behaviour against social and cultural templates – for example, 'reasonable parenting' – 'error making' can occur in social work decisions. Parton *et al.* (1997) describe one such use of common-sense reasoning that could induce 'error-making' – the practice of clarifying the expected features of parenting in a situation and using the presence or absence of these features to judge the possibility of abuse occurring. In my earlier research into parenting assessment (Woodcock, 2003) I found this practice occurring, whereby parenting was assessed against a series of expectations of behaviour.

A second answer might be that the social worker is once again responding to the parent's communication of strong feeling through processes of counter-transference. Indeed, the social workers involved in the forum theatre for the research study discussed how, at this point in the dialogue, the social worker seemed, once again, to be keen to provide a practical response to contain Maxine's expression of feelings (Practice Example 5.2, point 14: 'That's a really good way of doing it. A compromise...'). The social workers questioned whether and how this provision of a solution-focused response was appropriate. They were concerned that such a response might be seen as imposing their own opinion on to the service user, and as such it might not have felt responsive to individual need. They also wondered whether the solution-focused response might have been used as a cover-up or an avoidance tactic to side-step having to deal with a potentially uncomfortable and difficult discussion concerning access to normative services. In so doing, the social worker could be construed as operating another dynamic that was identified in the background literature as potentially occurring between a social worker and a service user in parenting assessment – the 'rule of optimism' (Dingwall, 1986; Parton, 1991). Prins (1999) described this dynamic in terms of a wish to see things moving forward, or improving, despite any evidence to suggest this might be happening. Certainly the social worker is quick to apply a solution-focused response because it is deemed to be 'more acceptable' to the service user. There are dangers in this, for while the social worker might feel reassured that he has achieved a degree of engagement with the parent, the more difficult work of uncovering and challenging difficult feelings and decisions remains undone. The following extract from the research transcript illustrates these points:

Johanna: If you were Makemba, why did you say 'it's a really good compromise'?

Social worker 1: I suppose because I just thought we hadn't heard the special needs bit before and that it might be a good place to start ....

Social worker 2: But was that 'a really good compromise' from Makemba's point of view or Maxine's?

Social worker 1: I don't know.

Social worker 3: But she seemed happy with it, like that was something she would agree to. She wasn't saying 'I don't want this.' She was sort of saying 'I've had this suggested to me...'.

Social worker 2: It just seems like its this classic thing that I sometimes do [*where*] it's a tricky situation and I'm out of my depth with knowledge ... which doesn't take very long! ... and I see a bit of an escape route and I think 'Oh this sounds really good.' I'm a bit of a Mr Fixit, so ... bang! I come in with a solution. It did sound a bit prescriptive, but, I mean, it's the sort of thing I do myself, that's why I recognise it. But I'm not sure whether it's what she wanted.

In summarising this set of points, the background literature and research transcript emphasises the degree to which a social worker influences the processes and outcomes of any parenting assessment. Thus a specialist communication skill which must be employed is that of 'identifying social worker's personal attitudes and preconceptions of parenting'. The following questions might enable a social worker to fulfil this:

- Am I operating a set of cultural and societal expectations about parenting behaviour?

- Am I viewing parenting as a relationship which is multiply determined and holistic?
- Am I viewing parenting in terms of promoting children's developmental welfare needs, and not just whether abuse and maltreatment is occurring?
- Am I seeking to support parenting as a means of safeguarding practice?
- Which of the factors influencing my judgements are to do with what's going on inside me – the influence of my 'self'?

Point 15 of Practice Example 5.2 is a critical moment. The social worker recognises he has fixated on his own agenda and concerns. He appears to recognise that work is not occurring between himself and Maxine, but rather it is, as Shulman puts it, 'the illusion of work'. Having recognised the illusion of work, he seeks to use the skill of 'achieving a shared purpose' once again ('You know, you've told me what the professionals think. It's really important for me to hear what it's like for you and your son, you know, your family. What's a day in your life like for you and Ben?') This 'open question' seeks elaboration, and again emphasises that he is prepared to hear and respect parental 'private' knowledge about the individual characteristics of an impairment and the individual way it affects family life. The rest of the dialogue demonstrates 'reflective listening' through empathising with feelings (5.2, point 16: 'Gives you a bit of time.'); but also, just as importantly, by using 'open questions' to ask for information about Ben's personality and individual response, which is framed in positive language (5.2, point 17: 'How is he when you leave him at playgroup – does he like it?'; 5.2, point 18: 'Does he like the other children?'; and 5.2, point 19: 'Things that he enjoys?'). This again illustrates the importance of using specialist communication skills of 'positive framing of development rather than using negative deficits notions' and 'demonstrating knowledge of the individual child'.

Conceptual ideas from systemic family therapy have been highlighted for work with families to make sense of the interconnections between parental problems, parenting, child well-being, and other social factors in the familial environment. Kroll and Taylor (2003) particularly emphasise the usefulness of the systemic framework as a way of viewing how substance use operates as a part of the family system and impacts on everyone else. They recommend the use of genograms and ecomaps as visual, symbolic tools to gain information about the world of families as experienced by the different family members. Arguably, such an approach would work well with families with disabled children. 'Open questions' and 'closed questions' would need to draw out the quality of the relationship between the parent and child, but also the relationship between each of them and the multitude of other social factors that co-exist and inter-relate with them. The systemic barriers experienced by parents would become easily identifiable, and it would be easier to operate the specialist communication skill mentioned above, of 'identifying, discussing and empathising with systemic barriers with parents'.

In summary, the specialist social work communication skills identified in this chapter have addressed the potential for misunderstanding and error-making when making judgements about parenting that emanate from within the 'self' and cultural and societal normative expectations of parenting. Systemic barriers must be identified and communicated. Second, the chapter has emphasised how important, yet difficult, it is to operate the specialist social work communication skills required to 'achieve a shared purpose' with 'hard-to-reach' parents. Significant emotional resources are required of a social worker to analyse interpersonal communication dynamics and to 'show empathy' within this context.

Professional Standards

This chapter will help you to meet the following National Occupational Standards:

Key Role 1: Prepare for, and work with individuals, families, carers, groups and communities to assess their needs and circumstances

Unit 1 Prepare for social work contact and involvement
Unit 2 Work with individuals, families, carers, groups and communities to help them make informed decisions
Unit 3 Assess needs and options to recommend a course of action

Key Role 2: Plan, carry out, review and evaluate social work practice with individuals, families, carers, groups, communities and other professionals

Unit 4 Respond to crisis situations
Unit 5 Interact with individuals, families, carers, groups and communities to achieve change and development and to improve life opportunities
Unit 6 Prepare, produce, implement and evaluate plans with individuals, families, carers, groups, communities and professional colleagues
Unit 8 Work with groups to promote individual growth, development and independence
Unit 9 Address behaviour which presents a risk to individuals, families, carers, groups and communities

Key Role 3: Support individuals to represent their needs, views and circumstances. Advocate with and on behalf of people

Unit 10 Advocate with, and on behalf of, individuals, families, carers, groups and communities

Key Role 4: Manage risk to individuals, families, carers, groups, communities, self and colleagues

Unit 12 Assess and manage risks to individuals, families, carers, groups and communities
Unit 13: Assess, minimise and manage risk to self and colleagues

Key Role 5: Manage and be accountable, with supervision and support, for your own social work practice within your organisation

Unit 16 Manage and be accountable, with supervision and support, for your own social work practice within your organisation
Unit 17 Work within multi-disciplinary and multi-organisational teams, networks and systems

Key Role 6: Demonstrate professional competence in social work practice

Unit 18 Research, analyse, evaluate and use current knowledge of best social work practice
Unit 19 Work within agreed standards of social work practice and ensure own professional development
Unit 20 Manage complex ethical issues, dilemmas and conflicts
Unit 21 Contribute to the promotion of best social work practice

CHAPTER

Working with People Who Use Substances 6

Summary of Specialist Communication Skills

- Tuning-in to social worker's personal attitudes and preconceptions of people who use substances
- Identifying social worker's personal attitudes and preconceptions of parenting
- Entering the world of substance-using families
- Making the child visible
- Addressing service user fears of stigmatisation
- Avoiding exhortations to change
- Motivating service users to decide to make changes, including components of:
  - providing affirmation
  - encouraging service user recognition of the divergence between their values or goals and the reality of their current behaviour
  - providing all options to encourage feelings of self-efficacy

Policy and background literature

In terms of communication issues arising from policy, the competencies needed to work in the field of substance use, and the knowledge and skills underpinning these competencies, are described in the 'Health and Social Care' National Occupational Standards (NOS) (Skills for Care and Development, 2008), and in particular in a group of standards taken from them known as the Drug & Alcohol National Occupational Standards (DANOS). These competencies state the need for professionals to 'promote effective communication for and about individuals'. Communication should be about substance use and its associated risks at a time, level and pace appropriate to the individual in order to maximise the likelihood of the individual understanding what is being said. Guidance, support and advice should be given to service users on ways in which methods of substance use and activities affected by it can be practised more safely.

People who use substances often have poor self-image, a very negative outlook on life and find small problems overwhelming. Physical addiction is only part of the problem, and difficult to disentangle from emotional, psychological and social elements (Kroll and Taylor, 2003). Indeed, it is important for social workers working with substance users to recognise the social factors contained within the aetiology, progression and maintenance of substance use. These concern developmental issues, effects of stress and the role of social support, peer group and other cultural influences, social exclusion and cultural stereotypes, prevention and treatment models (Skills for Care and Development, 2008).

When I was undertaking the work of identifying how these themes from within the literature relate to specialist communication skills, I found many to be relevant, but two key issues were particularly significant. These concerned: (i) the degree of stigmatisation; and (ii) the levels of secrecy and denial involved in substance use.

It is critical to understand how processes of 'denial' influence an understanding of levels of substance use and the impact of its use on well-being, as well as influencing the dynamics of the working relationship with a service user (Taylor, 1999). Denial is considered to arise from conflicted emotions between the desire to continue to be emotionally connected or 'attached' to a substance and the distress resulting from the behaviour and other consequences caused by the substance (Orford, 2001). If the conflicting emotions cannot be resolved, then confusion, panic and despair set in (Taylor, 1999). Thus the psychological operation of denial acts to prevent conflicting emotions coming to the surface. Orford (2001) also points out how processes of denial operate not just in an internal way, but also through an increased secrecy about the behaviour externally, such as in relationships with friends, family and support workers. As Kroll and Taylor (2003: 96) summarise: 'denial is a natural and self-protective response to pain', which when employed as a survival strategy resists demands to change. Unfortunately, in maintaining levels of secrecy and denial, other significant relationships start to be ignored, with family members, and particularly dependent children, being rendered 'invisible' (Kroll and Taylor, 2003). Continual relationship breakdown is a common feature and one that is likely to impact on the communication processes within the relationship with the social worker (Woodcock and Sheppard, 2002).

Social workers' professional judgements concerning problematic substance use can be influenced by personal attitudes and negative cultural stereotypes based on 'moral panics' (Forrester and Harwin, 2004). There is considerable stigma against people who have problems using drugs and alcohol, resulting in their marginalisation in society. The stigma exists despite the reality of drug use embracing legal as well as illegal activity, including recreational drug use, experimental drug use and prescribed drug use. Substance or chemical use is a feature of everyday life for most people. Alcohol is a frequent part of celebrations or relaxation, and many people take prescribed or unprescribed drugs for medical conditions. In any of these situations a person could lose control over their substance use, creating a number of risks to their health and safety, and that of their friends and family (Paylor, 2008).

The literature highlights the importance of achieving an empowering relationship in which to operate processes of change in behaviour involving substance misuse (Prochaska and DiClemente, 1983; Prochaska *et al.*, 1992; Velleman, 2001; Barber, 2002; Kroll and Taylor, 2003). As an example, Velleman's process of 'enabling change' has six stages: 'developing trust'; 'exploring the problem'; 'helping clients to set goals'; 'empowering clients to take action'; 'helping them to maintain changes'; 'agreeing with them when the time comes to end the counselling relationship'. DiClemente and Velasquez's (2002) model of change describes five key motivational stages that are often represented as a turning circle to indicate how a person may not pass through the stages in a particular order. These stages comprise: Precontemplation, Contemplation, Preparation, Action and Maintenance. Barber (2002) notes in operating the Prochaska and DiClemente (1983) model that workers must treat the individual with respect, take time and not be judgmental – 'not beating over the head with "you must change"'. Communication with 'precontemplators' of change will focus on reducing the value of substance use. If ambivalence or desire to change is evident, then the focus of communication should change as the service user is now in the 'contemplation' stage. Communication skills will be directed at eliciting individual decision-making.

When turning to the literature concerning parental substance use, I identified a number of practice dilemmas relevant to specialist communication. First, professional and cultural preconceptions exist about parental substance use, such as assuming that all parents who use drugs or alcohol will be a danger to their children (Cleaver *et al.*, 1999). Substance-using parents do not constitute a homogenous group (Taylor and Kroll, 2004). Many parents use alcohol and chemical substances and still parent effectively (SCODA, 1997; Harbin and Murphy, 2000, Buchanan and Young, 2002). However, there is an increasing body of evidence showing that parental substance use is linked to problems in child development and child maltreatment (Cleaver *et al.*, 1999; ACMD, 2003).

Second, the organisational context has been found to have an impact on effectiveness in assessing and treating parental substance misuse. This occurs despite all agencies who engage with substance-using parents being charged with a duty from The Children Acts (1989 and 2004 in England and Wales, and 1995 in Scotland) to assess the needs of children whose health and development might be at risk of being harmed. This duty was emphasised by the policy initiative *Hidden Harm* (Scottish Executive, 2004). Historically, problem substance use and child protection systems have developed separately and with different orientations, which have caused barriers for collaborative working (Taylor and Kroll, 2004). An organisational orientation towards child welfare has tended to prioritise the need to safeguard children over parental needs. In contrast, substance users have tended to be viewed as the primary focus of intervention if the professional orientation is treatment for substance use (Taylor and Kroll, 2004). The separation of organisational systems and orientations has meant that social workers, in general, lack training and confidence in working with the combined issues of substance use and parenting (Forrester and Harwin, 2004; Paylor, 2008).

Third, drug users have been found to express a common concern when they come into contact with services – fear that their children will be 'taken away' (Buchanan and Young, 2002; Taylor and Kroll, 2004). The fear of the initiation of child protection procedures can cause some parents to display erratic behaviour, such as avoiding contact with social workers. Taylor and Kroll (2004) identified that many of the difficulties professionals faced in gaining trust to achieve authentic information about lifestyle centred on secrecy and denial. Fear about how the agency might act on disclosed information caused parents to deny the reality of the impact of their substance use on their child, as well as failing to sustain engagement.

Finally, social work perceptions about parental substance use are inevitably influenced by perceptions of parenting more generally. The literature has focused on the influence of the constructions of parenting held by social workers themselves (Daniel, 2000; Holland, 2000; Woodcock, 2003). Feminist analyses have identified how workers make judgements about the role of 'mothers' and 'caring', resulting in the phenomenon of 'mother-blaming' (Turney, 2000). The interactive dynamic between the worker and the service user is also given attention by theoretical considerations of 'reflexivity' (Sheppard, 1998). Reflexivity exemplifies that parenting assessment is not just a technical activity but involves various underlying factors influencing practice, including beliefs and values about what is 'good enough' or 'not good enough'. Daniel's (2000) study emphasised in particular how beliefs were influenced by workers' experiences of their own parenting and their own children's development pathways. Howitt (1992) similarly suggested that workers assess parental behaviour against social templates (for example, 'reasonable parenting') resulting in 'error making' in social work decisions. Some of my own earlier research (Woodcock, 2003) confirmed that of Parton *et al.* (1997)

in finding social workers using common-sense reasoning devices to make decisions, usually in situations of uncertainty, such as when assessing risk of harm. In my research study this involved clarifying the expected features of parenting in a situation and using the presence or absence of these features to judge the possibility that abuse might occur. Clearly, if any social worker leaves his or her personal attitudes about parenting unexamined then he or she might reinforce the marginalisation already experienced by service users.

Practice application

Practice Examples 6.1 and 6.2 focus on the communication between a social worker (Iona) and two substance-using parents, Karen and John.

PRACTICE EXAMPLE 6.1

The Collins-Evans Family

Preparatory stage

Yesterday, John Collins (28 years old) and Karen Evans (25 years old), both describing themselves as 'white Welsh' ethnic origin, received a telephone call from a social worker from the city's Children's Services (Local Authority) to arrange an appointment to visit them and their three children: Caris (aged 8), Natasha (5) and Josh (18 months). A teacher from the children's school had contacted the social work team with a number of concerns about the well-being of Caris and Natasha. These included: the children frequently being late for school; the children being overtired and with poor concentration; Caris being quiet and withdrawn, and overly mature for her years such that she appears to parent Natasha. Two parents have told Caris's teacher, in confidence, that their father has a drug addiction which is out of control, and their mother has approached them for money to meet the household bills. The social worker wants to meet the whole family as part of her initial assessment of the children's safety and well-being.

The family live in a recently built local authority housing estate, located in a socially deprived area of a medium-sized city in the UK. The general practitioner notes that Karen has a history of depression and that she received advice about the dangers of alcohol consumption during her pregnancy with Josh. The couple relationship has broken down on a number of occasions in the past. Karen has a strained relationship with her mother, who lives locally. Her mother looks after the children one evening a week to give Karen a break. John lost contact with his family when he began using street drugs five years ago.

PRACTICE EXAMPLE 6.2

The Collins-Evans Family

Beginnings

Dialogue begins with the social worker visiting the family home, having telephoned the previous day to make an appointment to meet the whole family.

SW: Ms Evans? (*Karen nods slightly*) Hello, I'm Iona. We spoke on the phone yesterday. (*Smiles and offers to shake her hand*) It's good to meet you.

[1] *Karen*: Hello. Come in. Just in there. (*Gestures with her hand towards the living room where the rest of the family are sitting on sofas, then turns towards her partner, John*) Get your feet off there! (*Karen waves her hand in an agitated manner at John*) This is John.

[2] *SW*: Hello John, I'm Iona. (*Offers to shake John's hand.*) These your girls, Caris and Natasha? Hello. And Josh? (*Smiles at Josh, who is sitting on Caris's lap on the sofa*). Is it OK for me to sit down? Here OK? Thanks. As I said on the phone, I'm a social worker from Children's Services. I'm here to discuss the referral. I guess you've probably been wondering why I'm coming to see you. Maybe worried. I really believe in being open and honest and working alongside people. (*Pause*) Can we discuss the concerns the school have raised in the referral together? (*Pause*) I'm wondering ... have the children got some toys they could play with just while we talk?

Karen: Caris, take Natasha and Josh out to the garden to play.

Caris: Can we take some crisps? (*Karen nods and the children all leave*)

SW: Thanks Caris ... Do you know anything about the referral? Has the school discussed it with you?

Karen: The school phoned me today.

SW: What did the school say?

Karen: Well, just generally....

[3] *John*: (*Interrupts in a loud voice*) Look, what they said is I'm a druggie ... got a problem with me! I'm not doing anything that's affecting my kids.

[4] *SW*: OK. So they are saying you are using drugs. OK. What are they saying their concerns are about your use specifically?

John: Don't know.

►

▶

[5] *SW*: You see, my experience is that people who use drugs do it in different ways and different issues come up for people, and sometimes problems come up.

[6] *Karen*: It's about him taking drugs and keeping the kids off school.

SW: They're not getting to school…?

[7] *Karen*: I can't do everything. Getting them up, getting them to school. Tash can be a right one in the mornings….

SW: John, do you have any care of them? Do you ever take them to school?

John: From time to time.

SW: So, Karen, it sounds like you feel that you're left with the care of the children and you find it hard to get everyone up in the morning to get them to school. Are they quite overtired in the morning?

Karen: They don't seem to get tired in the evening and it takes ages to get them to bed. They're not out playing like the other kids round here. They don't use up their energy.

John: That's 'cos they get bullied.

Karen: I'm not surprised! They say their dad's a druggie! He spends £400 on it.

[8] *SW*: What are your thoughts and feelings about that, John?

John: They're just kids saying it at the end of the day.

[9] *SW*: John, it would help me understand more if you tell me what kinds of drugs you're using. (*Gestures with hands for John to say more*)

[10] *John*: Smack.

[11] SW: Have you got some support to help you manage your drug-taking safely?

[12] *Karen*: We've tried before for John to stop but it hasn't worked. Look, my kids are OK. I don't do anything.

[13] *SW*: I can see you're worried about me asking all these questions about the children. The reason I'm asking you and John these things

▶

▶

is to try and work out what impact your drug use has on your parenting. I'm not judging you for taking drugs but I will need to know more about the drugs you are taking and what happens to you when you take them. Where I can I want to support you both and work out how to support the children, so they are not affected in their daily lives by the drug use. Things like, are they upset by it? Are they missing school? Are you getting the income you need? Have you got friends to support you or are you lonely and tired? If you are not going to address your drug use, then we will need to provide much more help and support to the children. How does that sound to you? Can we work on this together?

[14] *Karen*: OK. We'll have to sort this out.

SW: That's really positive Karen... you know... that you want to think about this. First, John, I need to find out more about your drug use. Do you mind speaking with Karen here, or would you prefer to be on your own? I could arrange for you to meet a specialist drugs and alcohol worker to talk through the issues.

The background literature highlighted how social workers' professional judgements concerning problematic substance use can be influenced by personal attitudes and negative cultural stereotypes (Forrester and Harwin, 2004). 'Tuning in to social worker's personal attitudes and preconceptions of people who use substances' is a crucial first specialist communication skill for the social worker in preparation for the ways in which Karen and John might express their emotions during the meeting. There is a danger of the social worker assuming that Karen and John will inevitably be a danger to their children because they use drugs or alcohol. It is important to remember that the problematic substance use itself may not cause significant harm, but the particular way it impacts on parenting and the child's well-being needs to be identified (Cleaver *et al.*, 1999). An attitude that sees all drug use as dangerous will fail to distinguish between recreational use and problematic dependence. The social worker needs to prepare herself not to over-react or under-react to both types of use, whether relating this to Karen's use of alcohol or John's use of drugs (Gilman, 2000).

The social worker needs to tune in to how her personal attitudes might be orientated towards a particular model of addiction. An individualised (medical) model would view the parents' problematic substance use as resulting from biological or emotional disposition or sickness. In this case, the social worker will inevitably only perceive that the service users are at less risk of harming their health and well-being if they abstain from using substances.

This attitude, while commonly and often unconsciously held, will fail to take into account the number of environmental factors existing within the practice scenario. Indeed, abstinence is very difficult to maintain, and so the social worker might feel fairly pessimistic about its success. These attitudes of 'individual responsibility to abstain', individually based treatment and negativity or feelings of hopelessness about success will influence how well the social worker empathises with the service users' communication.

Personal attitudes might be orientated towards another dominant model – that of viewing drug use as the development of patterns of habitual behaviour that have become dysfunctional and unsafe because of triggers that are psychological or within the social environment (Paylor, 2008). Social workers with this set of attitudes will seek to see changes in the social environment, encouraging the individual to utilise harm reduction strategies and terminate the dysfunctional behavioural patterns. This attitude also propagates 'individual responsibility', but the focus is on the service user managing drug use through improvements in the psycho-social situation. The sheer number and complexity of different psycho-social factors within this practice scenario may cause similar feelings of pessimism about success, which could influence communication. Clearly, if any social worker leaves his or her own feelings and knowledge about substance use unchecked then he or she may exacerbate the marginalisation already experienced by service users.

This is not just a meeting to discuss substance use in isolation, but to work out the impact of the substance use on parenting and the children's welfare. The background literature identified how parenting assessments can be influenced by a social worker's personal constructions of parenting. Thus, at this preparatory stage of 'tuning in', the social worker needs to use the specialist communication skill of 'identifying social worker's personal attitudes and preconceptions of parenting'. In particular, the social worker needs to guard against holding a set of societal expectations about parenting behaviour as opposed to a multiply determined, holistic model, such as that set out within the *Framework for Assessing Children in Need and their Families* (DoH, 2000a) or the Standing Conference on Drug Abuse (SCODA) guidelines (Forrester and Harwin, 2004). Indeed, while in many areas women have achieved greater equality, oppressive gender stereotypes still pervade women's lives in relation to parenting. Cultural prescriptions of 'good parenting' expect mothers to know how to parent and to always provide 'sensitive and responsive' care regardless of social circumstance (Sheppard, 2000; Woodcock, 2003). Karen, as an alcohol-using mother in receipt of social work services is doubly vulnerable to 'mother blaming'. As Paylor (2008: 603) states: 'The female alcohol/drug user can be portrayed as a morally inadequate person failing to fulfil their duty as a "decent woman"'.

In addition to 'tuning-in to personal attitudes and preconceptions', the social worker should seek to 'tune-in' to the way in which the service users might express their emotions to her during their meeting. The background literature highlighted that drug users frequently expressed fear that their children would be 'taken away' which was evidenced through avoidance and other strategies of secrecy and denial (Buchanan and Young, 2002; Taylor and Kroll, 2004). In Practice Example 6.2, point 3, we see John communicating fear about how the social worker might act on disclosed information through his reticence to become involved in the communication and then his angry outburst that his substance use is having no effect on the children ('John interrupts in a loud voice: 'Look, what they said is I'm a druggie ... got a problem with me! I'm not doing anything that's affecting my kids.') Karen communicates the same fear but in a less confrontational manner, such as emphasising how the demands of their care are particularly high and her children are thriving (Example 6.2, points 7 and 12). In drawing on the basic communication skills described in Chapter 2, the social worker will need to achieve and communicate empathy for these fears when they arise, to enable the service users to feel understood, if they are to engage and retain them (Paylor, 2008).

The social worker needs to 'tune-in' to the likelihood that Karen and John have experienced multiple relationship breakdowns, and that, subsequently, they will have brought insecure relationship templates to their relationship, and indeed also to communication with her. Modern attachment theorists have explored the way that the mind processes interpersonal information to use as a psychosocial template for relationships (Howe, 2005). Relationships can confirm or refute those internal relationship models at any point across the lifespan. People with an insecure-ambivalent attachment relationship model will feel only conditionally worthwhile, uncertain of whether they will be understood and valued, and they therefore constantly seek to test out the emotional and physical availability of the social worker. Alternatively, they might provide responses that 'seek to please' as opposed to risking any indication of their true feelings. People with an insecure-avoidant relationship model, however, bring to the communication their experience of having their needs consistently ignored. They are mistrustful of the potential of the social worker to be helpful, preferring to rely on their own coping strategies, which generally involve remaining emotionally detached to avoid inevitable rejection. Their self-esteem is often very low – feeling unlovable and without worth. In 'tuning-in', the social worker could hypothesise from the number of relationship breakdowns that Karen and John might have developed either type of insecure relationship pattern and anticipate them communicating reluctance to explore their difficulties because of their mistrust of adults who are supposed to care for them. As before, the social worker will need to prepare to achieve and communicate empathy for this anxiety.

When first meeting the family, the social worker must employ four of basic communication skills discussed in Chapter 2: 'achieving a shared purpose (that is, 'being clear on role'); 'being clear on purpose'; 'reaching for feedback' and 'showing empathy'. As stated above, the authority the social worker brings through her legislative role can cause significant fear and mistrust, which could dramatically influence the communication. Consequently, the social worker must ensure that she 'shows empathy' to those feelings immediately they arise, to enable Karen and John to feel understood, and in control of their emotional and social selves (Howe, 1998; Agass, 2002; Ruch, 2005b). At point 1 of Practice Example 6.2 we see Karen potentially communicating this fear non-verbally through her agitated behaviour, and John demonstrates fear through his silent observation of events. The social worker 'shows empathy' for these anticipated feelings in her opening statement (Example 6.2, point 2):

> As I said on the phone, I'm a social worker from Children's Services. I'm here to discuss the referral. I guess you've probably been wondering why I'm coming to see you. Maybe worried. I really believe in being open and honest and working alongside people. (*Pause*) Can we discuss the concerns that the school have raised in the referral together? (*Pause*) I'm wondering ... have the children got some toys that they could play with just while we talk?

The social worker immediately goes on to demonstrate that the opening statement, including the demonstration of empathy, is not just an empty promise of honesty and openness in collaborative working. She emphasises that she wants to share the referral information with the parents, and, more than this, she wants to ensure that they have an equal understanding of the concerns being raised. The data from the research transcripts called attention to this practice as a way of communicating a desire for partnership working. It constituted an expression of seeking to 'work with' as opposed to 'doing to' service users, and was considered part of a dynamic that would alleviate anxiety about the social worker's authority role:

> *Johanna*: In your experience of this practice setting, is 'Are you going to take my children away' said straightaway? No? So you think this is at the back of their minds ... being worried?

> *SW*: Yeah, if this is a new referral, referred by education about their concerns, then that conversation could be ameliorated by actually saying to them – the parents – that the reason we have come to see you is to actually hear your views about the referral ... that ... you know ... we are not coming to judge you. We are coming because (a) it's your right to know we've had a referral; and (b) to get your views ... I can hear that you are anxious....

It may be that a demonstration of such collaborative working will encourage service users to give their feedback on the social worker's beginning attempts at 'achieving a shared purpose'. This enables movement towards achieving a shared agenda for work to occur. Certainly, in our practice example, the supportiveness of the statement could have precipitated John's revelation about his substance use and expression of feeling (Example 6.2, point 3). His communication of denial about the impact of substance use on his children's welfare could be understood as further communication of fear of the social worker acting on any disclosed information. However, in drawing on the background literature concerning the dominance of issues of secrecy and denial, it could also be understood as an early indication of John denying the existence of a substance use problem for himself or his family generally. Indeed, the presence of the social worker may be causing the previously mentioned internal intrapsychic conflict about his substance-using behaviour to come to the fore. Certainly his tone is angry, suggesting that he is struggling with his emotions.

This occurrence in the dialogue provides a good illustration of how the social worker needs simultaneously to adopt some objective distance as well as achieve emotional attunement to the thoughts and feelings being expressed. In Chapter 2, we referred to this objective distancing as operating a 'third ear', or a 'second head', with the social worker having in mind questions such as 'What is really going on in the communication here?'; 'Is the problem that he or she is describing the most immediate problem, or is there something more worrying?' In this situation, if the social worker considers the communication to be predominately about fear of her authority role, it would seem useful to *'use immediacy',* one of the basic communication skills discussed in Chapter 2, to allow the social worker to comment honestly and directly on what is occurring within the process between the social worker and the service user. An example of this would be: 'You know, John, I wonder if you are feeling worried about me being a social worker and whether you can trust me, and this means you are reluctant to share your concerns with me. What do you think, can we talk about this?'

However, the dialogue shows the social worker implementing an alternative interpretation – that John is showing early evidence of denial of his problem substance use. The worker responds with 'reflective listening' through 'paraphrasing' John's statement but in a calm, accepting and non-judgmental way ('OK. So they are saying you are using drugs. OK. What are they saying their concerns are about your use specifically?') In so doing, the social worker establishes a reality of the drug use and potential effects, as opposed to collaborating with any denial of it existing.

The social worker's legal duty is to make sense of the way the drug use is affecting the lives of all members of the family, the parenting being provided to the children and the children's well-being. The multiplicity and interaction of the problems experienced, such as mental health, finances and a lack of an emotional support network means that it is not easy to make connections between the substance use and the parenting and social circumstances. A holistic approach to understanding is vital. Also, it means that it is important to consider each family situation individually. When 'being clear on purpose', the social worker needs to communicate how and why she is taking a holistic and individual approach to the family situation. In naming this specialist communication skill I have chosen to adopt a phrase used by Aldridge (1999) to describe what a social worker should do to fully understand parental substance use, which is 'to enter the world of substance using families'.

I hope that the articulation of this skill will help social workers to be clearer about their purpose in working with substance-using parents and families. The background literature indicated that this lack of clarity of purpose has its roots in the problematic organisational context, in terms of the separation of organisational systems and orientations of being focused on child welfare or on substance use. These organisational separations have impacted upon social workers' knowledge and confidence in working with combined issues of substance use and parenting (Forrester and Harwin, 2004; Paylor, 2008). Indeed, this theme was evident at the forum theatre during the research study underpinning this book. The research transcript showed that social workers struggled with ways of describing their purpose in this setting. The following excerpt illustrates this confusion:

SW1: Wouldn't you just introduce yourself as the social worker and say you are 'the one you spoke to the other day on the telephone. I've come to discuss the call we had, and to sit down and talk to you about this, and hear your views. Is this OK with you? Can we sit down and talk somewhere?' Then talk about the obstacle – 'We've had a referral from education, regarding your substance use. Have you heard from them?'

SW2: I would do that a bit differently though, because the referral was about the child. I wouldn't say 'the concerns are about your substance use' but about 'the parenting capacity'. The concerns are about the impact of the substance use on the child.

Johanna: So how are you going to phrase it?

SW2: Yeah, I don't know.

A helpful way of communicating a preparedness 'to enter the world of substance-using families' is to adopt conceptual ideas from systemic family therapy that have been highlighted for work with families, to make sense of the interconnections between substance use, parenting, child well-being and other social factors in the familial environment (Kroll and Taylor, 2003). The systemic framework provides a way of viewing how the substance operates as a part of the family system and impacts on everyone else. Different levels of responsibility between family members can be identified, although care should be taken not to emphasise blame, or reinforce power or gender imbalances. Kroll and Taylor (2003) recommend the use of genograms and ecomaps as visual, symbolic tools to gain information about the world of families as experienced by the different family members. The tools address three of the main issues from the background literature about parental substance use. First, communicating in a way that 'makes the child visible' is critical for this practice setting. The placing of children on the genogram and ecomap as part of the family system ensures that they are visible and not hidden behind parental or professional preoccupations with the substance. Second, the significance of the relationship between the substance and the parent, and the consequential relationship between the children and the substance needs to be paid attention during the communication. The mapping of all family members on the ecomap, and including the substance as a 'family member', enables the quality of relationships to be explored. A mix of 'open questions' and 'closed questions' would be needed to draw out the quality of the relationship between the parent and child, but also the relationship between each of them and the substance. Finally, the use of the visual tools enables exploration of the role of the multitude of other social factors that co-exist and inter-relate with the substance use. For example, intergenerational patterns and significant life events can be explored within a genogram, and sources of support or tension within the extended family, friends and wider community can be investigated by using an ecomap.

Communication which demonstrates that professional interest is about the totality of the family experience and support of family members, as opposed to apportioning blame to one or more individuals is more likely to address service-user fears of stigmatisation. There is considerable self-disapproval as well as social disapproval in the use of the labels 'alcoholic' or 'drug addict'. As such it is important to communicate in a way that does not attribute this label. Practice Example 6.2 illustrates the social worker using the specialist communication of 'addressing service-user fears of stigmatisation'. At point 5, the social worker emphasises to the service user how her perspective of substance use is that it is not necessarily problematic, and that people who use substances are not one homogenous group but that each person and situation has individual characteristics ('You see, my experience is that people who use drugs do it in different ways and different issues come up for people, and sometimes problems come up.') She goes on to highlight her own non-judgmental attitude about drug use by exploring whether his drug use is 'managed' and 'safe' as opposed to a closed attitude of establishing whether it occurs or not ('Have you got some support to help you manage your drug-taking safely?'). At point 13, the social worker goes about 'addressing service-user fears of stigmatisation' by stating directly that she will not judge the service user for taking drugs ('I'm not judging you for taking drugs but I will need to know more about the drugs you are taking and what happens to you when you take them'). As before, she does not rely on empty words but gives illustrations of the types of issues she needs to consider with the parents in order to support them and the children.

Communication must go beyond non-attributing a label to the positive emphasis of personal choice and individual responsibility for deciding future behaviour (Miller and Rollnick, 2002). The premise underpinning motivational interviewing, identified in the background literature as a dominant approach in addiction treatment, is that the service user and social worker should identify how much of a problem the service user and family are having with the substance use, and whether or not to change. While social workers may wish to confront parents with the reality or truth of the problem substance use and the impact of that problem usage on the welfare of their children, the strategies of confrontation are more likely to cause a response of denial and/or be perceived as argumentative (Barber, 2002). As such, a key specialist communication skill for the social worker to adopt is to 'avoid exhortations to change'.

It is better if service users come to their own conclusions through social workers drawing the arguments for or against change from the service users themselves. I have chosen to refer to this as a specialist communication strategy of 'motivating service users to decide to make changes'. The three themes Barber considers to be interwoven through motivational interviewing would seem to be central components of this strategy. The first theme is for the social worker to 'provide affirmation' of the service user's statements and feelings. This is best achieved by using the basic non-verbal and verbal communication skills outlined in Chapter 2 of 'reflective listening' and demonstration of empathy through skills such as 'putting feelings into words', 'reaching for feeling' and 'use of silences' (Shulman, 2009). Barber (2002: 96) recommends a strategic use of these skills. While the social worker should demonstrate acceptance and 'a sense of being alongside' the service user, he or she should carefully select which service-user statements to reflect and explore. Of these statements, it is important to show positive confirmation about the need for change.

Practice Example 6.2, point 4, illustrates this specialist communication of 'providing affirmation' for change. As stated earlier, the social worker 'paraphrases' John's statement that he is 'a druggie' and that his usage has no effect on his children in a calm, accepting and non-judgmental way that establishes the reality of the drug use existing along with possible difficulties in that usage. She does not collaborate with any denial of it existing ('OK. So they are saying you are using drugs. OK. What are they saying their concerns are about your use specifically?') At point 5, the social worker offers information that drug use can affect people's lives in a negative way, but then asks an open question about John's usage. In so doing, she avoids showing any judgment about his behavior but begins to introduce the idea that John might benefit from considering how his drug-taking is potentially problematic. Barber refers to this type of open questioning as 'affirmative questioning'.

The second of Barber's themes can be summarised as 'encouraging service user recognition of the divergence between their values or goals and the reality of their current behaviour'. This requires the social worker to help the service user clarify his or her life goals as well as specific goals about substance use. 'Open questions' are important for enabling exploration of the service user's own perspectives. The social worker should provide feedback, in an individualised, empathic and non-judgmental manner about how the substance use is not conducive to those goals (Paylor, 2008). Finally, Barber specifies that social workers should seek to 'provide all options to encourage feelings of self-efficacy', to promote motivation. The service user needs to believe that there is a realistic possibility for change and that he or she has the capacity to solve the problem. This means that the social worker and service user should discuss all the different options that are available. Communication skills from Chapter 2 of 'summarising' and 'paraphrasing' will be useful in drawing information together to achieve more focus (and therefore more motivation) within this discussion.

The background literature suggests that the success of this specialist communication strategy of 'motivating service users to decide to make changes' is also dependent on the stage a person has reached within a process of change. In applying the cycle of change model (Prochaska *et al.*, 1992) to our practice example, it is possible to identify that Karen is at a stage of wanting to change the situation for the family. While she has not yet engaged in a discussion of her own alcohol use, she has made a clear statement that the substance use and parenting difficulties need to be addressed (6.2, point 14). Also, she showed continually through the dialogue that she is unhappy with John's drug use, and is prepared to discuss the level of the use and the way it impacts on the children's lives. She is moving through the 'contemplation' stage. Barber highlights that communication at this stage needs to focus on maintaining service-user co-operation and his or her own vision of the problematic aspects of the substance use (whether, in this example, it relates to her own or to her partner's use) and the options and capacity she has to make changes for the safety of each of the family members. John's communication indicates that he is a 'precontemplator' of change, showing neither ambivalence about his drug use nor a desire to change. In applying Barber's model, communication with John as a 'precontemplator' needs to focus on reducing the value of substance use, and working with Karen and the wider social network to reduce the stresses within the environment to lower the value of the drug-taking behaviour to John.

This chapter has identified how social work communication with substance users is influenced by wider tensions in society concerning problematising and stigmatising attitudes to substance use which have caused marginalisation of individual substance users and their families. The specialist social work communication skills identified and discussed in this chapter seek to provide a balance between 'care' and 'control'. These can be summarised as communication that represents authority and making supportive challenges for work, but at the same time attends to welfare concerns of promoting safety and well-being for all family members, and preventing marginalisation.

Professional Standards

This chapter will help you to meet the following National Occupational Standards:

Key Role 1: Prepare for, and work with individuals, families, carers, groups and communities to assess their needs and circumstances

Unit 1 Prepare for social work contact and involvement
Unit 2 Work with individuals, families, carers, groups and communities to help them make informed decisions
Unit 3 Assess needs and options to recommend a course of action

Key Role 2: Plan, carry out, review and evaluate social work practice with individuals, families, carers, groups, communities and other professionals

Unit 4 Respond to crisis situations
Unit 5 Interact with individuals, families, carers, groups and communities to achieve change and development and to improve life opportunities
Unit 6 Prepare, produce, implement and evaluate plans with individuals, families, carers, groups, communities and professional colleagues
Unit 7 Support the development of networks to meet assessed needs and planned outcomes
Unit 8 Work with groups to promote individual growth, development and independence
Unit 9 Address behaviour which presents a risk to individuals, families, carers, groups and communities

[B]Key Role 3: Support individuals to represent their needs, views and circumstances. Advocate with and on behalf of people

Unit 10 Advocate with, and on behalf of, individuals, families, carers, groups and communities
Unit 11 Prepare for and participate in decision-making forums

Key Role 4: Manage risk to individuals, families, carers, groups, communities, self and colleagues

Unit 12 Assess and manage risks to individuals, families, carers, groups and communities
Unit 13: Assess, minimise and manage risk to self and colleagues

Key Role 5: Manage and be accountable, with supervision and support, for your own social work practice within your organisation

Unit 14 Manage and be accountable for your own work
Unit 16 Manage, present and share records and reports
Unit 17 Work within multi-disciplinary and multi-organisational teams, networks and systems

Key Role 6: Demonstrate professional competence in social work practice

Unit 18 Research, analyse, evaluate and use current knowledge of best social work practice
Unit 19 Work within agreed standards of social work practice and ensure own professional development
Unit 20 Manage complex ethical issues, dilemmas and conflicts
Unit 21 Contribute to the promotion of best social work practice

(In addition to the GSCC National Occupational Standards for Social Work, readers may find it useful to access the Drugs and Alcohol National Occupational Standards (DANOS). Available at: http://www.skillsforhealth.org.uk/danos/)

CHAPTER

7 Working with People with Mental Health Problems

Summary of Specialist Communication Skills

- Promoting understanding of links between experiences and symptoms
- Tuning-in to experience the individual experience of mental distress
- Being open to communication at all levels
- Use of silences
- Giving time to process thoughts or feelings and respond
- Maintaining a non-threatening body position

Policy and background literature

The most recent policy directive concerning social work practice in this area (National Services Framework for Mental Health: DoH, 1999) provided a very limited message about social work communication skills. This occurs despite social work activity in this practice setting coming under the spotlight with increasing organisational change as local government social services departments integrate with Health and/or Social Care Trusts, and the creation of new roles for mental health social workers. In Scotland, social workers undertake the role of Mental Health Officers, and The Mental Health Act 2007 replaced Approved Social Workers (ASWs) with Approved Mental Health Practitioners (AMHPs) in England and Wales. Significantly for social workers, this widened the role to include other professions, such as occupational health workers, public health workers and nurses as well as social workers. There have been concerns that the knowledge and skills from the socially informed training of ASWs have not been sufficiently recognised, and that the place of social interventions might be compromised by a health perspective (Bowl, 2009).

Moreover, policy has required a more positive emphasis towards mental health as being concerned with health and developmental well-being rather than just illness (DoH, 1999; DoH, 2004a). Mental health should be viewed, not as a deficit static state, but as a state of developmental wellness, dependent on several factors that may change over time (HAS, 1995; Mental Health Foundation, 1999; WHO, 2001). Thus, 'mental health' is no longer just the province of specialist mental health workers operating within multi-disciplinary community and primary care settings and offering assessment, consultation or outreach to identify severe, complex need, or specialised services for severe, complex and enduring conditions. The broader definition of mental health services includes primary care professionals promoting mental health and initiating early intervention, and this includes social workers located in any practice setting. We conclude that, in terms of communication strategies, these should include increased positive emphasis and openness to mental health and well-being at every level of intervention.

Yet, entrenched derogatory Western stereotypes of mental health persist (Royal College of Psychiatrists, 1998; WHO, 2001, 2005). The inequality and discrimination faced by people with mental health problems has been highlighted in many of the recent policy documents in this area including the *National Service Framework for Mental Health* (DoH, 1999) and *National Service Framework Five Years On, NICE Guidelines for Schizophrenia* (NICE, 2002), the response of Crisis (Crisis 2003) to a consultation request from the Social Exclusion Unit (Crisis, 2003) and *Our Health, Our Care, Our Say* (DoH, 2006b). Unfortunately, professionals can perpetuate stigmatisation through feelings of fear of perceived unpredictability and aggression; or through an unwillingness to consider mental health as operating along a continuum of 'normal' human experience and clinical disorder, for fear of acknowledging their own vulnerability to such problems (Dogra *et al.*, 2002). Opposed to embracing the positivity behind the term 'mental health', it is still perceived as a derogatory term, with a tendency to avoid its use among professionals (Dogra *et al.*, 2002).

Many people find coming to terms with mental distress and diagnosis a long and difficult process. Their experience of stigmatising attitudes, home or financial insecurity and loss of relationships causes isolation and social withdrawal. Fear related to emotional and physical safety is pervasive (Mental Health Foundation, 2000). Research (Mental Health Foundation, 1997) highlights how the actions of 'seeking and achieving acceptance from others' is a vital element for survival because it provides a means of achieving self-acceptance. Many people with mental distress seek out and create their own 'accepting communities' with shared experiences and shared identity because of feeling alone and fearful on their own. Indeed, as an illustration, social work research has repeatedly identified the importance of the role of 'supportive confidantes' for depressed mothers. Thus, social workers need to communicate emotional support as 'being there for the service user', not just in terms of a physical presence, but to provide a sense of safety and security for the person in distress, and a sense of being unconditionally accepted. Service users cite the importance of their relationships with social workers as achieving a level of depth and consistency not achieved with other professionals (Mental Health Foundation, 2000; Bowl, 2009).

An orientation towards 'recovery' as opposed to becoming 'symptom-free' has been propounded by the service user movement as a way of dealing with the stigma of having a 'mental illness' and being labelled as being a 'mental patient' (NIMHE, 2005; Bowl, 2009). This entails focusing on strengths and encouraging inclusion through participation in social and occupational activities, such as attending leisure centres. Communication needs to be about developing strengths and abilities to build resilience while sustaining an optimistic perspective (Scottish Executive, 2006a, 2006b). An aspect of this person-centred perspective is for communication to be culturally sensitive, such as using phrases and idioms that are ethnospecific; attending to the relevance of traditional and cultural healing systems; and taking into account gender relations and the placing of individuals in their families (Al-Krenawi and Graham, 2000). Religious faith and spiritual beliefs are often cited by people with mental health problems as helpful factors by giving meaning to their lives and a reason to continue despite deep mental distress (Mental Health Foundation, 2000).

Mental distress frequently co-exists and interacts with other problems in everyday living, such as repeated relationship breakdowns, problems with substance use, social exclusion and criminal activity. Problems are likely to be multiple and compounded. From the research underpinning this book, an important communication issue for the social worker seems to be that of 'promoting understanding of links between experiences and symptoms' – both in terms of how past experiences affect current behaviour and symptoms, and how the problems in everyday living impact on symptoms. If these everyday problems could be attended to, then the symptoms could improve. Such complex and potentially dangerous situations require social workers to evaluate the risk of the person causing significant harm to him/herself and others, whether they need safeguarding from exploitation or harm, and whether they have the capacity to give informed consent to services and treatment (Mental Capacity Act, 2005). Social workers also have to judge appropriate limits to confidentiality. Sometimes compulsory powers are exercised to enforce detention. Communication skills are needed to obtain the information to make these judgements in the context of dealing with challenging and/or aggressive behaviour. Social workers need to be aware that their feelings about managing uncertainty and being 'agents of social control' could have an impact on the communication processes used with a service user.

The day-to-day lives of people with severe and enduring mental health problems are made harder by poor physical health, which only serves to increase the social exclusion they are already experiencing. Life chances in education, employment, housing and social networks are all affected. A particular concern is that much mental illness goes undetected. This is in part because of social exclusion and because of the tendency for physical health symptoms to be confused with mental health symptoms, thus allowing serious problems to remain untreated (Phelan, 2001). This masking of symptoms can be caused by assumptions made by health and social care staff involved in caring for people with severe and enduring mental health problems. For example, complaints of ill health such as lethargy and tiredness can be assumed to be what are termed the negative symptoms of psychotic illness, but they are also indicators of many of the physical health problems common among people with mental health problems. Similarly, staff can make inaccurate assumptions about the attitudes of people with mental health problems towards their own physical health. These commonly include assumptions that people with mental health problems are not concerned about weight gain, and do not have high levels of commitment to stopping smoking, eating healthily or engaging in physical exercise programmes. There is good research evidence to show that people with mental health problems are in fact at least as concerned about their physical well-being as anyone else (Osborn *et al.*, 2003). People experiencing severe mental ill-health have themselves complained that insufficient attention has been paid to their physical health (Petit-Zeman *et al.*, 2002).

The literature also highlights the inadequate recognition of mental health needs of people with physical impairments and disabilities even though they are even more likely to be users of mental health services. People with mental health difficulties are also more likely to have physical impairments as a consequence of accidents (Morris, 2004). Service users report how not getting an appropriate response for mental health needs causes fear; for example, staff interacted with them differently on discovering mental health difficulties, and/or medication for physical conditions had negative effects on mental health and vice versa. Through its 'Choosing Health' policy, the government has required workers to adopt 'a new approach' to the physical health care of people with mental health problems by tackling health and social inequalities (DoH, 2004b). Social workers need to ensure that their communication covers both mental health needs and physical health and impairment.

In relation to working with older service users with mental health needs, there is a wide literature available offering guidance for working with people with dementia and other cognitive impairments. This is covered in more detail in Chapter 10, which deals with 'Working with Older People'. Put simply, a person's basic tools of communication, such as speech and memory, may be impaired, so people with dementia often have some difficulty communicating via language because they feel a lot of pressure through having to think quickly, particularly where higher-order concepts are employed (Proctor, 2001; Reid *et al.*, 2001; Tibbs, 2001). There is a need for social workers to obtain as much factual information as possible before the visit, and to be clear on the purpose of the visit in terms that make sense to both user and carer. Generally, it is better to make a number of short visits than a single long one. Research by the Joseph Rowntree Foundation (Allan, 2001) emphasises how a range of communication techniques and approaches (for example, pictures, word cards) should help workers to understand client views and preferences.

Practice application

The background literature indicated that overarching emotions of fear, distress and anger have a significant role in this practice setting, with the corresponding need for social workers to tread carefully and sensitively to avoid scaring and alienating service users. Suspicion and mistrust may not only be born of negative marginalisation from society and services but may also be a symptom of the mental illness itself. It is distressing, frightening and isolating to experience mental pain. The social workers from the research study identified that these constitute barriers to overcome at the inception of any communication with individuals suffering mental distress. (See Practice Example 7.1.)

Preparing to demonstrate empathy for that communication of feeling, through using the basic communication skill of 'tuning-in' is therefore vital (see Chapter 2 for a discussion of this). Indeed, Wilson *et al.* (2008: 318) state that social workers must not only be 'emotionally available' to communication by service users of their mental pain, but also expect that communication to occur at a number of levels, including internally within the social worker. Thus, in this area of specialist practice, when using the skill of 'tuning-in', the social worker needs to engage with concepts from the psychoanalytic and psychodynamic literature concerning projection, transference and counter-transference (see Chapter 2 for an explanation of these). 'Tuning-in' will facilitate the first stage of a meaningful 'person-centred' communication with service users, as

PRACTICE EXAMPLE 7.1

Graeme

Preparatory stage

Graeme is a single, homeless man, 36 years of age, who presented himself at the drop-in facility of a local community mental health centre a week ago. Such was his mental distress and physical condition that he could hardly speak. He was cold and hungry. He simply handed over a sheet of paper that had his name written on it with the address for the centre. The approved mental health professional on duty immediately provided a hot drink and a sandwich. Short-term accommodation was arranged for Graeme at a local charity-run homeless shelter. Graeme appeared fearful and mistrusting of staff at the shelter. He stayed in his room, and spoke very little. Graeme has not seen his general practitioner for several years as he finds the surgery environment difficult to manage. He says he will attend an appointment next week. His general practitioner has treated him for anxiety and severe depression in the past.

The approved mental health professional who arranged the accommodation for Graeme is a 48-year-old male social worker, Dave Smith. Dave visited Graeme at the shelter on a second occasion this week, and found him to be highly anxious. Today he is visiting to continue assessing Graeme's mental well-being and vulnerability. He has to begin to make medium-term plans with Graeme, for his immediate treatment, accommodation and the form of future support services, whether informal or formal in nature.

opposed to an 'illness-focused' one (Bowl, 2009). Service users have stated that this approach builds relationships as it demonstrates the social worker being interested in the service user's needs as a person and not as an 'object of concern' (Cree and Davis, 2007). As such, I have decided to call this early specialist communication skill 'tuning-in to experience the individual experience of mental distress.'

A central dimension to this specialist skill is to engage in reflexive processes by 'tuning-in' to 'self'. This requires the social worker to reflect on how well he or she might receive the feelings being transferred by the service user, and whether there might be any barriers. Crucially, for this practice setting, the social worker must seek to identify how their own preconceived notions and cultural stereotypes (based on their own experiences and biography) of 'mental health problems' might influence their judgement, or indeed their behaviour, in tolerating painful feelings being shared and the service user's personality coming forward. Indeed, the background literature has highlighted that professionals can perpetuate stigmatisation through feelings of fear of perceived unpredictability and aggression; or through an unwillingness to consider mental health as part of a continuum of 'normal' human experience and clinical disorder. This might occur as a result of fear of acknowledging the social worker's own vulnerability to such problems (Dogra *et al.*, 2002). Questions should be considered, such as 'Who, where or what did they, themselves, experience when they suffered their most troubled, anxious experiences?' Identifying and recalling his own feelings will help the social worker identify with some of the difficult feelings that Graeme is likely to transfer. Wilson *et al.* (2008: 318–19) neatly summarise the point:

> Think – perhaps there have been times when you have felt so worried and anxious you really could not 'hear' what anyone else had to say; or times when you felt so emotionally low that reassurance and encouragement just had no effect on you; or even times when you were so convinced that everyone disliked and hated you that you 'snapped their heads off' when they tried to come close. Now think again – suppose that such a state of mind were deeper and much more lasting than the experience you had. Perhaps that brings us closer to understanding part of what it is to 'have a mental health problem', and what the particular challenges are in terms of communication.

Having 'tuned-in', we find, at the beginning of Practice Example 7.2, the social worker giving his opening statement – part of the basic communication skill from Chapter 2 of 'achieving a shared purpose'.

PRACTICE EXAMPLE 7.2

Graeme

Beginnings

The social worker, Dave, is meeting Graeme in one of the consultation rooms in the homeless shelter. This is the second time that Graeme has met Dave this week, but the first time Graeme has been able to talk with Dave about his well-being. Earlier in the week, Graeme had presented a lot of mental distress, and had been hungry, cold and sleep deprived.

[1] *SW*: Hello Graeme. Good to see you again. It's been a few days since we last spoke. Shall we sit here?

Social worker moves one of the chairs at about a 45-degree angle, and about a metre away from the other chair, possibly so that he could look more easily into Graeme's face. Graeme is silent and sits down.

►

▶

	SW:	How are you doing today?
	Graeme:	OK.
[2]	*SW*:	Do you feel like you are recovering a bit? (*Graeme nods*) That's good. We need to talk, the two of us, about how to help you in the situation you are in … help you feel better … you know…. For us to do that, I need to understand more about you … what you might need. Are you OK with that?
	Graeme:	You want to ask questions?
[3]	*SW*:	Well, yes, if you can talk to me about what's going on for you in your life, how you feel about it, then I might be able to understand and help you. I won't judge you in any way.
	Graeme:	What do you want to know?
	SW:	The other day you said you were struggling to find food when you were on the streets.
	Graeme:	Just rummaging through bins, Sunday roast, chicken sandwich, just anything I could find really.
	SW:	So how long were you doing that for?
[4]	*Graeme*:	(*Shakes his head*) About ten months. Well, it was all right at first. I had a bit of money, you know. I just didn't want to live in a house. I wanted to get away from things.
	SW:	What did you want to get away from?
	Graeme:	Life.
	SW:	Any particular part of life?
[5]	*Graeme*:	I don't know where to start.
[6]	*SW*:	Wherever you want to start.

Silence for about ten seconds. Graeme is leaning forward, head down, rubbing his hands over the back of his head. Social worker is sitting with legs apart, arms resting on knees but hands clasped, slightly leaning back.

	Graeme:	Every day there was trouble. Always fighting and arguing. I just wanted to get away from it.

▶

▶

SW: Fighting and arguing. Was that someone in particular, or in general?

Graeme: Just everyone.

SW: Everyone. Family? Friends? People you know?

[7] *Graeme*: Family. I was drinking to get away from all the arguing. I thought that by walking every night it would be all right and better. But then you realise that you are constantly looking over your shoulder. It's not as safe as you think.

[8] *SW*: It sounds like it's quite painful ... and that when you're walking, checking over your shoulder, is it like you're running away from something? (*Motions with hands*)

[9] *Graeme*: (*Puts his hands up to cover his eyes, rocks forward and back in his seat*) I don't run from anything. (*Silence. Social worker sits still*) You'll never understand me.

[10] *SW*: The more you talk about it, the more I can try and understand. You seem upset and angry. If you don't want to talk to me about it, then that's fine. It's completely your choice. (*Pause*) But I can try to get to know you and get to know the situation better.

Graeme: So now you want to be my friend. I come here off the streets. Tell you my deepest, darkest secrets? (*Sits back and looks social worker in the eye*)

SW: I'm a social worker. You've been talking about strained relationships, being without a home ... I hope, in talking to me about your life at the moment, you can have a better understanding of what's going on for yourself, and what needs to happen for things to be better.

Graeme: Oh, I understand what's going on because I've had to live with it all my life! And then you come in and you try to take it over!

Graeme moves around on his chair. He looks directly at the social worker. Social worker sits quietly and still in the same position

SW: Do you think I'm taking it over? Taking control?

Graeme: What do you need to know about me? You need to know nothing about me.

▶

▶

Silence: *Graeme sits forward, running his hands over his head. Silence continues.*

Graeme: Spent eighteen months drinking. I don't want to think. I drink to stop thinking. I walk to stop thinking. So why would I come in here to think about everything I want to forget?

SW: (*Moves forward. Puts hands clasped together in front of his legs*) It's obviously upsetting and painful, Graeme. I don't want you to feel pressurised in any way. Do you want some space now? Look, I'm at the centre most mornings. You can always contact me whenever you feel you want or need to talk. I want to be helpful to you. I guess it's too soon today.

The service user immediately responds with dialogue that seems to be communicating the anticipated fear about what information to reveal ('You want to ask questions?'). The social worker immediately 'shows empathy' for this fear by using the basic communication skill of 'putting feelings into words' ('Well, yes, I guess it might be hard'), but also emphasising that he will be non-judgmental about the information the service user might offer ('I won't judge you in any way'). In doing this he attends to a potential obstacle that might have arisen concerning the service user's fear of stigma, and mistrust of this worker. Shulman's (1998, 2009) name for an impediment to trust is the 'intimacy obstacle'. Dealing with the obstacle in this direct but empathic way means that there is a greater chance of having a shared agenda for the rest of the communication. Certainly, the remainder of the social worker's opening statement seeks to show the service user the benefits of doing the work together, and tries to create the right kinds of conditions for work to occur ('Well, yes, I guess it might be hard, but if you can talk to me about what's going on for you in your life, how you feel about it, then I might be able to understand and help you. I won't judge you in any way.')

The social worker then goes on to try to make sense of Graeme's state of mind through listening carefully to the way Graeme describes his experience of his everyday life. Skills in good 'reflective listening' are usefully employed. In this case, the social worker uses 'open questions' alongside 'paraphrasing', such as:

Graeme: I wanted to get away from things.

SW: What did you want to get away from?

Graeme: Life.

SW: Any particular part of life?

The social worker uses several of the service user's own words as part of the paraphrasing, and it seems to have some success in showing that the social worker is listening to and accepting the service user's perspectives. The 'open questions' seek clarification to check for shared meanings and obtain further details. Often this use of the service user's own words is called 'reflecting back' or 'mirroring'.

Graeme: Every day there was trouble. Always fighting and arguing. I just wanted to get away from it.

SW: Fighting and arguing. Was it someone in particular, or in general?

Graeme: Just everyone.

SW: Everyone. Family? Friends? People you know?

Graeme: Family. I was drinking to get away from all the arguing.

'Reflective listening' involves receiving thoughts and feelings made clear by the narrative but also revealed through tone of voice and attitude, and non-verbally through gesture and body position. Thus 'listening' needs to be carried out in tandem with 'observing' non-verbal behaviour, as well as experiencing the thoughts and feelings internally to fully attend to the service user's total communication. Whatever the channel of communication ('listening', 'observing', 'feeling') or level of communication ('internally', 'interaction' or 'structurally'), the social worker needs to receive these feelings in an open, warm and receptive manner.

By way of illustration, a critical point in Practice example 7.2 is when we see the social worker communicating empathy for the anxiety and anger expressed by Graeme as a result of his painful feelings becoming difficult to control (8.2, points 7–10). The empathy is needed to enable Graeme to feel understood, and in control of his emotional and social self (Howe, 1998; Agass, 2002; Ruch, 2005b). In Chapter 3, I considered how Bion's (1962) concept of 'containment' is frequently used to describe this process, summarised by Agass (2002: 127) as

> not simply putting up with or absorbing whatever unpleasant or uncomfortable feelings the client stirs up in us. It is a much more active process of struggling to 'contain', understand and work through our own emotional responses in the hope that this will enable our clients to do the same for themselves.

The availability of this communication medium is critical for service users seeking to communicate their mental pain, as they may find that their thoughts and feelings are 'crowding in' and dominating consciousness to the extent that ordinary communication may be difficult (Wilson *et al.*. 2008). 'Being open to communication at all levels' is therefore an important specialist communication skill.

Wilson *et al.* (2008) recommend that social workers are sensitive to the particular, and often complex, ways a service user might employ to communicate their state of mind. For example, metaphors and images may be used. In our practice example, Graeme uses an image of himself walking the streets to 'get away' from his painful thoughts. The social worker picks up on the image being used and asks Graeme to explain a little more about what he is 'running from'. Graeme denies 'running away' verbally, but his body language tells the social worker that whatever it is he is 'running from', it is emotionally painful for Graeme and he is trying to hide it. It is an image that they might both use at a later time.

The social worker appears unabashed by Graeme's anger. His demonstration of 'containment' is evident in the way he communicates non-verbally, such as his 'use of silences', the way he 'gives time to process thoughts or feelings and respond', and the way he 'maintains a non-threatening body position' by remaining still and open. Each of these constitutes a specialist communication skill for this practice setting and will be considered in turn.

The skill of 'using silences', regardless of how difficult and uncomfortable the communication may have been, is important for developing a working relationship with a service user with mental health problems. Sitting alongside and just 'being' with the service user demonstrates support and acceptance. 'Being' indicates respect by allowing difficult thoughts to remain unspoken until the service user thinks it is an appropriate time to disclose them, whereas 'doing' demands work to be done on those feelings when the service user is unwilling or unable to do so (Wilson *et al.*, 2008). Often, social workers need to practice 'the art of being' as they are used to interpreting situations and problem-solving (Kroll, 1995). Holding back and giving the service user choice and control over what to work on respects person-centred rights of dignity, consideration and rationality.

Silences also enable the social worker to 'give time to process thoughts or feelings and respond'. This thinking time might be required by either the service user or the social worker. Indeed, the social worker must take steps to prevent becoming so immersed in the content of the narrative that he or she fails to engage the specialist communication skill of 'being open to communication at all levels'. They might miss seeing the feelings that are being revealed unconsciously by attitude, gesture or tone of voice as the service user pursues his or her line of thought. A short period of silence can enable what I referred to in Chapter 2 as operating a 'third ear' or 'second head' to adopt some objective distance at the same time as achieving emotional attunement to the thoughts and feelings being expressed. Questions to enable analysis of the interaction could be held in mind, such as, 'What is really going on in the communication here?', 'Is the problem he or she is describing the most immediate problem or is there something more worrying?', 'What is the nature of the obstacle to our communication?' and 'What skill should I use next?'

'Maintaining a non-threatening body position' is critical in situations where service users are demonstrating anger and a loss of self-control. Koprowska

(2005: 149) recommends that social workers include non-verbal behaviours in managing aggressive situations and containing angry feelings. These were considered in Chapter 3 but are repeated here to emphasize their usefulness within these situations:

- Ensure you are standing or seated at a slight angle and not 'square on', but at least a one-and-a-half arm distance away.
- Look at the person's face, making frequent but not continuous eye-contact.
- Show an interested and relaxed facial expression, but do not smile.
- Keep your arms relaxed, away from your hair, face or around your body (as this can be interpreted as being impatient, anxious, or seductive).
- Keep your hands open and in view with palms up to indicate negotiation.
- Keep the tone of your voice of low-register and calm.

It does not matter that there was not a lot said during the meeting. The fact that the social worker stayed with Graeme, and accepted his behaviour as displayed, and his feelings as communicated, gave Graeme an important message that Dave will not reject his difficulties and pain. The consistency of the relationship between service user and social worker is considered vital if service users are to reveal their deeply hidden reasons for mental distress (Bowl, 2009). Service users have reported how their relationships with social workers achieve a level of depth and consistency not achieved with other professionals.

In summary, the specialist social work communication skills in this chapter have focused on the social worker achieving a level of emotional attunement sufficient to 'hear', and demonstrate empathy for, the service user's communication of mental pain. Crucial to this were specialist communication skills to overcome possible obstacles arising concerning the service user's fear of stigma and mistrust of the social worker. These skills communicated acceptance and support, as well as helping the service user to link past experiences to current behaviour and symptoms, and how the problems in everyday living impact on symptoms.

Professional Standards

This chapter will help you to meet the following National Occupational Standards:

Key Role 1: Prepare for, and work with individuals, families, carers, groups and communities to assess their needs and circumstances

Unit 1 Prepare for social work contact and involvement

Unit 2 Work with individuals, families, carers, groups and communities to help them make informed decisions
Unit 3 Assess needs and options to recommend a course of action

Key Role 2: Plan, carry out, review and evaluate social work practice with individuals, families, carers, groups, communities and other professionals

Unit 4 Respond to crisis situations
Unit 5 Interact with individuals, families, carers, groups and communities to achieve change and development and to improve life opportunities
Unit 6 Prepare, produce, implement and evaluate plans with individuals, families, carers, groups, communities and professional colleagues
Unit 9 Address behaviour which presents a risk to individuals, families, carers, groups and communities

Key Role 3: Support individuals to represent their needs, views and circumstances. Advocate with and on behalf of people

Unit 10 Advocate with, and on behalf of, individuals, families, carers, groups and communities

Key Role 4: Manage risk to individuals, families, carers, groups, communities, self and colleagues

Unit 12 Assess and manage risks to individuals, families, carers, groups and communities
Unit 13 Assess, minimise and manage risk to self and colleagues

Key Role 5: Manage and be accountable, with supervision and support, for your own social work practice within your organisation

Unit 14 Manage and be accountable for your own work
Unit 16 Manage, present and share records and reports
Unit 17 Work within multi-disciplinary and multi-organisational teams, networks and systems

Key Role 6: Demonstrate professional competence in social work practice

Unit 18 Research, analyse, evaluate and use current knowledge of best social work practice
Unit 19 Work within agreed standards of social work practice and ensure own professional development
Unit 20 Manage complex ethical issues, dilemmas and conflicts
Unit 21 Contribute to the promotion of best social work practice

Working with Adults with Disabilities

CHAPTER 8

Summary of Specialist Communication Skills

- Using the whole communication spectrum
- Actively looking for the channels of communication that the person is using
- Validating and recognising 'private' knowledge of the individual nuances of the impairment as applied to a person
- Communicating empathy for the experience of systemic barriers
- Taking time

Policy and background literature

Legislation and policy for working with adults with disabilities exhorts augmented skills in communication (*Valuing People* (2001); *Independence, Well-being and Choice* (2005); Disability Discrimination Act (2005); *Our Health, Our Care, Our Say* (2006b), Disability Discrimination (Northern Ireland) Order 2006). Indeed, the policy highlights that social workers should be working with service users, not just as active participants but as expert partners in assessing a wide range of needs and designing care plans to maximise independence (DoH, 2001, 2005, 2006b). Their work must be 'person-centred', achieved through treating service users with dignity, as individuals, and enabling choice about care. Developments have built on the Direct Payment Schemes of the 1990s to the use of 'Individual Budgets', 'self-assessed need' and 'self-directed support' (Boxall *et al.*, 2009; Sapey, 2009). Moreover, the principles underpinning the Mental Capacity Act (2005) require social workers to presume that service users have the capacity to make decisions unless it has been established that they lack that capacity. This indicates the need for social workers to use particular communication skills to explore issues of 'decision-making capacity'. Indeed, one of the items within the functional test that is applied to ascertain capacity for decision-making concerns the ability of the service user to communicate their decision effectively. The social worker needs to be alert to all the different forms and channels of communication a service user may be using, or be encouraged or enabled to use.

The requirement for social workers to facilitate a safe relationship from which to explore feelings and opinions concerning choice, risk and protection is also underlined by government measures to specifically address the abuse of vulnerable adults, such as the *No Secrets* guidance (DoH, 2000b); *In Safe Hands* (National Assembly for Wales, 2000); *Safeguarding Vulnerable Adults* (Social Services Directorate (N.I.), 2006); the Safeguarding Vulnerable Groups Act 2006 and Adult Support and Protection (Scotland) Act, 2007. These policies and resulting practice guidance place a responsibility on the social worker to investigate and take action when a vulnerable adult is believed to be suffering abuse at the hands of carers or other people in their social environment. Risk-taking and managing risk is a normal part of everyday life for anyone. However, research has found that, while staff working with people with disabilities recognise risk management as an essential aspect of nomal life, these views tended to conflict with those of parents or carers, who wanted the person to be protected from such daily dangers (Mitchell and Glendinning, 2007). Carers' perspectives are not always consistent with those of the service user. Meaningful communication within a relationship that reflects a 'partnership of expertise' with the service user (GSCC, 2005) and seeks to facilitate the 'best interests' of that individual (Mental Capacity Act 2005) will ensure more individually focused, person-centred considerations of choice, risk and safeguarding. Despite these policy exhortations, the practice experience of social workers, and lived experience of service users, show that this specialist area of social work is undervalued and is accorded a low priority in terms of resources.

The literature points to the need for social workers to operate with an appropriate theoretical model of disability – 'the social model of disability' – where the assumption of impairment is that of normality. This stands opposed to a focus on the physical limitations of impairment, which is often accompanied by a desire to promote adjustment to a perceived 'normal' world occupied by the able-bodied (Oliver and Sapey, 2006). The social model of disability argues that such attitudes constitute barriers which, when (a) internalised; (b) are reproduced behaviourally; and (c) become institutionalised, create disabling psycho-social and structural inter-relationships and environments for people with impairments (Thomas, 2007; Sapey, 2009). In relation to communication, society places a high value on the written and spoken word. However, the more appropriate social model of disability recognises the importance of not framing communication strategies on the basis of this privileged reality but respecting how the other person senses, perceives and communicates about their world. The Disability Discrimination Act 2005 places a duty Upon organisations and professional workers to be proactive in setting in motion this 'positive communication'.

Valuing People (2001) identified that people with learning and/or sensory disabilities do not have a single recognised set of language tools but are dependent on professionals to use individually tailored communication technologies involving additional forms of communication such as objects, pictures, signs, gestures and symbols. In addition, the policy and other literature supports the need for workers to employ a 'common language' or 'total communication system' that uses a range of communication media to encourage inclusion in communication at any level or point of professional encounter with a service user.

Research surrounding communicating with people with aphasia similarly emphasises an attitude to interaction that is 'authentic', with people prepared to engage with each other, and to find mutually intelligible and accessible forms of communication (Parr *et al.*, 2004). This literature identifies how people need additional time to process information; formulate and express ideas; and negotiate choice and decisions. Workers often displayed ignorance about ways to react to a communication disability or language impairment, yet changes to structures and processes make a difference, such as rearranging a meeting to a time when an individual is most alert; providing paper to explore ideas pictorially; ensuring quiet and minimising distractions (Parr *et al.*, 2004).

The literature suggests that the social worker should prepare to empathise with the social barriers faced by people with impairments and their carers (Barnes, 1991). In my previous published research about specialist communication with parents of children with disabilities, I found that while social workers sought to understand parenting behaviour in social terms, it was not sufficient, as it required the *social model of disability analysis* to emphasise the influence of systemic barriers on families' abilities to function in their social environment (Woodcock and Tregaskis, 2008). By 'adding on' a practical application of the social model of disability approach, I achieved a greater appreciation of the ecological context of the everyday living environment. Moreover, the research revealed that social workers needed to be prepared to discuss and contain strong feelings of pain and frustration being presented by service users with disabilities caused by the influence of those systemic barriers in their lives. There was a high emotional content to the discourse, with a resulting impact on the listener. Systemic barriers included a service failure to take the specific needs of individuals and families into account, in favour of a 'one size fits all' model. Another service failure was to provide 'joined-up services' for individual needs. For example, one child was recommended activities by a speech therapist which involved sitting upright, but the child could not sit up independently and occupational therapy would not supply the chair needed because the child was not on their list. Barnes (1991) would explain these systemic barriers occurring because services are developed primarily to meet the normative needs of the provider, and take insufficient account of the diverse needs of client groups. The effect of such normative provision on disabled people's lives is described more extensively in Barnes (1991).

Practice application

Drawing on the social model of disability, a key issue for the social worker (in Practice Example 8.1) is to identify the barriers in society that are impacting on the social worker's communication with Sue, and seek to overcome them.

PRACTICE EXAMPLE 8.1

Sue and Steve Preston

Preparatory stage

Our practice example shows a number of meetings between Sue, a 32-year-old woman, her husband Steve (35 years old), and their new social worker. Two years ago, Sue survived a stroke which caused a lasting impairment to her brain function and speech. Since the stroke she tires more easily when moving around their home. Steve has become a full-time carer for his wife. The last review of Sue's care was six months ago. Steve is described by the various health professionals involved in Sue's life as being very protective of his wife and essentially operates a gatekeeping role in relation to visitors and professionals, from a well-meaning position of seeking to shield Sue from getting upset. Both Sue and Steve are distressed about the impact of the impairment on their lives. Sue was very young to have suffered a stroke. Their loss at not fulfilling the hopes and plans they had made together is palpable. There is an air of pessimism about the future.

A first step is to acknowledge that barriers are likely to be located within himself as attitudes and behaviour (Marchant and Page, 2003). The social worker must start from an attitudinal position which is that Sue has a right to be communicated with and be facilitated to express decisions concerning her life (Wilson *et al.*, 2008). The social worker needs to find out as much as he can about the way in which Sue communicates, and value that means of communication. Importantly, it is the responsibility of the social worker to determine this (Morris, 2002; Wilson *et al.*, 2008). This suggests another attitudinal position, summarised by Wilson *et al.* (2008: 323) as 'a point where we believe the person has something to say and then think creatively about how this can be achieved.' Communication could use different methods and formats beyond that of verbalisation, such as body language but also pictures, symbols, signs and media packages. Moreover, the background literature identified how the use of several methods in tandem encouraged a more thorough understanding for both parties – 'a total communication system'. Given this, I have chosen to refer to two skills for this specialist communication strategy: 'actively look for the channels of communication that the person is using' and 'using the whole communication spectrum'. The social worker in the practice example needs to ensure that he has the knowledge and skills to use the different methods of communication. Therefore, planning his communication strategy during this preparatory stage will be essential to increase his confidence and skill.

In promoting Sue's right to be communicated with and facilitating expression of her thoughts and feelings, the social worker must consider how he will respond if Sue's carer, in this case her husband Steve, communicates for her. In addition to attending to her right for privacy and to be communicated with in her own right, the background literature identified how carers' perspectives are not always consistent with those of the service user. The social worker needs to be both confident and empathic in dealing with the likelihood of Steve communicating for Sue. This will include recognising how his behaviour might be a response to the experience of systemic barriers in their lives. Instead of seeing Steve's 'gatekeeping' behaviour as over-protectiveness, a social model of disability approach would consider whether this was about his attempts to overcome systemic barriers to his wife receiving effective help, such as reducing her feelings of depression, or preparation for significant life changes (leaving familiar surroundings to go for rehabilitation or treatment, or example). The basic communication skill of 'tuning-in' will prepare for delivering an empathic and challenging response to his communication should it arise. In Chapter 2, I described how Shulman (2009) identifies 'tuning-in' as a vital communication skill for identifying and dealing with thoughts and feelings, particularly if expressed indirectly, to enable service users to feel 'listened to' and understood. Thus, when first meeting with the family, the social worker must employ the four parts of the basic communication skills listed in Chapter 2: 'achieving a shared purpose', that is:

- 'being clear on role';
- 'being clear on purpose';
- 'reaching for feedback'
- and 'showing empathy'.

Practice Example 8.2, points 1–4 begins with the social worker seeking to be 'clear on purpose' with Sue's husband, Steve.

PRACTICE EXAMPLE 8.2

Sue and Steve Preston

Beginnings

[1] *SW*: Hello. Mr Preston?

Steve: Yes.

SW: Great. I'm Ewan Jones, a social worker. I wrote to your wife to arrange an appointment today. You wrote to us saying that a review of services was needed for your wife. I'd like to get a bit of an understanding from you both of what it's like for her and you at the moment ... starting with your wife and then both of you. May I come in?

[2] *Steve*: Yes, in here. Thanks. You can sit down here. Right, OK.

They sit down on sofas at right angles to each other. The social worker looks around for Mrs Preston in order to begin. Mr Preston sits forward, rubbing his hands in an agitated manner, waiting for the social worker to start talking.

Steve: What is it you need to know, then?

[3] *SW*: Uh, what I want to do is to see if the situation of six months ago is still the same today. I'm just going to try and get some up-to-date information from you and your wife about how your wife's recovery is going, and how she is managing various things in everyday life at the moment.

Steve: Are you going to make a change, then?

SW: What we need to do together, what we need to work on, is to find out from your wife, and from you, what are the things that are affecting you both, and what we can do is to see if we can help at all with your wife's situation, OK?

Steve: What? So how do you want to help?

[4] *SW*: (*Leans forward in his seat, elbows on thighs and opens his hands out, palms showing*) Yes, I'd like to help ... I can see you are worried about your wife. Well, it would be finding out things like 'What's the impact of your wife's condition at the moment?' and 'What's going well or not going well day-to-day?' and 'Are the services working out for her?'

Steve: Well, she gets tired more easily so she's, uh, you know, she used to be really extrovert, but now she's just kind of really going back

▶

►

into herself. You know, not being able to go out much. It's really difficult for her to communicate as well as it's really affected her speech.

[5] *SW:* Is your wife around, Mr Preston? It really feels as though we should have her here too. It just feels as if we're talking about her, and her views are, like, really the most central.

Steve: She's sleeping. She gets tired, you know, she gets tired a lot. You know, it's so difficult to arrange a time for people to come around, and when she's feeling well enough to talk, and you know, we're both around. When she goes to sleep, I try to go to sleep as well. It's the only time I've got. Or, I'm catching up on everything else that needs to be done in the house, um, so it's really kind of, it's really tricky, so ... you know, all different people, like nurses and that, they talk to me and... yeah, treat me like I'm an expert and I'm meant to know everything about the whole illness, and to be honest, I don't know how my wife is reacting, and I don't know what to do, but I do my best.

[6] *SW:* I'm sure you do. (*Pause*) Is there a particular time of day that's better for your wife when we could meet? You know, sometimes when people have had a stroke they find they have a bit more energy at a particular time of the day.

Steve: Yeah, kind of, early afternoon is all right, you know, but it depends, you know, it changes from day to day. I mean it tends to be kind of early afternoon she's all right. First thing in the morning she's not great. She's taken her medication so it's got to have time to kick in. She doesn't, you know, since she's not been out she's not comfortable talking in front of too many people. Certainly not talking to many people for any length of time. She's aware of her disability, and she knows that other people are aware of that and, you know, I don't know how that makes her feel. I can only imagine. And then people ask me questions you know, I can only second guess.

[7] *SW:* How do you find it best to communicate with your wife? I'll try to do the same....

Steve: Well, we can, you know, we can talk to each other, but it's a lot ... it's drawn out a lot more. Her words are slurred a lot so it's really difficult sometimes to grasp what she's saying. I mean I know you get better at it. You know, it's been two years now, but I'm still kind of starting to understand her more now. It's just you know, where she gets really bad days, and I'm really stressed, that we don't talk so well.

►

▶

[8] *SW*: OK, so I must make sure I have plenty of time. What about writing things down or drawing things … does that help?

[9] *Steve*: Sometimes. You could try, but she's not stupid. It's an injury. She's not mentally ill. She's brain damaged through a stroke, and not … you know … her behaviour's been affected because of brain injury, but it's not a mental health problem.

[10] *SW*: No, I promise you Mr Preston, I will not speak to your wife as though she's stupid. It's just important that she contributes as much as she can to the meeting. I want to make sure I do everything I can to communicate as well as possible. (*Silence for ten seconds*) You know, you have a right to an assessment as a carer too. You are doing so much here. Would it be OK for us to meet up on our own too, after we've met with your wife?

Steve: Um… I don't know… obviously if you ask me the same questions in front of her then you know, it makes it really difficult for me. I know you need to talk to her, but I don't want to be put in the situation where I have to lie in front of my wife. You know, I've got my feelings, but you know, I don't want her getting more upset when….

SW: If there's anything you find particularly difficult to raise when she's there, then perhaps it would be good if we could meet up again after that to talk about your needs so that we can support you?

Steve: No, I'm OK, I'm fine, but I need to make sure that she's getting the best, you know, that's all we need to do, we just need to start with that. Like I say, I don't want to be put in the situation where she finds out how difficult it is for me and, you know, how tough it can be trying to keep everything together. I know she knows, but I don't trust myself emotionally, you know, to try and keep it together in front of her, and you know, that's tough… so… I can see what you're saying… I can see where you're coming from, but, um, I don't know. Maybe if you spoke to her and I came in at the end, that might make me feel better.

[11] *SW*: OK. Great, then that gives your wife the opportunity to talk to me on her own. I have to make sure that happens. When I come, we'll just see if your wife is happy with those arrangements as well. Can we arrange a date at this stage when I can come back and meet your wife?

Steve: Yeah, this week, or…?

SW: Yes, this week if it's convenient.

▶

▶

Steve: OK, uh... Thursday's quite good, usually... I would say about half twelve. She won't be able to... any earlier on. Can I tell Sue that things are going to get sorted? Are you guys gonna get on top of it now?

SW: Well that's the pian, obviously to come along and find out what she actually wants in the future, to see what we can actually do. But obviously if she's not feeling well on that day... Well, what I'll do is I'll give you a ring about a quarter of hour before I'm due to come over and see how she's feeling. Is that OK?

Steve: Are you actually going to turn up?

[12] *SW*: Yes I will, yeah. (*Writes appointment in diary*)

Steve: It just there's so many workers who say they are coming but just don't turn up. They expect us to deal with all this stuff, you know.

[13] *SW*: I can only apologise for the sort of experiences you've had, but I certainly will turn up.

While the social worker had sought to meet Sue first, as anticipated, Steve wants to communicate with the social worker ahead of his wife. He is communicating anxiety about whether this new social worker will be able to effect any positive changes in his wife's situation and, related to this, whether any communication with his wife with simply cause her further upset. The way Steve communicates this is indirect, both through seeking clarification and reassurance of the social worker's purpose and method for working, and non-verbally such as by his agitated body language in Example 2.2. The relevant section from the dialogue (8.2, points 3–4) is provided here to illustrate this:

SW: Uh, what I want to do is see if the situation of 6 months ago is still the same today. I'm just going to try and get some up-to-date information from you and your wife about how your wife's recovery is going, and how she is managing the various things in everyday life at the moment.

Steve: Are you going to make a change, then?

SW: What we need to do together, what we need to work on, is find out from your wife, and from you, what are the things that are affecting you both, and what we can do is to see if we can help at all with your wife's situation, OK?

Steve: What? So how do you want to help?

SW: (*Leans forward in his seat, elbows on thighs and opens hands out, palms showing*) Yes, I'd like to help … I can see you are worried about your wife. Well, it would be finding out things like 'What's the impact of your wife's condition at the moment?' and 'What's going well or not going well day-to-day?' and 'Are the services working out for her?'

In this section we see how the social worker recognises that Steve's communication could relate to his experience of systemic barriers. He takes time to explain the purpose of his work, and through using the basic communication skill (from Chapter 2) of 'putting feelings into words' he demonstrates that he has 'listened reflectively' to Steve's worries about his wife's emotional well-being ('Yes, I'd like to help … I can see you are worried about your wife'). His statement is mirrored by his body language changing to a more 'open' and receptive position, which emphasises a wish to engage with Steve on that matter (*'Leans forward in his seat, elbows on thighs and opens hands out, palms showing'*). This seems to constitute a specialist communication skill of 'communicating empathy for the experience of systemic barriers'.

While the social worker recognises that Steve's communication could relate to his experience of systemic barriers, he must not become so focused on this particular explanation that he fails to see the possibility of others. One explanation for Steve's reluctance for the social worker and other professionals to see Sue on her own is that he may be worried that she might disclose information that he is causing her significant harm. The policy guidance mentioned above concerning safeguarding vulnerable adults emphasises that social workers must recognise that people with disabilities are particularly vulnerable to abuse, whether by strangers or by carers. Physical impairment and/or learning difficulties can render a person more vulnerable to being exploited as a victim of physical, emotional or sexual violence. Furthermore, as noted in earlier chapters, many of the communication systems that disabled people use do not have a wide range of words, signs or symbols to describe feelings, parts of the body (such as genitalia) or acts of maltreatment (Wilson *et al.*, 2008).

The social worker seeks to ensure that he pays attention to Sue's rights to dignity and to be communicated with about her needs by refusing to take the conversation any further without her being present. He follows the policy guidance concerning safeguarding vulnerable adults and mental capacity to make sure that Sue has the opportunity to express how she feels about her life situation, particularly whether she feels safe from harm (8.2, point 5: 'Is your wife around, Mr Preston? It really feels as though we should have her here too. It just feels as if we're talking about her and her views are, like, really the most central', and point 11: 'Great, then that gives your wife the opportunity to talk to me on her own. I have to make sure that that happens.')

In arranging the subsequent meeting with Sue, the social worker uses the opportunity to uncover the best communication method to use with her (8.2, points 7–8). He asks Steve for his perspective on what works best in communication with Sue. In doing so, Ewan operates the specialist communication skill of 'actively look for the channels of communication that the person is using'. He also initiates the idea of using non-verbal forms of communication, demonstrating that he is willing to apply the principles of 'total communication' and think more creatively about the different media he could use in addition to verbalisation. This demonstrates the specialist communication in 'using the whole communication spectrum':

SW: How do you find it best to communicate with your wife? I'll try to do the same...

Steve: Well, we can, you know, we can talk to each other, but it's a lot... it's drawn out a lot more. Her words are slurred a lot so it's really difficult sometimes to grasp what she's saying. I mean I know you get better at it. You know, it's been two years now, but I'm still kind of starting to understand her more now. It's just you know, where she gets really bad days, and I'm really stressed, that we don't talk so well.

SW: OK, so I must make sure I have plenty of time. What about writing things down or drawing things... does that help?

Another aspect to this section of the dialogue is the social worker's preparedness to discuss the impairment in a frank and more individualised manner, rather than a generalised application from formal knowledge of the impairment. The social worker demonstrates the same communication strategy when he draws on his formal knowledge about the impairment to identify that medication may cause it to be more difficult for Sue to concentrate at particular times of the day , but he does not assume that this is necessarily the case for Sue. Rather, he seeks to understand the way that the impairment may impact upon Sue in an individual way (8.2, point 6: 'Is there a particular time of day that's better for your wife when we could meet? You know, sometimes when people have had a stroke they find they have a bit more energy at a particular time of the day.')

In my earlier research with parents of disabled children, I indicated that it will be felt to be more supportive to service users, through being more inclusive to their individual needs, if a specialist communication approach is taken that seeks to 'validate and recognise "private" knowledge of the individual nuances of the impairment as applied to a person' (Woodcock and Tregaskis,

2008). Social workers need to open themselves up to hearing *new* knowledge about the individual characteristics of an impairment, and the individual way it affects family life. My research found that some professionals were either unable or unwilling to do this, which suggested that the problem lay with the disabling attitudes of the professionals concerned. This presents another example of the way barriers in society impact on communication with people with impairments.

This specialist communication theme of 'validate and recognise "private" knowledge of the individual nuances of the impairment' dominated in the research transcripts of the forum theatre used as a practice setting for this book. The qualifying social workers showed continued respect for the service user's expert knowledge in relation to her impairment or disability. They acknowledged that their understanding of an impairment or specific disability was likely to be fairly low-level, and, as disability affects each individual uniquely, that the only people who could truly have an in-depth and longitudinal understanding of the minutiae of the situation were the service users themselves. As such, partnership emerged as a strong theme throughout the research of the communication in this practice setting. Recognition of the service user's expertise meant that the service user was consulted about the appropriateness of all possible actions throughout a meeting.

The third dominant theme arising from the research transcripts for this book concerned the way in which *promises* were used in this practice setting. While the issue of commitment emerged in other practice settings, the social workers demonstrated the skill of recognising the need for a more personally meaningful commitment to service users with disabilities who were feeling let down by social care and social work services. While the social workers did not use the term 'systemic barriers' to describe the use of promises to empathise with feelings of disappointment, the specialist communication skill of 'communicating empathy for the experience of systemic barriers' did seem to be what they were describing. An illustration of the use of promises in this way can be seen in Practice Example 8.2 at the point where the social worker seeks to empathise with Steve's worries that his wife might be distressed by his communication (as seen at point 9), while emphasising simultaneously that he will treat Sue with dignity and respect (8.2, point 10: 'No, I promise you Mr Preston, I will not speak to your wife as though she's stupid'). Also, at the end of the practice example, he responds to Steve's communication of mistrust that he might be 'like all the others' and 'let them down' by promising that he is different from the previous workers (8.2, point 13: 'I can only apologize for the sort of experiences you've had, but I certainly will.') He uses non-verbal communication to additionally emphasise the point by immediately writing the appointment in his diary in full view of Steve (8.2, point 12). The qualifying social workers in the study for this book noted that promises carried weight and therefore should not be given lightly, but if used appropriately would build trust and rapport with the service user. There were two aspects to this theme: making realistic promises to build trust; and the importance of not making promises that cannot be kept.

In Practice Example 8.3, the social worker is meeting Sue. He seeks to create an atmosphere for the communication of thoughts and feelings by engaging in 'reflective listening'. In Chapter 2 it was described how 'reflective listening' conveys the assurance of warmth and concern while paying attention to the service user's communication, whether through narrative or via non-verbal instances of feeling that illuminate their perception of, and response to, their difficulties and their situation. This helps the person to

PRACTICE EXAMPLE 8.3

Sue and Steve Preston

Work phase

SW: Hello again, Mr. Preston.

Steve: Hello. Come in. Sue's in the living room. Do you want a cup of tea, or...?

SW: Tea would be great. Milk and sugar, thanks. Shall I go on in to see Sue?

Steve: Yes, hang on (*Walks past the social worker and leads him into the living room. He walks over to Sue and waves his hand towards the social worker*) Sue, the social worker's here... er... Ewan....

[14] *SW*: Yes, Ewan Jones. (*Smiles and walks towards Sue*) Good to meet you. Are you happy for us to meet here together this afternoon?

Sue: (*Nods her head*) Yes.

SW: I have come to talk to you about how to help you and your husband. He wrote to me saying you wanted a review of the services provided.

Sue: (*Nods her head*) Yes.

[15] *SW*: I'd like to talk with to you on your own first. I need to hear your views. (*Pause*) Steve said he would join us later. Is that OK with you? (*Sits down opposite Sue. Looks directly at Sue's face*)

►

▶

Sue: (*Nods her head*) Yes.

Steve comes in with two cups of tea and places them on the table next to Sue.

Steve: I'll be in the kitchen for a bit, getting dinner ready. I'll come back when you're finished.

SW: Thanks. Uh, Mrs Preston… Sue, is that OK? (*Looks at Sue's face and she nods*) I know you had the stroke two years ago. It must have been a tough time. (*Sue nods her head. Silence for about five seconds*) Tell me about the things you feel you need help with at the moment.

Sue: Uh, moving... (*Waves arm, gesturing around the room*) ...going out.

SW: You mean getting around the house? Going outside?

[16] *Sue*: Yes…uh…(*Sighs*)

[17] *SW*: Erm, Sue, I've got these flash cards with me in my bag here. They are really good... helps us to talk about problems you may have. Look, they have pictures, see? (*Pause*) If I show you them one at a time, perhaps you could tell me if the picture shows something you would like help with? (*Pause*) Have you seen them before?

Sue: No. (*Leans forward, looks interested*)

SW: OK, look at this, what about walking? (*Shows a card*)

Sue: (*Nods*). Yes, slow. Steve.

SW: Steve helps you? (*Sue nods*) It's slow, but you walk without problems? (*Sue nods*) OK, so not great, and I can see that it's worrying you.

SW: (*Shows a second card*) What about getting up and washing?

Sue: No. Steve.

SW: Steve helps you to get up and washed in the morning? Are you OK with that, or would you like some one else to come and help you?

Sue: No. Steve.

SW: OK. You would prefer Steve to help.

▶

▶

[18] *Sue*: Yes. Steve... (*Sue becomes tearful*) Helps me... housework....

[19] *SW*: You're upset Sue. Tell me, what's wrong?

Sue: Steve...

Sue cries quietly. Silence for twenty seconds. Social worker sits quietly.

[20] *SW*: Sue, you're really sad... Can we talk about it? Look at these cards. Do any of these pictures show why you're upset?

Sue: (*Picks picture of man and woman smiling and hugging*). Steve.

[21] *SW*: Does this show you being happy with Steve?

Sue: (*Nods*) *Yes.*

SW: Do you want me to get Steve?

Sue: (*Nods.*)

[22] *SW*: OK. I'll just get him. Look, our tea's getting cold! Here you are. (*Gives Sue the cup of tea and then goes out to the kitchen*)

SW: Steve, erm, Sue's got a bit upset. She'd like you to come back in. Is that OK?

Steve: Yeah. Upset? She does get tearful. It's frustrating for her.

They walk back into the living room.

feel able to disclose information or worries without fearing being blamed or misunderstood.

The social worker begins by ensuring that he is sitting opposite Sue, so that both can see the other's face clearly and pick up any non-verbal communication to aid understanding (8.3, point 15). As part of the basic communication skill described in Chapter 2 – 'achieving a shared purpose', he says he recognises that Sue might wish to have Steve present to provide communication support, but also explains why he would like to speak to her on her own, to hear her view of her situation. He uses short sentences and allows for pauses to give Sue time to mentally process the content of what he is saying, and time to formulate her answers (8.3, points 14–16). This specialist communication skill of 'taking time' is vital to gaining shared understandings. The skill gives Sue confidence that she will not need Steve present to help with communication at the meeting and so it goes ahead.

As the meeting unfolds it becomes apparent to the social worker that Sue is becoming frustrated by being unable to explain the different issues she is experiencing in her life (8.3, point 16). At this point, the worker introduces the flash cards as an additional medium for communication. In doing so, he operates the specialist communication skill of 'using the whole communication spectrum' (8.3, point 17: 'Erm, Sue, I've got these flash cards with me in my bag here. They are really good... helps us to talk about problems you may have. Look, they have pictures, see? (*Pause*) If I show you them one at a time, perhaps you could tell me if the picture shows something you would like help with? (*Pause*) Have you seen them before?') The social worker goes on to utilise this 'total communication' while maintaining an adult style of interaction. He makes use of 'closed questions' other than 'open questions', as he has seen how Sue finds it easier to respond with 'yes' or 'no' answers (8.3, points 17–18). This demonstrates the importance of 'actively looking for the channels of communication that the person is using'.

The specialist communication strategy appears to have some success in facilitating Sue's expression of thoughts and feelings. At point 18 of the dialogue she communicates strong feelings of distress and frustration.

Sue: Steve... (*Sue becomes tearful*) Helps me…housework.

SW: You're upset Sue. Tell me, what's wrong?

Sue: Steve...

Sue cries quietly. Silence for twenty seconds. Social worker sits quietly.

SW: Sue, you're really sad... Can we talk about it? Look at these cards. Do any of these pictures show why you're upset?

At this point the worker shows empathy for her distress by 'putting feelings into words' and asks an 'open question' to seek clarification of why she is feeling upset (8.3, point 19: 'You're upset Sue. Tell me, what's wrong?'). He uses an 'open question' because he is aware that there could be many reasons for her distress, including that of being in danger of harm. Policy guidance for safeguarding adults warns against the use of questions that could be construed as being 'leading'. It is apparent, however, that Sue needs additional communication support to explain and explore her distress. The social worker offers the flash cards again, which contain a number of different scenarios, including some pictures of a person being intimidated or harmed by another person (8.3, point 20).

Arguably, the cards could still be considered as being 'leading' through offering only a selection of possible responses. Certainly, there are limitations to the method. However, the cards do offer Sue a wider vocabulary than she has access to at present. In the event she chooses a card that indicates an expression of love between a man and a woman. The worker is careful not to assume that the scenario depicted on the card has the same meaning for Sue as it does for him. The picture could still have been interpreted as a scene of exploitation. Again, he uses 'closed questions' to check with Sue about what the scenario means to her (8.3, point 21: 'Does this show you being happy with Steve?')

This chapter has identified specialist communication skills required by the social worker to work as an effective partner to service users in determining very complex issues and ethical dilemmas about safeguarding and the protection of vulnerable adults, choice and independence. Consideration was given to how barriers to communication can be caused by individual life experiences, dominant cultural expectations and beliefs about disability in society. A key element of the specialist social work communication strategy was to use language that identified and addressed these societal and systemic barriers and focused on the individual nuances of an impairment for a person in their life situation.

Professional Standards

This chapter will help you to meet the following National Occupational Standards:

Key Role 1: Prepare for, and work with individuals, families, carers, groups and communities to assess their needs and circumstances

Unit 1	Prepare for social work contact and involvement
Unit 2	Work with individuals, families, carers, groups and communities to help them make informed decisions
Unit 3	Assess needs and options to recommend a course of action

Key Role 2: Plan, carry out, review and evaluate social work practice with individuals, families, carers, groups, communities and other professionals

Unit 4	Respond to crisis situations
Unit 5	Interact with individuals, families, carers, groups and communities to achieve change and development and to improve life opportunities
Unit 6	Prepare, produce, implement and evaluate plans with individuals, families, carers, groups, communities and professional colleagues
Unit 7	Support the development of networks to meet assessed needs and planned outcomes

Unit 9	Address behaviour which presents a risk to individuals, families, carers, groups and communities

Key Role 3: Support individuals to represent their needs, views and circumstances. Advocate with and on behalf of people

Unit 10	Advocate with, and on behalf of, individuals, families, carers, groups and communities
Unit 11	Prepare for and participate in decision-making forums

Key Role 4: Manage risk to individuals, families, carers, groups, communities, self and colleagues

Unit 12	Assess and manage risks to individuals, families, carers, groups and communities

Key Role 5: Manage and be accountable, with supervision and support, for your own social work practice within your organisation

Unit 14	Manage and be accountable for your own work
Unit 15	Contribute to the management of resources and services
Unit 16	Manage, present and share records and reports
Unit 17	Work within multi-disciplinary and multi-organisational teams, networks and systems

Key Role 6: Demonstrate professional competence in social work practice

Unit 18	Research, analyse, evaluate and use current knowledge of best social work practice
Unit 19	Work within agreed standards of social work practice and ensure own professional development
Unit 20	Manage complex ethical issues, dilemmas and conflicts
Unit 21	Contribute to the promotion of best social work practice

CHAPTER

Working with Refugees and Asylum Seekers

9

Summary of Specialist Communication Skills

- Experiencing service user feelings
- Using the whole communication spectrum
- Tuning-in to the fear and uncertainty over citizenship
- Demonstrating cultural acceptance

Policy and background literature

The provision of support to people seeking asylum and those gaining refugee status is a growing area of social work practice, where the role of the state in assessing asylum and the cultural climate within the UK of racist attitudes regarding egalitarian co-existence present particular communication issues for social workers. In communicating with asylum seekers, social workers need to recognise the pervasiveness of the legal framework over their lives, where they live in an atmosphere of fear, anxiety, control and uncertainty caused by the role of the state in assessing their application for asylum (Fell, 2004). Their overriding concern is to prove that their 'case' meets the requirements of the 1951 UN Convention.

The psychological distress that asylum-seekers experience as a result of their traumatic pre-migration experiences, such as rape, torture, bereavement and mourning (Parker, 2000; Kohli, 2006), will also affect communication processes. For unaccompanied minors, this psychological distress is particularly severe and often communicated through problematic behaviour. The literature points to a compounding number of stressors experienced by asylum-seekers and those granted refugee status: isolation, insecurity, fear and a struggle to cope with unsettlement, often related to the asylum legal process (Daycare Trust, 1995; Rutter, 2003). The experience of racist attacks often causes social withdrawal. Economic hardship and confusion combined with wariness concerning from whom to seek advice and help regarding housing and schooling is frequent.

These issues point to a need for communication to help asylum-seekers feel less marginalised and gain some degree of inclusion (Fell, 2004). Central to this is overcoming issues of trust and the reluctance to approach professionals for help for fear that it might be reflected back to the Home Office and prejudice their application for asylum. Active listening, availability and the ability to be a stable point of contact is recognised as important in relation to establishing trust (Comley, 1998; Fell, 2004). The use of more comprehensive communication strategies than simple verbal language in conveying warmth, understanding and acceptance is significant (Morales and Sheafor, 2001; Koprowska, 2005). Where verbal communication takes place, it needs to be at a slower pace, avoiding complex or ambiguous grammar, and a repeated check made for understanding (Koprowska, 2005). Cultural awareness and sensitivity is significant within these strategies. Definitions of family and change are not necessarily the same for the asylum seeker as for the host (Fell, 2004; Devore, 2001). Indeed, it is critical to guard against any stereotyping of values or practices of members of ethnic groups (Parker, 2000; Jones, 2003). Warnings surrounding 'cultural relativism' in social work practice are well-versed and relevant here (see Chapter 1 for further discussion).

Access to English language support and interpreters is important, yet the literature also points to the conflict and potential dangers inherent in the role of both formal and informal interpreters. Green *et al.* (2005) highlight that while there have been improvements in the availability and quality of interpreting services across health and social care, many service users rely on informal sources to make contact, appointments and attend consultations and meetings. Studies identify that informal interpreters are often preferred by families because they offer emotional and practical support, they are readily available and provide a greater understanding of the service user (Rhodes and Nocon, 2003; Green *et al.*, 2005). Yet, the majority of the literature focuses on the inappropriateness and potential ineffectiveness of informal interpreters, particularly child interpreters (Ebden *et al.*, 1988; Flores *et al.*, 2003). The reasons cited are that children may not have sufficient sophistication within the languages to interpret accurately, and they may lack emotional maturity to manage sensitive and distressing information about health problems. However, Cohen *et al.* (1999) and Green *et al.* (2005) identify normative ideology underpinning this perspective concerning the social construction of childhood in Western societies and the relative inappropriateness for children to 'take on' such adult responsibility. Green *et al.*'s study of the perspectives of child interpreters' found that the children rarely considered themselves as being 'exploited' or that their translation was 'inadequate'. Rather, they saw themselves as skilled mediators, bridging the communication gap between two adults. The contribution they made to their family gave them a sense of self-esteem. Difficulties arose when there were differences in the normative expectations of their role in the family, such as young men being asked to translate about their mothers' reproductive health problems, or young women being asked to investigate whether their parents are being compliant with medication instructions.

Care needs to be taken to establish the 'ethnic reality or experience' of the individual concerned (Devore, 2001). Indeed, an important aspect of communication seems to be that of a readiness to listen to and validate asylum seekers' and refugees' accounts of their past experiences (Parker, 2000; Devore, 2001; Fell, 2004). The availability and skills of the social worker in listening to these accounts, but at the same time being able to communicate information about help with practical issues, such as schooling, appropriate housing and finance seems to be successful in work with refugees (Parker, 2000; Fell, 2004). Related to this, the literature supports the importance of social workers addressing racism and racist experiences (Fanning, 2004; Dominelli, 1992). Social workers are expected to have learnt ways to counter unfair discrimination, racism, poverty, disadvantage and injustice. However, the literature highlights that professionals avoid dealing with issues of race and culture, finding them uncomfortable to discuss (Abney, 2002; Alexander-Floyd, 2008). Given that this area of practice is replete with instances and attitudes of hostility, then social workers need to develop strategies to counter such racism at both interpersonal and structural levels.

Practice application

The background literature states that the overriding concern for asylum-seekers is to move from non-citizenship to greater citizenship by being recognised as a refugee under the 1951 UN Convention (Fell, 2004). Thus a central concern for the social worker in Practice Example 9.1 should be to identify how societal barriers relating to this uncertainty over citizenship have an impact on her communication with Maria, and seek to overcome them. To this end it is important for the social worker to recognise that a significant barrier is likely to be an atmosphere of fear, anxiety, control and uncertainty caused by the role of the state in assessing Maria's application for asylum. Maria is likely to meet the social worker with suspicion and trepidation that, rather than a social worker, she might be an official from the Home Office, and fearing that any disclosed information might be referred to the Home Office and affect her asylum claim. Thus it is important for the social worker to engage in 'tuning-in' to prepare to 'show empathy' for the way that Maria might express these feelings during their meeting. In doing so the worker will be more able to demonstrate that she is not adopting a role that is controlling or hostile, but rather seeking to be accepting, available and willing to listen and understand Maria's thoughts and feelings. So critical is this preparatory empathy for this practice setting, that it seems important to emphasise the specialist communication strategy as being one of 'tuning-in to the fear and uncertainty over citizenship.'

PRACTICE EXAMPLE 9.1

Maria

Preparatory stage

Maria, aged 32,and her two children (Milosh, aged 13 and Gordana, aged 10) are a Roma family from Kosovo who came to the UK seven months ago seeking asylum. With Maria's permission, her general practitioner referred the family to the duty social worker of the local Advice and Assessment (Intake) Social Work Team. The general practitioner is treating Maria for depression. He feels that the victimisation she is experiencing from neighbours, alongside the problematic behaviour of her son Milosh and negative reports from school are exacerbating Maria's mental health problems. The general practitioner feels that urgent social work intervention is needed to support the family functioning and prevent further deterioration of Maria's mental health.

Maria, her husband and two young children were among the 120,000 Roma people who had to leave Kosovo as a consequence of a series of wars in the former Yugoslavia in the late 1990s. Over the last few years, Roma people who fled to neighbouring countries such as Hungary, Slovakia and the Czech Republic have been attacked with firebombs, stabbing and beating. Many of the attacks have been aimed at families and children. There are lingering feelings of hostility among the majority population in Kosovo in relation to Roma people as they often speak Serbian and are accused as having collaborated with Serbian forces.

A specialist communication strategy of 'demonstrating cultural acceptance' is significantly important, given that the aforementioned legal framework reflects a more general cultural climate in the UK of racist attitudes regarding egalitarian co-existence. There are regular reports of racist discrimination, stigma and disadvantage being experienced by asylum-seekers, refugee groups and other migrant workers and the families of minority ethnic groups (Cohen, 1994; Parker, 2000). Where appropriate, the social worker must be prepared to discuss examples of racism and attitudes of hostility that Maria may have experienced and believes has an impact on the safety of her family and home situation. Clearly, though, the social worker should not assume that racism is a necessary element of Maria's situation, as to do so would itself be racist (Jones, 2003). However, being aware of and sensitive to cultural differences among the people a social worker serves is considered to be a vital element of cultural competence (Compton *et al.*, 2005). This involves recognising that all cultures can supply strength to people and, equally, can oppress or create liberation for their members.

Given that the background literature has highlighted that professionals often find issues of race and culture uncomfortable to discuss (Abney, 2002; Alexander-Floyd, 2008), it is important that the social worker reviews her own deficits in knowledge and skills in relation to cultural competence at this preparatory stage (Devore, 2001). Devore (2001: 36) cites Miley *et al.* (1998: 39) in identifying how such self-examination should cover the four areas of personal identity, spiritual beliefs, knowledge of others, and cross-cultural skills. She highlights the following questions as being helpful within this analysis:

- Have I been a racist or a recipient of racist attacks?
- What privileges do I accrue because of my ethnicity or gender? Am I religious?
- What ethnic dispositions influence my identity?
- What am I doing to increase my knowledge about people in other ethnic groups?

Answering such questions will be essential to increase social worker confidence and skill in 'demonstrating cultural acceptance'. Social workers will learn about themselves as members of an ethnic group and its accompanying cultural norms and values, as well as increasing knowledge about other groups (Devore, 2001). Thus, in relation to this example, as part of this preparatory self-examination, the social worker should identify the cultural norms and values that frequently exist among Roma populations from Central Europe. Examples of such norms include the respect shown to traditional purity laws. Women often wear long skirts to cover their bodies from the waist down as these parts of the body are considered more private and 'less pure'. Times of menstruation, childbirth and postpartum periods are similarly considered impure, with cleanliness rituals adopted and women withdrawing from collective gatherings at these times. Men and women tend to adopt gender roles, with women being the primary caregivers and homemakers. Marriage tends to occur at an earlier age, and with other members of the Roma population. Sexual relationships before marriage are generally forbidden. Roma people tend to adopt the religion of the majority population in which they are living, and in Central Europe this is frequently the Christian or Muslim faith.

Having an awareness of these cultural norms and values will prepare the social worker to be sensitive to cultural differences and variations in patterns and styles of communication with Maria. While many Europeans experience eye contact as signalling openness, trust and honesty in communication, Muslim women sometimes find such direct eye contact to be insulting. If Maria is a practising Muslim she may avoid appointments coinciding with appointed times for prayer. If she adopts the traditional Roma norms and values concerning purity and gender roles, she may be offended by the social worker being dressed in clothes that accord her body far less covering. Depending on whether it is a time of less purity, she may be unable to leave the house to attend an appointment, or indeed avoid touching the social worker, such as by shaking hands. However, it is equally important that the social worker recognises that these norms, values and patterns of communication may not be replicated within Maria's family. In 'demonstrating cultural acceptance', she must not assume homogeneity in the values and practices of any ethnic group (Parker, 2000). For example, Maria and/or her children may have chosen to adopt some or all of the cultural norms of the majority ethnic population of the country or region in which she and her children now live. As Compton *et al.* (2005: 190) state: 'we are born into some cultures and we may adopt others ... many [service users] routinely draw from several cultures and multiple roles'. They consider communication improves when social workers view cultural identification as being not being primarily about race, ethnicity and religion, but seek to hear from service users about what they believe to be the most important contributing factors to their personal and cultural identities.

The social worker needs to 'tune-in' to another societal barrier that has an impact on communication, and that concerns the way in which society places a high value on the written and spoken word. This creates a disadvantage for people who do not speak the language of the majority population as their first language. In the case of our practice example, the social worker must start from an attitudinal position, which is that Maria and her children have a right to be communicated with in their first language and be facilitated to express decisions concerning their lives. Arguably, the use of an interpreter is crucial in enabling Maria to express her thoughts and feelings more accurately. However, the background literature has highlighted that the use of interpreters is not without its difficulties. Indeed, while interpreters are used far more extensively in social work practice, there are many cases where it is not possible to obtain the services of an interpreter, such as in emergency or unplanned situations, or where it is difficult to match the dialect of a language, or where the service user declines the service. Moreover, it is important to recognise that communication strategies with Maria should not be framed only on the basis of the written and spoken word, but respect how Maria senses, perceives and communicates about her experiences. Communication could use different methods and formats beyond that of verbalisation, such as body language but also pictures, symbols and signs. As with so many of the practice settings within this book, adopting a specialist communication strategy that 'uses the whole communication spectrum' will help to overcome the societal barriers to communication.

Practice Example 9.2 shows the social worker employing the four parts of the basic communication skill from Chapter 2 of 'achieving a shared purpose' (that is, 'being clear on role'); 'being clear on purpose'; 'reaching for feedback' and 'showing empathy'.

PRACTICE EXAMPLE 9.2

Maria

Beginnings

Social worker knocks at the door. Maria calls through the door.

[1] *Maria*: Who is that?

SW: Er, Mrs Kovac. My name's Angela Moore. I phoned you this morning.

Maria: Phoned? Who are you?

SW: Angela Moore. (*Bends down to letter box to speak more quietly*) I telephoned you this morning. (*Says even more quietly*) I'm the social worker.

Maria: Social worker. Come in. (*Opens the door*)

SW: Hello, Mrs Kovac? (*Raises her hand in a gesture of greeting*)... Nice to meet you. I'm Angela, from the social work office at Central Hall, a social worker. Um... your doctor was worried about you. I might be able to help. Do you mind if I call you Maria?

Maria: Yes, Maria.

SW: Where shall we sit?

They sit down on two dining-room chairs. The social worker moves her chair more towards Maria so that Maria can look into her face.

SW: Maria... do you know why I've come to see you today?

Maria: Um (*Points to left*) um... my roof?

[2] *SW*: (*Maintains eye contact, speaks slowly and clearly*) We can look at the roof, but first, it's about how you are... and how your children are... and whether we can help you in any way... OK?

▶

▶

[3] *Maria*: OK. (*Nods slowly in a nervous way*)

[4] *SW*: (*Continues to speak slowly and clearly*) You seem a bit worried.... I want you to know that I'm not from The Home Office, OK? And I'm not from the police... I'm from Social Services... do you understand Social Services?

Maria: No.

[5] *SW*: It's um... we try to help people... all sorts of people... not just people from other countries. We have older people, younger people... so lots... lots of people we try to help... OK? And what I want to do is see what help you need today.

Maria: Mmm...

SW: The doctor is worried about you Maria... The doctor said you were very sad... finding it difficult... Can we talk about it? (*Pause*) Is that OK?

Maria: Mmm...

[6] *SW*: Your English is very good, but perhaps you need a bit more help with your English? (*Pause for ten seconds*) Maybe an interpreter is a good idea?

[7] *Maria*: Well, no, my children... they help me.

SW: They help you. Your children... how old are they? (*Indicates differences in height with hand*)

Maria: At school... thirteen. Ten.

SW: Their English... have they learnt it at school?

Maria: Yes.

SW: And your English... how have you learnt your English?

Maria: Through my children.

SW: Through your children?

Maria: Yes, and speaking....

SW: And speaking in this country?

▶

▶

Maria: Yes.

SW: You've been here for seven months?

Maria: Yes.

SW: Do you like this country?

Maria: It is good.

SW: It is good?

Maria: Yes.

SW: What do you not like about this country? (*Shakes head*)

Maria: (*Tilts head, indicating she does not understand*)

[8] *SW*: What do you not like about this country? (*Shakes head and makes negative hand gestures*) What is bad with this country?

Maria: Um… Home Office?

SW: The Home Office? You don't like them?

Maria: No.

SW: You're waiting to hear from The Home Office whether you can stay?

Maria: (*Nods*) Yes… yes.

SW: You would like to do that? (*Nods*) You would like to stay here?

[9] *Maria*: Yes… Um… (*Waves arm…face reddens...she appears upset, tearful*) My husband…

[10] *SW*: (*Leaning forward*) It's OK… (*Silence for ten seconds*) Is it difficult for you to talk about that? (*Maria nods; silence for another ten seconds*)

SW: Do you want to talk to me about that? (*Pause*)

Maria: (*Nods; is upset*) I am… a little…(*Silence for twenty seconds*)

SW: Your husband? Is he back in Kosovo?

Maria: Yes. (*Nodding and crying*)

▶

▶
[11] *SW*: That must be very painful for you (*Reaches out and touches Maria's arm*) and your children to be in a strange country. Are you missing your husband? (*Maria nods and is very tearful*)

SW: Do you want a tissue? (*Maria shakes head*) Would you like to talk about that now... or later perhaps?

As anticipated, Maria seems to be communicating feelings of apprehension at speaking to the social worker. The 'tuning-in' activity revealed that this is likely to be related to the authority that the social worker brings through her legislative role and professional status. Maria's body language shows anxiety (9.2, point 3: *'Nods slowly in a nervous way'*), and her answers seem confused about the exact role of the social worker, and the purpose of the visit. The social worker uses the skill from Chapter 2 of 'putting feelings into words' to 'show empathy' for Maria's feelings of apprehension, and begins to find a way of better 'clarifying her role' by asking Maria to provide her understanding of the work of a social worker (9.2, point 4: 'You seem a bit worried.... I want you to know that I'm not from The Home Office, OK? And I'm not from the police... I'm from Social Services... do you understand Social Services?*'*) It is likely that the social worker will need to continue to 'show empathy' for these feelings throughout their meeting. This will continue to demonstrate that she is not adopting a role that is controlling or hostile but seeking to be accepting, available and willing to listen and understand Maria's thoughts and feelings.

Point 5 of Practice Example 9.2 illustrates the difficulty in explaining the role of a social worker in circumstances where there is no equivalent welfare system within the cultural experience of the other person. The language difference and difficulties between Maria and the social worker compound the problem in achieving a shared meaning. The opportunity for misunderstanding and miscommunication is great. Indeed, it is frightening enough for Maria to speak to a person in authority about her mental health and social situation, without the additional demands of communicating in a second language with the accompanying worry over misunderstanding. The social worker quickly realises this and offers to arrange for an interpreter for a subsequent meeting (9.2, point 6). Maria refuses this offer, preferring to involve her children as interpreters (9.2, point 7). The matter of seeking translation services through informal sources such as bilingual children, extended family, friends or other members of the cultural community caused considerable debate among the social workers involved in the research study for this book. Indeed, the same debate occurs in the background literature, which was summarised earlier.

The social worker needs to ensure that she is conversant with the advantages and disadvantages of using formal and informal interpreters. This should include recognising that an immediate aversion to allowing Maria's children to interpret might reflect the aforementioned Westernised societal ideology concerning an inappropriateness for children to adopt such a level of adult responsibility. It is important that the social worker takes into account the specific cultural and social role definitions that influence Maria in making this decision to request that her children act as interpreters. It may be viewed as an expected part of the usual set of economic and social relations of the family, which frequently provides the children with self-esteem and a sense of pride in the family. However, it would be wrong to consider these values and family norms solely within the context of Maria's culture. This would constitute an extreme form of cultural relativism (Compton *et al.*, 2005). The decision must also be made on the basis of whether the behaviour meets the legal conditions set out within the Children Acts 1989 and 2004 to safeguard and promote the welfare of children in need, including ascertaining their perspectives on those decisions in their own right.

In the research transcripts for the study underpinning the book, the theme of non-verbal communication, while present in all other transcripts, came very much to the fore; similarly, the role of feelings emerged as being significant. While in most of the other practice settings, non-verbal communication skills play a supporting role to what is communicated linguistically, when working with this particular service user whose use of English was limited, the spoken word took a lesser role and the importance of non-verbal communication skills emerged. The social workers identified that, where language is perhaps a barrier, the use of non-verbal techniques can offer support and encouragement as well as facilitating communication. Aside from non-verbal communication, the qualifying social workers also highlighted other ways of trying to adapt verbal communication to make it easier for the service user to understand, such as using short, non-complex sentences and repetition. This repeated check for understanding demonstrates the basic communication skill, discussed in Chapter 2, of 'reflective listening', which describes how a social worker, in attending to the service user's narrative and non-verbal communication of thoughts and feelings with warmth and concern, might encourage that person to feel more able to disclose information or worries without fearing blame or misunderstanding. Points 7 to 9 of Practice Example 9.2 illustrate this communication strategy. 'Closed questions', which are short and non-complex, allow Maria time to process the information and formulate the appropriate answer ('Your children... how old are they?'; 'You've been here for seven months?') The social worker uses occasional 'open questions' but keeps them short and avoids using higher order concepts or grammatically ambiguous words ('How have you learnt your English?', 'What is bad with this country?')

The specialist communication strategy appears to have had some success in facilitating Maria's expression of thoughts and feelings. At point 9 of the dialogue (9.2) she communicates strong feelings of distress through her body language. This continues until point 12.

[9]	*Maria*:	Yes… Um… (*Waves arm…face reddens...she appears upset, tearful*) My husband…
[10]	*SW*:	(*Leaning forward*) It's OK…. (*Silence for ten seconds*) Is it difficult for you to talk about that? (*Maria nods; silence for another ten seconds*)
[11]	*SW*:	Do you want to talk to me about that? (*Pause*)
	Maria:	(*Nods; is upset*) I am… a little…(*Silence for twenty seconds*)
	SW:	Your husband? Is he back in Kosovo?
	Maria:	Yes. (*Nodding and crying*)
[12]	*SW*:	That must be very painful for you (*Reaches out and touches Maria's arm*) and your children to be in a strange country. Are you missing your husband? (*Maria nods and is very tearful*)
[13]	*SW*:	Do you want a tissue? (*Maria shakes head*) Would you like to talk about that now… or later perhaps?

At point 10 the social worker 'shows empathy' for Maria's distress in non-verbal ways by 'using silences' and verbally providing reassurance that she will support Maria with these feelings ('It's OK'; 'Is it difficult for you to talk about that?'). In Chapter 7 the skill of 'using silences' was described, and it is an important skill for developing a working relationship with a service user expressing mental distress. Sitting alongside and just 'being' with the service user demonstrates support and acceptance. 'Being' gives respect by allowing difficult thoughts to remain undisclosed until an appropriate time for the service user, whereas 'doing' demands work to be done on those feelings when the service user is unwilling or unable to do so (Wilson *et al.*, 2008). Conceptually, the process provides 'containment' of painful feelings which have become difficult to control. Containment is described as an active process by which the social worker experiences the difficult feelings transferred by the service user and then seeks to work on those feelings to help the service user feel more understood, more 'in control' and less isolated (Agass, 2002).

Interestingly, the qualifying social workers in our research study, who were participating in the enactment of this role-play as forum theatre, found this point in the communication to be critical. While at this stage of the interview they had no knowledge of Maria's pre-migration experiences or those relating to settlement, they felt her projection of sadness and pain within themselves. Feelings emerged as a larger theme in this practice setting than the others considered for the book. It is likely that this is because this service user was being victimised, was isolated and was visibly upset and emotional. The social workers noted the importance primarily of helping this person to feel less sad and scared, with practical assistance being almost a secondary consideration (though still vital). As this service user also had a limited ability to communicate and was scared, the social workers identified a feeling in themselves of their own helplessness coupled with tremendous empathy for the service user. The theme of 'experiencing service user feelings' can be classified as a specialist communication skill, because the empathy for the service user in their role as social worker (especially when the limits of what they could do in their role were felt as helplessness) was clearly contributing to the development of reflexive practitioners.

The impact of this transference meant that, at point 12, when the social worker uses Shulman's (2009) skill of 'putting feelings into words' to verbally demonstrate empathy for Maria's feelings (9.2, point 12: 'That must be very painful for you and your children to be in a strange country') some of the qualifying social workers (within the forum theatre) encouraged the use of non-verbal communication to further emphasise the demonstration of empathy (9.2, point 12: '*reaches out and touches Maria's arm*'). They continued to debate the decision whether or not to have physical contact with the service user, as it might have a strong influence successful communication. As noted earlier, the cultural norms and values of some cultural groups indicate that some service users would be offended by such a gesture. Indeed, some social workers were not prepared to risk any allegations of inappropriate behaviour.

Repeatedly, the social worker uses 'open questions' to encourage Maria to talk about her feelings because she is aware that there could be many reasons for Maria's distress, including that of being in danger of harm from racist violence in a variety of forms (9.2, point 11: 'Do you want to talk to me about that?'; 9.2, point 13: 'Would you like to talk about that now… or later perhaps?').

As noted earlier, the background literature identified how asylum seekers experience psychological distress as a result of their traumatic pre-migration experiences, such as rape, torture, bereavement and mourning (Parker, 2000), as well as isolation, insecurity, fear and stress in coping with unsettlement, which is often related to the asylum process (Daycare Trust, 1995; Rutter, 2003). As stated earlier, an important aspect of specialist communication is that of listening to and validating to asylum seekers' and refugees' accounts of their past experiences. The worker should demonstrate acceptance of Maria's 'world view' or 'private voice' about her experiences. Fell (2004: 119) makes the point that social workers, who have the privilege of cultural and economic capital, professional status and citizenship, will find it difficult to envisage ever being able to empathise with 'those who have suffered more than we may ever have to'. We are outsiders to those personal stories and, as such, we should give validity to personal accounts and learn from them.

In summary, this chapter has highlighted the degree to which the wider social and political context in which social work communication occurs can cause barriers that impede the effectiveness of that communication. I have identified how a specialist social work communication strategy of attending to service users' fears and uncertainty over whether they will granted citizenship or not is crucial. Of equal importance is that of communication which demonstrates cultural acceptance and validity to lived experiences, given that the legal framework reflects a more general cultural climate within the UK of racist attitudes regarding egalitarian co-existence.

Professional Standards

This chapter will help you to meet the following National Occupational Standards:

Key Role 1: Prepare for, and work with individuals, families, carers, groups and communities to assess their needs and circumstances

Unit 1 Prepare for social work contact and involvement
Unit 2 Work with individuals, families, carers, groups and communities to help them make informed decisions
Unit 3 Assess needs and options to recommend a course of action

Key Role 2: Plan, carry out, review and evaluate social work practice with individuals, families, carers, groups, communities and other professionals

Unit 4 Respond to crisis situations
Unit 5 Interact with individuals, families, carers, groups and communities to achieve change and development and to improve life opportunities
Unit 6 Prepare, produce, implement and evaluate plans with individuals, families, carers, groups, communities and professional colleagues

Key Role 3: Support individuals to represent their needs, views and circumstances. Advocate with and on behalf of people

Unit 10 Advocate with, and on behalf of, individuals, families, carers, groups and communities

Key Role 4: Manage risk to individuals, families, carers, groups, communities, self and colleagues

Unit 12 Assess and manage risks to individuals, families, carers, groups and communities

Key Role 5: Manage and be accountable, with supervision and support, for your own social work practice within your organisation

Unit 14 Manage and be accountable for your own work

Key Role 6: Demonstrate professional competence in social work practice

Unit 18 Research, analyse, evaluate and use current knowledge of best social work practice
Unit 19 Work within agreed standards of social work practice and ensure own professional development
Unit 20 Manage complex ethical issues, dilemmas and conflicts
Unit 21 Contribute to the promotion of best social work practice

CHAPTER

10 Working with Older People

Summary of Specialist Communication Skills

- Use the whole communication spectrum
- Actively looking for the channels of communication the person is using
- Validation
- Mirroring, emphasising or exaggerating non-verbal communication without being patronising
- Taking time
- Using short, simple sentences

Policy and background literature

Since the end of the 1990s, social work practice with older people has taken place within the context of a changing UK national policy agenda, originating with the modernising social services agenda (DoH, 1998; Scottish Office, 1999) and developed by the 'National Services Framework for Older People' (DoH, 2001; Welsh Assembly Government, 2006). The 'new philosophy' of social care provision brought about by these changes requires social workers to engage with particular communication skills (SSI, 2002). Indeed, the policy highlights that social workers should be working with the service user as an active participant in assessing a wide range of needs and designing care plans to maximise independence. Their work must be 'person-centred', achieved through treating service users with dignity, as individuals, and enabling choice about care.

Indeed, the principles underpinning the Mental Capacity Act (2005) require social workers to presume a service user has the capacity to make decisions unless it has been established that they lack that capacity. This indicates the need for social workers to use particular communication skills to explore issues of 'decision-making capacity'. In addition, policy states that social workers should work with the service user, carer and other agencies to accomplish a timely single assessment process (DoH, 2001; SSI, 2002).

A central underpinning principle is that of combating ageism. Standard One of the National Service Framework for Older People expects social work and social care staff to meet a minimum standard of 'rooting out age discrimination' (DoH, 2001). More recently, this has been reinforced by European legislation to prevent age discrimination within employment, which came into force in the UK in 2006 (Directive 2000/78/EC). The social work literature emphasises how social workers must actively resist ageism, both in terms of their own attitudes and from other sources. An often quoted definition of ageism is 'the social process through which negative images of and attitudes towards older people, based solely on the characteristics of old age itself, result in discrimination' (Hughes and Mtezuka (1992), in Thompson, 1995).

The final raft of policy changes relevant to social work communication skills for working with older people concern the government measures to address specifically the abuse of vulnerable adults, such as the 'No Secrets' guidance (DoH, 2000) and the Safeguarding Vulnerable Groups Act 2006. These policies and resultant practice guidance place a responsibility on the social worker to investigate and take action when a vulnerable adult is believed to be suffering abuse. The indication is for social workers to ensure that their communication is not geared exclusively towards obtaining tangible outcomes such as service referral, but facilitating a safe relationship from which to explore feelings and opinions.

The wider literature relating to communication with older people relates almost entirely to working with people with dementia, people who have experienced a stroke, or those who have developed loss of sight and/or hearing. The themes identify particular communication challenges and skills necessary to promote collaborative, person-centred work with a person whose vision and/or hearing and/or cognitive abilities are becoming progressively diminished.

A common theme from across the literature was to recognise that it can take a person considerable effort to concentrate on verbal information being provided and then to put a sentence together (Buijssen, 2005). A repeated theme was to 'give the person time', as the person is likely to need more time to process information and formulate a response. Similarly, it is better to engage in frequent, shorter meetings than a single protracted meeting. Also, the use of short and simple questions and statements helps concentration and clarity (Buijssen, 2005).

A second common theme from across the literature was to recognise that, as the use of language becomes difficult, there is a need for communication to occur in ways that do not solely involve words but use the whole communication spectrum. The onset of dementia or sensory impairment is usually gradual, and not always recognised by the service user or social worker. As such, the service user may already be relying on non-verbal communication and not actually identify that they are doing so. Thus social workers need to show skill in emphasising or exaggerating non-verbal communication without being patronising (Bender *et al.,* 1987). For example, social workers need to check that their body language, such as facial gestures, reflects the content of what they are saying (Bounds and Hepburn, 1996). They need to be ready to write things down. They need to ensure that the physical environment does not provide a distraction, by ensuring good light, sitting close and 'face on' to the service user so that their lips, and indeed, their facial expression, can be read easily (Bounds and Hepburn, 1996).

A related theme across the literature concerned the importance of physical contact for older people. The literature highlights how many older people do not experience much physical contact, and a light touch on the arm, or a hand being squeezed can be a useful and emotionally powerful means of non-verbal communication (Bender, 1987). Equally, it is important to attend to cultural differences and cultural conventions, as a person may find aspects of non-verbal communication, such as physical contact or eye contact, to be intrusive or disrespectful (Bender, 1987; Alibhai-Brown, 1998). Indeed, the potential for cultural misunderstanding is a repeated theme across the literature. As opposed to adopting ageist attitudes, some cultural groups see old age as inevitable and to be valued (Alibhai-Brown, 1998). It is important for social workers to learn the formalities that are important to different cultural groups, such as respect for minority ethnic elders, but also the more subtle, understated forms of communication, which a worker could misread as a lack of concern (Alibhai-Brown, 1998). There may be culturally-based attitudinal differences to problems. For example, the use of the term 'dementia', and/or the care and treatment of it, is not shared and agreed across all cultural groups. Indeed, in this respect Bowes and Dar (2000) refer to the need for workers to develop 'linguistic and cultural communication'.

Over and above these communication issues, the literature identifies further skills in working with people with dementia. As people move through phases of dementia, with their cognitive and language skills altering in different ways, they develop a heightened awareness of non-verbal communication, and experience a particular preoccupation with the emotional aspects of their lives (Kitwood, 1997; Killick and Allan, 2001; Buijssen, 2005). Thus there is a need for social workers to seek out the channels of communication the person is using – to look for the feeling that is being articulated, even though the words may not be making any sense to the worker (Buijssen, 2005; Bounds and Hepburn, 1996). This skill of seeing everything that a person with dementia does as meaningful is described by Chapman *et al.* (1994) as 'validation' and is contained within the 'care mapping approach'. It requires the worker to actively listen and watch the communication; to try to understand the feeling; and then to find a way to communicate with that person about the feeling. The literature points to three additional skills that can help a worker to achieve this. The first is 'mirroring' (Killick and Allan, 2001). This involves focusing on the service user's movements and reflecting back what the person does in the style that they used. Frequently, this might involve physical contact, such as a squeezing a hand, or giving a hug (Killick and Allan, 2001; Burnside 1986). The second is the use of 'reminiscence' or 'biography' (Chapman *et al.*, 1994). Memories of the past are stored longer than those of the present. Through evoking some of these memories, it is possible to 'make contact' with the person and 'put them at ease' (Buijssen, 2005). The third is to make use of creative arts, as these provide a medium for the expresion of wishes and feelings in a way that does not involve words (Killick and Allan, 2001). On a more day-to-day contact level, research by the Joseph Rowntree Foundation emphasises how a range of communication techniques and approaches (for example, pictures, word cards) may help workers to understand service user views and preferences (Macer *et al.,* 2009). Indeed, people with dementia can experience much additional frustration and upset because others do not take the time to communicate effectively with them. Often this can lead to an increase in either apathy and depression, or the kind of non-verbal communication that is often described as 'challenging behaviour'. Dementia does not remove the capacity to have opinions or preferences, or the capacity for feelings and emotions.

Practice application

At the beginning of Practice Example 10.1 we find the social worker 'tuning-in' to the service user, Doug, as a vulnerable adult. This begins with the social worker writing to Doug to arrange a visit and telephoning to ensure that he has received the information. And the social worker telephones an hour before the visit to remind him of her imminent arrival. These seem mundane, and not extraordinary, steps, but they are important in terms of service user safety, on two levels.

First, the service user needs to be assured that it is the social worker and not a stranger at their door. Crimes against vulnerable older people on their own doorstep, such as mugging, theft and violence, have increased in recent years, creating a fear of the 'knock on the door'.

Second, the social worker needs to begin facilitating a safe relationship from which to explore feelings and opinions, as he or she has the responsibility to investigate and take action when a vulnerable adult is believed to be suffering abuse. Moreover, it is about treating the service user with dignity and respect as an individual by creating a relationship for the service user to be an active participant, enabling choice in decisions. Trust is unlikely to develop if the service user is unable to differentiate the social worker from any of the other care professionals involved in the service user's life. Hence, it is important to ensure that the service user is clear about the social worker's name and role in advance of his or her visit; just prior to their arrival; and on arrival. The provision of ID at the door is a critical part of that process (as it is in any practice situation with any service user).

This point concerning the confusion experienced by service users about the numbers of different care professionals in their lives and the parameters of their differing roles is illustrated in our practice examples (for example, 10.1, points 2–5). Doug comments that the care professionals 'just turn up'. He is unsure of what each professional actually does, except that 'they' get his pension for him. Importantly, this not only communicates the confusion mentioned earlier concerning the number and roles of professionals, but also a degree of vulnerability concerning his own safety.

In fact, the dialogue goes on to reveal that he gains some reassurance of the legitimacy of their presence by their behaviour in sharing a cup of tea with him. He seeks to do the same with the social worker. Indeed, the social workers in our research study identified the need for the social worker to pick up on this nonverbal communication cue for reassurance.

The need for social workers to 'actively look for the channels of communication the person is using' – to look for the feeling that is being articulated – is a point supported by the background literature, and as such consitutes a specialist communication skill in this setting. If, as Chapman *et al.* (1994) state, the social worker 'validates' this communication as being as meaningful as a verbal expression of wishes and feelings, then he or she must not only actively listen and watch the communication to try to understand the feeling, but also then to find a way to communicate with that person about the feeling. 'Validation', therefore, becomes an important specialist communication skill. In our practice example, the social worker uses this skill by going to buy some milk and making a cup of tea to share with the service user. This is a crude and basic illustration of the skill of 'mirroring', with the social worker focusing on behaviour and reflecting back what the person does in the style that they use. Killick and Allan (2001) and Burnside (1986) note that 'mirroring' more frequently involves physical contact, such as squeezing a hand, or giving a hug.

PRACTICE EXAMPLE 10.1

Doug

Preparatory Stage

Doug is a 76 year old White Eastern European man who lives on his own in a block of flats within an inner-city residential area. The social worker is about to visit Doug in order to review his care plan with him. Doug has limited mobility and so receives home care services on a weekly basis (shopping and cleaning). He enjoys volunteering at the local day centre, and arranges transport to participate in this. Doug has infrequent contact with his family. The social worker, Clare, is 45 years old, white British, and has recently moved to the area from London.

Beginnings

Social worker knocks at door. Doug walks slowly toward the door, carefully placing one foot in front of the other, and opens the door.

Doug: Ooh, hello (*Friendly tone*).

[1] *SW*: Hello there, Doug, it's Clare, the social worker. Remember? I phoned today to say I was coming. Here's my ID. (*Offers ID card to Doug)* May I come in?

Doug: Oh, er, yes, come in.

Doug walks slowly towards the living room.

SW: Need any help there, or are you OK?

[2] *Doug*: No thanks, I'll manage. I'd make you a cup of tea, but I haven't any milk.

SW: No, I've just had one, thank you.

Doug: Silly of me, really. I'm dying for a cup.

SW: Is there anyone who can help you get some milk?

Doug: No, not really, I asked this young care worker who comes around. I said to her 'can you go and get some' and she said no. Silly. I don't understand it.

SW: So you asked her to go and get some stuff for you and she wasn't happy to do that?

Doug: Something to do with the Council, she said. I don't understand what she means.

▶

▶

SW: So you're doing without a food shop at the moment?

Doug: I've got a few bits in. Don't need much. I could do with a cup of tea though.

SW: Want me to make you a quick cup of tea?. OK without milk?

Doug: No, urgh!

SW: I'm going to get you some milk. If I go out to get it, will you be all right to get up and let me in again, or do you want to give me your key, to let myself in?

Doug: Here's the key. Thank you. Good of you. (*Social worker leaves and returns with milk*)

[3] *SW*: Hello Doug. (*Walks over to Doug*) Is it OK to change my mind and have a cup with you now?

Walks past Doug to kitchen. Brings tea cups over to Doug and sits down across from him.

SW: So, how are things going for you at the moment?

Doug: Fine. You don't want to moan too much, do you?

SW: That's what I'm here for – to listen to any moans you've got at the moment.

Doug: Where do I start?

SW: Let's go back to that care worker who's not able to get milk for you. What's she doing for you?

Doug: I don't know, she turns up, she sits down for ten minutes and then she goes out, you know. She is allowed to get my pension … which helps … but I can't get to the shops.

SW: So she goes and gets your pension, but not any milk? What else does she do?

Doug: Don't know. To do with the Council. Ridiculous though, isn't it, you don't expect it! (*Voice gets louder, tone agitated*)

SW: Doesn't sound sensible. Maybe it's something she thinks she can't do but really she can. Are you happy for me to have a word with her?

▶

► *Doug*: You're in the same department, I don't know why you can't just talk to each other? (*Voice still sounding louder, starts rocking forward and back, agitated*)

SW: Actually, I don't work in the same department but I'm happy to have a word with them.

Doug: I don't know, do I? Expect you two know what you're doing. No one talks to each other. (*Louder voice*) It's silly. (*Said more quietly*)

SW: I can understand that. I'm happy to go back and have a word.

Doug: Yes, that's what I need. These are things I need.

Silence for a few seconds.

SW: Doug, you may remember ... a previous social worker drew up a care plan with you. I had a look at a copy of it before I came. It says what the care worker should do.

Doug: (*Looks down at piles of papers down by his feet*) So many papers. I try to keep it as organised as I can.

[4] *SW*: Don't worry about looking for it now. What would help me would be to know what happens during the week. Who comes to see you? What do they do for you?

Doug: They just turn up. (*Still looking down*)

SW: Every day?

Doug: Once a week if I'm lucky.

SW: On the care plan it says once a week to pick up your pension.

Doug: (*Looks up, but not at social worker*) Kids come round. Got their own families now. It's difficult for them.

SW: They probably still care what happens to you, though?

Doug: You'd think so, but kids these days ... It all changes. (*Looks down again*)

[5] *SW reaches across to Doug and touches his shoulder. Silence for a minute.*

As Practice Example 10.1 develops it becomes evident that Doug is demonstrating diminished cognitive abilities. When the social worker asks questions about the responsiveness of the service he is receiving from the care professionals, Doug becomes agitated, frustrated and cross (10.1, between points 3 and 4: 'Don't know. To do with the Council. Ridiculous though, isn't it, you don't expect it! (*Voice gets louder, tone agitated.*)'; 'You're in the same department. I don't know why you can't just talk to each other? (*Voice still sounding louder, starts rocking forward and back, agitated*)'; 'I don't know, do I? Expect you two know what you're doing. No one talks to each other. (*Louder voice.*) It's silly (*Said more quietly.*)') Doug is confused by the role and tasks of those different professionals, and probably just as confused about the role and purpose of the social worker sitting in front of him. The background literature identifies that, in moving through phases of dementia with cognitive and language skills altering in different ways, people develop a heightened awareness of non-verbal communication, and experience a particular preoccupation with the emotional aspects of their lives (Kitwood, 1997; Killick and Allan, 2001; Buijssen, 2005). Potentially, this explains why the detail of the work carried out by the care professionals is not mentioned by Doug. The information he provides to the social worker about the work carried out for him in his home is about the feeling he gets when the care professionals share a cup of tea with him. Retaining knowledge about the detail of those services is less important to him. Hence he becomes frustrated with the social worker questioning him about those services.

Information provided by Doug later in the interview also sheds light on the communication behind his agitated behaviour at this beginning stage. Doug states he has received social work services in the past. This relates to his childhood experiences of living in a children's home because of parental neglect and physical abuse. We know from the background literature that memories of the past are stored longer than more recent ones. Doug's memories of those events may have been evoked by the social worker's visit. The feelings aroused by those memories may be causing him emotional pain. His agitation and anger may be an external demonstration of a psychological defensive response to the evokation of those memories and associated feelings. Certainly, between points 4 and 5 in Practice Example 10.1 Doug becomes quiet and contemplative, disengaging from the social worker and demonstrating closed body language.

Interestingly, the social workers in our research study, who were participating in the enactment of this role-play as forum theatre, found this point in the communication to be critical. While at this stage of the interview they had no knowledge of his childhood experiences, they felt the projection of anxiety, fear and pain within themselves. In Chapter 2 it was shown how social workers need to attend to such transference processes occurring between the service user and social worker. The feelings being evoked within the social worker give clues to the communication of the service user. Moreover, in attending to those feelings, the social worker can provide understanding and containment. In our practice example, however, it may not be sufficient or appropriate simply to utilise the basic communication skill of 'putting feelings into words' (such as 'Are you worried about me being here, Doug?'). Rather, in acknowledging Doug's potentially heightened awareness of non-verbal communication, it is important for the social worker to check that her body language, such as her facial gestures, reflects the content of what she is saying. A specialist communication skill, in this respect, is therefore that of 'emphasising or exaggerating non-verbal communication without being patronising'. In Practice Example 10.1, point 5, the social worker did this by reaching across to Doug and lightly touching his shoulder. In doing so, she again used the skill of 'validation' to acknowledge the feelings being communicated and sought a way to communicate with Doug about the feeling.

The qualifying social workers in the research study highlighted that the decision whether or not to have physical contact with the service user was important, as it might have considerable bearing on successful communication with the service user. On the one hand, the qualifying social workers recognised that the demonstration of physical comfort can communicate with the service user in a way that words cannot. However, they also stated that touching the service user would put them in a very vulnerable position concerning possible allegations of inappropriate behaviour. For some this was not something they were prepared to risk, and clearly, some service users would be offended by such a gesture. Some qualifying social workers were less absolute in their decision on this issue. Evidently, personal decisions have to be made regarding where to draw the line in one's own individual practice. It seems important to note that the service users we interviewed for the research study told us that they missed having physical contact with another person, and they wished that sometimes a social worker would just give them a hug. This position is supported by the background literature which highlighted how non-verbal communication can be useful and powerful to an older person who does not experience much physical contact (Bender, 1987).

Thus, even at this early stage, Practice Example 10.1 illustrates the significant importance of the social worker allocating sufficient time to promote communication that might occur in ways that do not solely involve words, but use the whole communication spectrum. This suggests two specialist communication skills: the importance of 'taking time'; and the need to 'use the whole communication spectrum'.

The specialist communication skill of 'taking time' was found to be crucial in the second part of our practice example (10.2), mainly because the unfolding communication showed the negative consequences of 'not taking enough time'! From points 7 to 10 we find lengthy, dense dialogue, with Doug becoming increasingly agitated. Unfortunately, the social worker starts to rely solely on verbal communication as opposed to continuing the skill of 'actively looking for the channels of communication that the person is using'. The pace of each retort becomes faster and faster, until at point 8 the social worker interrupts Doug and at point 10 it becomes evident that there are two agendas to the meeting, as opposed to a 'shared agenda' ('Doug, I did make an appointment with you. I don't want to get into an argument with you. What I'm trying to do is find out what we can do to make things better for you.') Chapter 2 identified that in situations where two agendas seem to operating, it is important for the social worker to ask him/herself the questions 'Is there an obstacle present?' and 'What kind of obstacle is it?' Having identified the obstacle, the social worker can try to address it. In this way, the communication channels will be clearer and the work more purposeful.

PRACTICE EXAMPLE 10.2

Doug

Work phase

[6] *SW*: Doug, you seem a little anxious about me being here. Is there anything that's worrying you about me being here?

Doug: No, we worry about a lot of things, don't we? (*Silence for about ten seconds*) I'd like to get out more. There's only my volunteering. Got to be back … people coming round and … well ….

SW: What do you do with your volunteering?

Doug: I go down to the Help the Aged place. It's great down there. It's really good.

SW: So how many days a week is that?

Doug: It's only once a week. Gets me out of the house.

SW: Sounds like you enjoy it. Would you like to do more of that?

Doug: It's finding it … the hours aren't a problem … hard to get out of the house. I get couple of hours, but the rest of the time I'm stuck in. Not nice.

▶

► *SW*: So, the volunteer that helps you get to Help the Aged ... could we help you to get more support for more days at Help the Aged, perhaps? It helps to get out and chat to people, doesn't it?

Doug: It's your independence back. It's so important. You get used to having independence and when you can't do small things, it's difficult.

Silence for ten seconds.

SW: Is there anything else that's worrying you at the moment?

Doug: Bit of tidying up. I can't bend down either ... and then it's difficult to get back up (*Laughs*). It's tough, really tough.

[7] *SW*: How would you feel if someone gave you a hand with the tidying up?

Doug: Don't want people moving all my stuff around. You know, it's not.... (*Waves his arms at the papers at his feet*)

SW: But if you give them directions?

Doug: They don't listen. They move, walk around and 'they've got to do it'. Oh no. More hassle than it's worth sometimes.

SW: Anything you particularly need them to do? (*Silence for ten seconds*) I understand that you don't want your things moved because they are personal, but do they cause you any problems when you are getting around?

Doug: No, they're all right.

SW: Have you had any falls or anything...

Doug: No, I'm still all right. I can still manoeuvre around the house. It's when you go outside. Pavements are not even flat these days, it's....

[8] *SW*: (*Interrupts*) Back to the papers. I understand you don't want a carer ... but what about if your family helped you to move them aside?

Doug: No, they're very busy. Sometimes can't get round every week. It's not something ... it's my place. I want things left as they are. They will be all right. I don't want things moved around.

►

▶

SW: I'm sorry. I understand that. I didn't mean to tell you where to put them and if you think I did, I apologize.

Doug: You wait for weeks for an appointment. Someone just turns up. You open the door and there's someone new standing there. I don't even remember about you coming round today. Did you tell me?

SW: I did tell you. Yes. You've obviously forgotten, but it really doesn't matter.

[9] *Doug*: Well, I don't forget everything. People think that as you get older your brain goes. I still know what I mean. Every now and then you forget the odd word. Things don't fit into place as they used to.

Silence for a minute.

SW: What would be the one thing we could do to help you at home?

Doug: People just telling me when they're coming round. Not just turning up. More regular visits. People don't come round regularly. They turn up when they want to.

SW: At the moment you have someone round once a week to get your pension for you?

Doug: She's useless. Just sits there … drinks my tea.

SW: One person gets your pension for you. You're saying that you need someone else to get your milk and tea for you. A more regular shop?

Doug: Yes, that would help.

SW: How often would you need that? How many days a week?

Doug: Every couple of days … and it gets so lonely up here. Would be nice if someone could take me out. All I hear is departments shifting….

SW: You're saying you want to get out more?

Doug: Yes, been trying to say that … get people to do that for ages. No one ever seems to listen to me.

SW: I'm listening to you now. What I'm trying to say is ... not take you here, there and everywhere, but to find out where you….

▶

Doug: Don't want to go here, there and everywhere! Just up the road is fine.

SW: Where's 'up the road'?

Doug: Walk round the block, going out for lunch and things. No one seems to care. 'Got too many people on the books', that's all I get.

SW: I don't think it's 'too many people on the books'. It's that your circumstances have changed in the last few weeks.

Doug: Don't understand why people come round ... don't make appointments ... and when they come round, they can't do anything! It's silly, isn't it!

[10] *SW*: Doug, I did make an appointment with you. I don't want to get into an argument with you. What I'm trying to do is find out what we can do to make things better for you.

Doug: I've said, haven't I? Not just to you but to other people who come round.

SW: What you've said to me is you want to get out up the road, to have a walk round. I need to find out how we manage that, whether it's us that gets someone to do that, or whether there's someone you'd like to do that with you ... friends or family?

Doug: Family are not around. They are very busy people. I thought Social Services were there to help. Then you come round, want to move my stuff, get my family, volunteers to come round....

SW: I'm not saying to bring volunteers round. What I'm saying is, who would you like to come round? If you'd like family and you'd like me to speak to them, that's fine. If not family, then that's fine. I need to find out who you'd like to do that.

Doug: What about the carer that comes round, can't she take me out? No. She doesn't come back with bread and milk. It's silly. Wouldn't trust her.

SW: Well, I'm going to go back to the office to sort that out and make sure she's doing what she's supposed to be doing. If you don't get on with that carer, she wouldn't be the right person to do it.

Silence for about a minute.

SW: Doug, it's obviously difficult at this time to decide what to do. What about if I come back tomorrow?

► *Doug*: You actually going to come back tomorrow? Because they say they'll come and then they don't.

SW: Is 11 o'clock all right?

Doug: Yes, OK.

SW: I'll phone fifteen minutes beforehand to say I'm on my way.

THE NEXT DAY

SW: Hello, Doug. It's Clare. (*Offers ID card*)

Doug: Yes, come in. (*Doug walks slowly towards the living room, gradually placing one step in front of the other*)

SW: Since yesterday, have you had any thoughts on who you'd like to come round and take you out?

Doug: Still don't know why you can't come round. You're here now.

SW: We can go for a walk now if you want?

Doug: Yes, could go now. How long have you got?

Social worker picks up her coat….

In this case, the obstacle seems to stem from both parties experiencing increasing frustration at being misunderstood. It is probably the case that Doug experiences this frustration frequently during a number of conversations. Hence his frustration and anger rise quickly. This is an example of communication that is so often labelled 'challenging behaviour'. Interestingly, this point in the communication presented another moment at which the qualifying social workers in the research study, participating in the enactment of this role-play as forum theatre, felt the projection of anxiety, fear and pain within themselves. Surprisingly, projection seemed to come from both directions, with the social workers empathising with the frustration and anger of both Doug and the social worker. We might understand the feelings being projected from the social worker as 'counter-transference'. In Chapter 2 it was outlined how counter-transference has been used to describe the reaction set off in the worker as a result of being receptive to a service user's transferred feelings. These emotions are considered to be a helpful guide to understanding transferred feelings that are unexpressed. Equally, though, the reaction could be negative. The social worker could be transferring feelings from his or her own past experiences and applying them inappropriately to the service user or his/her problem. The social worker needs to check whether his or her responses are valid according to what the service user is communicating, or whether it is the social worker reacting to what they are bringing to the situation.

The specialist communication skill of 'taking time' will contribute towards lessening Doug's frustration and facilitating his understanding, if combined with the skill of 'using short, simple sentences'. While the social worker's questions sought to show respect, they were often very long, included more than one sentence at a time and used higher order concepts. Questions that start with 'why' and 'how' create difficulties for service users with diminished language and cognitive skills, as these types of questions require detailed, lengthy and explanative responses. It would take great effort by that person to concentrate on how to put such a response together and then to deliver it (Buijssen, 2005).

I would argue that there is a second, related obstacle at this point. This concerns a statement frequently repeated by Doug throughout the dialogue in Example 10.2 – for example, at point 9: 'Well, I don't forget everything. People think that as you get older your brain goes. I still know what I mean. Every now and then you forget the odd word. Things don't fit into place as they used to.' Whenever a statement is repeated it should become clear to the social worker that it is important to the service user. Doug seems to want to communicate to the social worker that his diminishing cognitive ability is a concern to him. Indeed, the theme appears in a less direct way when he states that 'people just turn up' and expresses anger, vulnerability and confusion at their 'sudden appearance' at his door. The awareness that one's cognitive skils are diminishing is a frightening feeling and could be understood as a communication obstacle surrounding a societal taboo area of diminishing cognitive ability. Drawing on the basic communication skills from Chapter 2, the social worker needs to deal with the obstacle through doing what Seden (2005: 26) refers to as 'listening to the base line (what is not openly said but possibly is being felt)'. Verbal communication using Shulman's (2009) skills of 'reach for feeling' and 'putting feelings into words', alongside the previously mentioned specialist communication skill 'emphasising or exaggerating non-verbal communication without being patronising' will be useful for drawing out those feelings that are not on the surface or are difficult for Doug to express. This will provide 'validation' of Doug's repeated concerns, which he raised as indirect cues and hidden communication throughout the practice example.

The background literature suggests that the non-verbal techniques should extend to writing things down or using flash cards. The specialist communication strategy should be to 'use the whole communication spectrum'. The social worker in Practice Example 10.2 does not use such examples of visual communication alongside the verbal communication. However, at the end of the practice example we find the social worker using non-verbal communication to achieve rapport and trust in the relationship by offering to go for a walk with Doug. In doing so, she returns to the skill of 'actively looking for the channels of communication the person is using'. The action shows that she has listened to Doug's wishes to go out, but also that she has responded to his anxiety about whether he can make his communication understood. Thus, once again, the specialist communication skill of 'validation' is supremely important.

In summary, social workers who work with vulnerable older people, particularly in the statutory sector, do so in the context of agency pressure that prioritises task-orientated, outcome-focused practice within tight time-scales. In this chapter I have identified how social work communication with vulnerable older people is complex, emotionally challenging, and covers as vast a range of potentially problematic issues as with any other person. The focus must be on the processes of the work and not just on outcomes. A specialist communication strategy that actively seeks out and validates the meaning provided by different forms, media, channels and content of communication by a service user is critical.

Professional Standards

This chapter will help you to meet the following National Occupational Standards:

Key Role 1: Prepare for, and work with individuals, families, carers, groups and communities to assess their needs and circumstances

Unit 1 Prepare for social work contact and involvement
Unit 2 Work with individuals, families, carers, groups and communities to help them make informed decisions
Unit 3 Assess needs and options to recommend a course of action

Key Role 2: Plan, carry out, review and evaluate social work practice with individuals, families, carers, groups, communities and other professionals

Unit 4 Respond to crisis situations
Unit 5 Interact with individuals, families, carers, groups and communities to achieve change and development and to improve life opportunities
Unit 6 Prepare, produce, implement and evaluate plans with individuals, families, carers, groups, communities and professional colleagues

Unit 7 Support the development of networks to meet assessed needs and planned outcomes
Unit 9 Address behaviour which presents a risk to individuals, families, carers, groups and communities

Key Role 3: Support individuals to represent their needs, views and circumstances. Advocate with and on behalf of people

Unit 10 Advocate with, and on behalf of, individuals, families, carers, groups and communities
Unit 11 Prepare for and participate in decision-making forums

Key Role 4: Manage risk to individuals, families, carers, groups, communities, self and colleagues

Unit 12 Assess and manage risks to individuals, families, carers, groups and communities

Key Role 5: Manage and be accountable, with supervision and support, for your own social work practice within your organisation

Unit 14 Manage and be accountable for your own work
Unit 15 Contribute to the management of resources and services
Unit 16 Manage, present and share records and reports
Unit 17 Work within multi-disciplinary and multi-organisational teams, networks and systems

Key Role 6: Demonstrate professional competence in social work practice

Unit 18 Research, analyse, evaluate and use current knowledge of best social work practice
Unit 19 Work within agreed standards of social work practice and ensure own professional development
Unit 20 Manage complex ethical issues, dilemmas and conflicts
Unit 21 Contribute to the promotion of best social work practice

Conclusion

Social work communication skills are employed in the current social and political welfare context in the UK, in which social work is tightly regulated and managed using performance indicators and quantifiable outcomes. Individual social work service users are categorised through bureaucratic procedures using stringent eligibility criteria and processes for resource allocation. Richards *et al.* (2005: 409) summarise neatly the ethical dilemma facing social work educators of communication skills within this context:

> Should we teach students to communicate in a way that conforms to the priorities and pressures of current practice? Or should we retain the focus on inter-personal skills and on engaging with the worlds of service users?

This book is committed unashamedly to the latter perspective. Logically, it is difficult to take any other perspective on board when, as we saw in Chapter 1, the most dominant models in social work practice are founded on inter-relational frameworks and a personalisation agenda that focuses on respect, choice and joint participation with service users. However, having said that, the book has endeavoured to equip social work students to engage with the realities of practice across some of the range of social work practice settings they might find themselves working in. Thus, in the nine chapters relating to different social work practice settings, an attempt has been made to formulate theoretical linkages between:

1. The communication issues identified by social work service users as central for effective communication.
2. The communication issues identified by policy and dominant themes within the existing literature for that setting.

3. The communication strategies uncovered by social workers as responding effectively to those issues.

In the case of points 2 and 3, existing literature on communication skills was used to augment the author's recently conducted empirical research. This research sought purposefully to identify social workers' communication skills from the first base of the reality of their practice actions and practice learning. Experiential learning (Schön, 1983) was used as a research methodology, with forum theatre methods being used to observe and analyse social worker communication while they were 'in action', as well as collating their critical reflections 'on the action' immediately after it occurred. A crucial dimension to the study was that the knowledge sought through the 'reflection-in-action' was embodied and not derived solely through abstract thought. I was as interested in how the social workers were feeling, in a physical sense, in response to service-user communication and the requirements of the practice setting, as in their thinking processes.

The recognition of a connection between thoughts and feelings is a repeated theme in the discussion of specialist social work communication skills throughout the book. This was perhaps unsurprising, given that a relationship-based theoretical approach was taken to these discussions. A major premise of this approach is that social workers must be attuned to the ways in which feelings might be expressed because, as complex beings, we find that our rational thoughts are shaped by our emotions, and often express our thoughts through our feelings (Wilson *et al.*, 2008; Ruch, 2009). In relation to each different practice setting, examples of basic 'universal' communication skills have been used to prepare social workers to expect feelings to be a medium of communication – and to prepare for the manifestation of those feelings as they might arise within a specific practice setting. *'Tuning-in'* (Shulman, 2009) was a skill found to be relevant to all settings in this respect. However, the background literature and service-user perspectives identified that particular emphasis needed to be placed on this component of communication skills in certain practice settings. The required emphasis on the operation of this skill within these settings meant that a more specific label was given to the skill that summarised the purposes for its use. In this respect, it moved from being a basic communication skill to being a specialist communication skill in certain settings. Thus 'tuning-in to experience the child's world' was identified for working with children; 'tuning in to social worker's personal attitudes and preconceptions of people who use substances' was highly relevant for substance users; and 'tuning in to experience the individual experience of mental distress' was highlighted as essential for working with people with mental health problems.

A second theoretical position adopted by the book is that, until both thoughts and feelings are identified (and often actually 'felt' in an affective sense through transference) then those perspectives will not be 'heard' or understood by social workers. As psychodynamic processes of 'containment' are considered to be crucial for achieving this attention to thoughts and feelings (Bower, 2005; Ruch, 2009) there was discussion and illustration of its use within each of the chapters related to the different practice settings. Again, some settings seemed to require more discussion and application of its use than others. In some cases, this finding emanated from the analysis of the background literature, which emphasised strongly a particular theoretical approach or issue affecting or likely to affect the way in which containment of thoughts and feelings was communicated. In these cases, a label was applied to the specialist skill to depict this. Thus, in working with children, the specialist skill of 'containing a child's feelings by providing and being a safe place in which feelings can be explored' was highlighted. In the case of work with substance users, social workers will need to 'address service user fears of stigmatisation', and when working with people with mental distress there is a need for 'being open to communication at all levels'. However, in some practice settings, specialist communication skills for containment were identified following processes of transference within the classroom itself in response to the feelings being elicited within the qualifying social workers by the forum theatre. An example of this learning and identification process was in relation to working with refugees and asylum-seekers, where the specialist skill of 'experiencing service-user feelings' was identified.

The demand for greater clarity of the aims and purposes of social work assessment and ongoing intervention meant that communication skills for 'achieving a shared purpose' for the social worker and service user meeting were operated in each of the practice settings. The background literature and service-user perspectives for each of the different practice settings identified that the authority that the social worker brings through social and legal mandates causes a power differential and barrier to communication that has to be overcome. In some settings, this authority role caused particular dynamics within the communication, with specific communication skills identified to deal with them. Thus, in relation to working with children, there was need for a 'child-centred contract' to ensure a shared understanding of the social work role and purpose. Two practice settings demonstrated particular communication dynamics of secrecy and denial in response to the authority role of the social worker. First, work with young people engaging in offending behaviour was considered to require specialist skills of: 'communicating consequences in a non-threatening manner'; 'developing early rapport'; and 'defending service user rights' to overcome authority obstacles. Second, in relation to work with substance-using parents, it was identified as vital to 'enter the world of substance using families'.

One of the theoretical premises of the book was that a practical application of the social model of disability approach provides greater appreciation of the impact on communication of obstacles relating to normative expectations and required social work communication strategies than can be achieved by the relationship-based approach alone. A repeated theme in all the practice settings was that communication skills are needed to address attitudinal barriers within social workers themselves. Frequently, this should involve taking an attitude that: (i) does not privilege expert knowledge but seeks to validate private perspectives wherever reasonable; and (ii) does not privilege particular forms and media of communication. Thus, in working with people with disabilities, specialist communication skills were identified concerning the need to 'validate and recognise private knowledge of the individual nuances of the impairment as applied to a person', and 'use the whole communication spectrum'. On a similar theme, working with children and young people required the need to 'identify, validate and use the child's medium of communication', and when working with older people specialist communication involved skills of 'actively looking for the channels of communication that the service user is using', 'validation' and 'using the whole communication spectrum'. 'Taking time' was a specialist skill across many practice settings, but in work with children and young people it was identified as a sub-skill of 'showing respect'. The background literature and service-user perspectives of some practice settings in particular identified how social workers need to find a communication mechanism whereby they identify and discuss systemic barriers with service users, expecting such communication to be in both direct and indirect ways. This was a particular feature of working with parents, where the following specialist communication skills were considered relevant: 'identifying the social worker's personal attitudes and preconceptions of parenting'; 'identifying, discussing and empathising with systemic barriers with parents'; 'identifying a practical response of seeking to overcome systemic barriers'; 'positive framing of development than using negative deficit notions' and 'demonstrating knowledge of the individual child'.

It is important not to be uncritical about the claims to knowledge made in this book. This is only a beginning exploration of the theoretical linkages between service-user perspectives, policy, key theoretical concerns and practice strategies that affect communication in different practice settings. It is not possible to claim that all the aspects of the diversity of social work practice and service-user experiences have been explored here. The individuality of service users in relation to gender, ethnicity, class, age, personality and other important characteristics that might impact upon communication processes is missing. Related to this, I have located the specialist communication skills around the administrative bureaucratic categories of social work agencies and policy literature as opposed to the self-definitions that service users may use. In a book of this length, I have only been able to highlight key issues using the policy, existing literature and research study as a guide. The research study itself examined the communication practice strategies of a limited number of social workers at the point of qualification from a social work degree programme in a medium-sized city in England. Between five and thirty qualifying social workers attended each of the performances of the forum theatre research method. Moreover, those qualifying social workers involved in the study volunteered their time and, as such, we might expect them to be sufficiently comfortable with research procedures to present a bias to this preference in their insights. Thus it is not possible to make claims that the research findings can be generalised to all social worker–service user meetings in a particular type of practice setting.

These concerns apart, it is hoped that the exercise of using an innovative research methodology alongside existing literature to uncover tentative theoretical insights in a developing conceptual practice area is useful. The analysis, in linking the different sources of information, sought to gain a more holistic understanding of specialist social work communication skills and issues. Pawson *et al.* (2003) identify that social workers can only make judgements on the 'best evidence' that is available, ensuring that this evidence is integrated with the personal accounts of service users about their situations. Arguably, this is what I have achieved here. Moreover, in making the research and analytical processes clear, including the provision of illustrative examples of the application of the skills to practice, I hope to have achieved the potential for some degree of 'transferability' (Lincoln and Guba, 1985) for readers to decide whether theoretical concepts can be transferred to their particular social work practice context.

This last section considers the implications for social work education and training. First, one of the key successes of the forum theatre as a teaching and learning method was that it enabled the qualifying social workers to think about and tolerate on an emotional level the ambiguous, anxiety-making, difficult experiences and communication that occurs within the reality of practice settings. It seems vital for social workers to be given regular opportunities to engage in critically reflexive processes that enable them to reflect on action with other workers in an emotionally safe place that allows connection in an embodied way with the thoughts and feelings raised. While forum theatre might not be to everyone's taste, other models have been developed in professional development contexts within the UK that encourage social workers to stop coming to premature conclusions about service-user situations, but rather to tolerate uncertainty and explore multiple perspectives, including self-examination about pre-conceived assumptions (Fook, 2007; Ruch, 2009). Such models can be applied within group learning contexts. For example, Ruch (2009) describes the application of a three-stage model with groups of social workers, containing consistent members and a facilitator, who meet on a regular basis to present and reflect on an issue from their practice. In brief, in stage one, the presenter explains the issue from practice that is concerning or interesting them. Meanwhile, the rest of the group are invited to engage in 'emotional listening', which Ruch (2009: 354) describes as 'learning simply to be and to listen and desisting from doing and writing'. Attention needs to be paid to the way the issue is framed in language and the feelings evoked. In stage two, the group explores which aspects attracted more personal attention, and possible reasons for the significance. Emphasis is given to encouraging multiple perspectives and not seeking immediate solutions. This time, the presenter engages in 'emotional listening'. Finally, in stage three, the presenter re-enters the discussion, exploring how the different perspectives might enable a more informed response.

The need to create and sustain safe, containing learning environments, such as described in Ruch's model and achieved here in the forum theatre, in which social workers can reflect critically on 'self' cannot be emphasised enough. This book has discussed how it is that so much about good communication is the removal of barriers, and that so many of the barriers in communication lie within the individual worker. As individuals located within a social context, we take in societal and cultural stereotypes and radiate them outwards, which unfortunately creates systemic barriers and further marginalisation for our service users. The teaching and learning of specialist communication skills must include opportunities for learners to engage with the examination of 'self' to acquire self-knowledge or self-awareness of attitudes. An approach that looks for the similarities and differences in personal characteristics and social circumstances between the social worker and service user will be helpful. A search for differences ensures that preconceived assumptions are not applied on the basis of homogeneity of experience, as well as demonstrating respect and curiosity for the individuality of those experiences and situations. A search for similarities discourages a 'them and us' divide between social workers and those with whom they work. For example, when working with a service user who is having difficulty with his or her mental health, it is important for the social worker to remember that they, themselves, are also in a state of mental health wellness. It is simply a matter of degree.

My final point is to encourage the greater use of creative teaching and learning technologies to uncover and rehearse specialist communication skills through 'reflection in action'. So much of social work practice learning relies on critical reflection that occurs at a point after the event. In so doing, the totality and reality of the exact practice moment is lost. It is difficult to think of situations where it is appropriate for social workers to stop in the middle of interactions with service users and have their communication strategies, thoughts and feelings examined. Creative technologies, such as forum theatre, using well-designed simulation in safe, containing learning environments, offer a good alternative. Drama allows learners to become a character that can feel more real and enable identification with profound areas of experience. But at the same time, some distance is achieved because it is not real but playing a role (Kaptani and Yuval-Davis, 2008). Thus the knowledge gained from such technologies is embodied and critically reflective but not solely abstract thought – components that are crucial for relationship-based practice. Lishman (2009: 207) calls for social workers 'to learn, to reflect and to consolidate their communication skills in a reflective and evidence-based way.' This book has taken early steps towards achieving this in relation to specialist communication skills for social workers.

Research Appendix

Background

This research responds to the challenge for educators to:(i) better integrate communication skills training with practice learning, to prepare social workers for the real-life challenges of practice; (ii) begin to bridge the knowledge gap of relevant 'specialist social work communication skills' to meet real-life challenges in different practice settings; and (iii) increase service-user involvement in the design and delivery of such work (Diggins, 2004; Trevithick *et al.*, 2004).

Innovatively, I felt that Stage 3 social work students at the very point of qualification could be supported to bridge the previously mentioned knowledge gap themselves by using a 'bottom-up' method towards learning, with the student actively discerning theoretical linkages to the real-life challenges and actions of their practice learning settings. This meant observing and analysing their communication while they were 'in action', as well as collating their critical reflections 'on the action' immediately after it occurred. Experiential learning (Schön,1983) was used explicitly as a research methodology, with forum theatre methods being employed to gather this 'reflection-in-action' in a way that paid as much attention to how the social workers were feeling, in a physical sense, in response to service-user communication and the requirements of the practice setting, in addition to their abstract thinking processes.

Boals' (1979) method of Forum Theatre is rarely reported in social work (Houston *et al.*, 2001), but is ideally suited to facilitate conscious recognition of collective problems (in this case identifying specialist communication), and developing realistic and dialogical strategies for action. Indeed, the method, which involves the dynamic involvement of the audience with three main characters in an unfolding drama sketch, provides a space in which debate can take place. The three main characters usually consist of a protagonist whose role is to represent the experience of the group; an antagonist who embodies an oppressor role; and a 'facilitator' who acts as a link between the actors and audience by providing commentary on the unfolding drama and inviting response and intervention. For our purposes here, the delineation between the social worker (as oppressor) and service user (as oppressed) was not so strictly drawn, as clearly social workers seek to fulfil requirements to be anti-oppressive. Yet, the roles *were* useful in aiding identification of how practice actions (that is, communication strategies) might be experienced as being oppressive and unhelpful. An additional important component of the method was to compare social work perceptions with service-user perceptions regarding the type and nature of communication skills required. This draws on my own recent research findings (Woodcock and Tregaskis, 2005) that, using a combined model – in seeking both a social work perspective and service user 'insider' (social model) perspective of relevant communication skills in differing settings – was found to produce a more holistic and ecological analysis, as issues were considered at personal, cultural and structural levels, and drew on data from both parties to the communication process.

Methods

A group of qualifying (Stage 3) undergraduate social work students (n = 55) were divided into specialist interest groups corresponding to eight different practice settings: children; parents; older people; adults with disabilities and their carers; people with mental health difficulties; asylum seekers and refugees; young offenders; and people who misuse substances. Each group was assigned to attend one or more of the eight Specialist Social Work Communication Skills workshops corresponding to their practice setting. It was the function of these workshops (each lasting two hours) to engage the students in the Forum Theatre method. Attendance was good, not least for the reason that the students were going to make use of the data as part of an assessment to complete their programme of study.

The method, as undertaken here, involved two paid and experienced actors performing a scripted role-play to the audience of students in each workshop. In addition, a facilitator (the author) invited students to interact with the actors, ensuring that: (i) interaction and discussion occurred alongside the role-play; and (ii) that the discussion focused on communication issues, and the type and nature of communication skills relevant for particular settings. Such prompts included: 'Why was that issue mentioned?'; 'What's going on?'; 'What's going well, and why?'; 'What's not going well, and why?'; 'Do you want to ask them anything?' Different scripts were written to reflect the 'typical, everyday' issues of communication between a service user and a social worker in different practice settings. The scripts were written by one of the actors and the author, in consultation with volunteers from a Service User Consultative Group recruited by the relevant University. This service user involvement was important as the author wanted the data yielded by the method to encompass both service user and practitioner perspectives. The debates were recorded using a camcorder to capture the detail of the verbal articulation of the communication issues and skills raised, and any non-verbal communication arising during the role-play interaction. The recording was transcribed, analysed and copies sent to all students, to enable them to use the information when writing up their assignment.

Outcome measures of effectiveness

Effectiveness was measured in relation to how far and in what way students evidenced the following outcome measures in (i) the transcript of the workshop session; (ii) the detail of their summative assessment; and (iii) responses to a semi-structured questionnaire at the pre- and post-stages of the intervention/method:

> identified specialist communication skills for different social work practice settings; identified the differences and similarities between service user and social work perceptions of issues of communication, and the type and nature of the communication skills required; used theory, research evidence and practice experience to analyse the role-play of real-life illustrations of the dilemmas and challenges in communication between social workers and service users; and engaged in reflective processes about their practice learning experiences concerning communication skills (evidenced by consideration of what went well, what did not go well, and where improvements might be made)

The short, semi-structured questionnaire contained a combination of closed and open-ended questions to facilitate student reflection of issues of communication and the type and nature of communication skills required by their practice setting. Students received and responded to it before the workshop. After the workshop, students were presented with a copy of their completed questionnaire with additional questions seeking their perspective on whether and how their understanding of 'specialist communication skills' and their theoretical underpinning had improved, and the way and extent to which the teaching method had helped this. They were then asked to revisit their answers in light of this analysis.

Analytical tactics of constant comparative analysis (Woodcock and Tregaskis, 2008) were used to identify and compare 'instances' that demonstrated experiences, definitions or perspectives of communication issues and skills as they appeared at any point across the four data sources. This involved categorising and labelling ('open coding': Strauss and Corbin, 1990) potentially theoretically relevant concepts and relationships, then questioning emergent themes by making connections between service user concerns and (student) social workers' concerns and responses, seeking to elicit the range and dimensions of the categories and relationships ('axial coding': Strauss and Corbin, 1990). The students gave independent and anonymous feedback regarding their perspectives of the usefulness of the Forum Theatre method in helping them to elicit specialist social work communication skills in their practice settings.

Ethical considerations

The author attended a Service User Consultative Group meeting to discuss information and engender trust and a stake in the project. An information sheet was emailed or handed out to all students, explaining the project process, the right to withdraw, details of how to contact the author, and an undertaking that participants' names would be confidential to the research team and that all information relating to service users considered in the students' work would be sufficiently anonymised to prevent identification. It was stated that where information revealed a person as being at risk of significant harm, that information would be passed on to relevant social work personnel. A consent form was used. As Forum Theatre is a dynamic and emotive learning experience, participants might well have been left with some unresolved feelings, and as such contact details for counselling services were provided at each workshop.

Bibliography

Abney, V. (2002) 'Cultural Competency in the Field of Child Maltreatment', in J. Myers, L. Berliner and J. Briere (eds) *The APSAC Handbook on Child Maltreatment*, London: Sage.

ACMD (Advisory Council on the Misuse of Drugs) (2003) *Hidden Harm: Responding to the Needs of Children of Problem Drug Users. Report of an Inquiry by the Advisory Council on the Misuse of Drugs*, London: The Home Office.

Agass, D. (2002) 'Countertransference, Supervision and the Reflection Process', *Journal of Social Work Practice*, 16: 125–33.

Agazarian, Y. A. (1997) *System-Centred Group Psychotherapy*, New York: Guilford Press.

Aldgate, J. and Bradley, M. (1999) *Supporting Families Through Short Term Fostering*, London: The Stationery Office.

Aldridge, T. (1999) 'Family Values: Rethinking Children's Needs Living With Drug-using Parents', *Druglink*, 14: 8–11.

Alexander-Floyd, N. (2008) 'Critical Race Pedagogy: Teaching About Race and Racism through Legal Learning Strategies', *Political Science & Politics*, 41(1)183–8.

Alibhai-Brown, Y. (1998) *Caring for Ethnic Minority Elders: A Guide*, London: Age Concern.

Al-Krenawi, A. and Graham, J. R. (2000) 'Culturally Sensitive Social Work Practice with Arab Clients in Mental Health Settings', *Health and Social Work*, 25: 9–22.

Allan, K. (2001) *Exploring Ways for Staff to Consult People with Dementia about Services*, York: Joseph Rowntree Foundation.

Armstrong, D. (2004) 'A Risky Business? Research, Policy, Governmentality and Youth Offending', *Youth Justice*, 4(2): 100–16.

Armstrong, K. L., Fraser, J. A., Dads, M. R. and Morris, J. (2000) 'Promoting Secure Attachment, Maternal Mood and Child Health in a Vulnerable Population: A Randomized Controlled Trial', *Journal of Paediatric Child Health*, 36: 555–62.

Audit Commission (2004) *Youth Justice 2004: A Review of the Reformed Youth Justice System*, London: Audit Commission.

Banks, S. (2001) *Ethics and Values in Social Work*, Basingstoke: Palgrave Macmillan.

Barber, J. G. (2002) *Social Work with Addictions* (2nd edn), Basingstoke: BASW/Palgrave Macmillan.

Barn, R. (2007) 'Race, Ethnicity and Child Welfare: A Fine Balancing Act', *British Journal of Social Work*, 37: 1425–34.

Barnes, C. (1991) *Disabled People in Britain and Discrimination: A Case for Anti-discrimination Legislation*, London: Hurst & Co.

Batten, A. (2009) *Youth Justice – The Next Steps*, London: National Autistic Society. Available at: http://www.nas.org.uk/nas/jsp/polopoly.jsp?d=2529&a=3826.

Bell, M. (1999) 'Working in Partnership in Child Protection: The Conflicts', *British Journal of Social Work*, pp. 437–55.

Belsky, J. and Vondra, J. (1989) 'Lessons from Abuse: The Determinants of Parenting', in D. Cichetti and V. Carlson (eds) *Child Maltreatment: Theory and Research on the Causes and Consequences of Child Abuse and Neglect*, Cambridge: Cambridge University Press.

Bender, M., Norris, A. and Bauckham, P. (1987) *Groupwork with the Elderly: Principles and Practice*, Bicester: Winslow Press.

Bion, W. (1962) *Learning from Experience*, London: Heinemann.

Bishop, D. (2008) 'An Examination of the Links between Autistic Spectrum Disorders and Offending Behaviour in Young People', *Internet Journal of Criminology*. Available at: http://www.internetjournalofcriminology.com/Bishop%20-%20Autistic%20 Spectrum%20Disorders%20and%20Offending%20Behaviour%20in%20Young%20 People.pdf.

Blom-Cooper, L. (1985) *A Child in Trust: The Report of the Panel of Inquiry into the Circumstances of the Death of Jasmine Beckford*, Brent, London Borough of Brent.

Boal, A. (1979) *Theatre of the Oppressed*, London: Pluto Press.

Bounds, J. and Hepburn, H. (1996) *Empowerment and Older People*, Birmingham: Pepar Publications.

Bowes, A.M. and Dar, N.S. (2000) 'Researching social care for minority ethnic older people: Implications of some Scottish research', *British Journal of Social Work:* 30: 305–21.

Bower, M. (2005) *Psychoanalytic Theory for Social Work Practice: Thinking Under Fire*, London: Routledge.

Bowl, R. (2009) 'PQ Social Work Practice in Mental Health' in P. Higham (ed.) Post-Qualifying Social Work Practice, London: Sage.

Bowlby, J. (1962) 'Preface' in M. L. Ferard and N. K. Hunnybun (1962) *The Caseworker's Use of Relationships*, London: Tavistock.

Boxall, K. and Speakup Self Advocacy and Eastwood Action Group (2009) 'Learning Disability' in P. Higham (ed.) *Post-Qualifying Social Work Practice*, London: Sage.

Brandon, M., Thoburn, J., Lewis, A. and Way, A. (1999) *Safeguarding Children with the Children Act 1989*, London: The Stationery Office.

Brandon, M., Howe, A., Dagley, V,, Salter, C. and Warren, C. (2006) 'What appears to be helping or hindering practitioners in implementing the Common Assessment Framework and Lead Professional Working?', *Child Abuse Review*, 15(6): 396–413.

Bray, M. (2007) *Sexual Abuse: The Child's Voice: Poppies on the Rubbish Heap*. London: Jessica Kingsley.

British Agencies for Adoption and Fostering (1984) *In Touch with Children*, London: BAAF.

British Agencies for Adoption and Fostering (1986) *Working with Children*, London: BAAF.

Bronfenbrenner, U. (1979) *The Ecology of Human Development: Experiments by Nature and Design*, Cambridge, Mass.: Harvard University Press.

Brown, G. and Harris, T. (1978) *Social Origins of Depression: A Study of Psychiatric Disorder in Women*, London: Tavistock.

Buchanan, J. and Young, J. (2002) 'Child Protection: Social Workers' Views', in Klee, H., Jackson, H. and Lewis, S. (eds) *Drug Misuse and Motherhood* Routledge: London.

Buckley, H. (2000) 'Child Protection: An Unreflective Practice', *Social Work Education*, 19: 253–63.

Buijssen, H. (2005) *The Simplicity of Dementia*, London: Jessica Kingsley.

Burnard, P. (2003) 'Ordinary Chat and Therapeutic Conversation: Phatic Communication and Mental Health Nursing', *Journal of Psychiatric and Mental Health Nursing*, 10: 678–82.

Burnside, J. (1986) *Working with the Elderly: Group Process and Techniques*, Sudbury, Mass.: Jones & Bartlett.

Butler-Sloss, E. (1988) *Report of the Inquiry into Child Abuse in Cleveland 1987*, London: HMSO.

Cameron, H. (2008) *The Counselling Interview: A Guide for the Helping Professions*, Basingstoke: Palgrave Macmillan.

Case, S. (2007) 'Questioning the "Evidence" of Risk that Underpins Evidence-led Youth Justice Interventions', *Youth Justice*, 2007(7): 91–105.

Chand, A. (2000) 'The Over-representation of Black Children in the Child Protection System: Possible Causes, Consequences and Solutions', *Child and Family Social Work*, 5: 67–77.

Chapman, A., Jacques, A. and Marshall, M. (1994) *Dementia Care: A Handbook for Residential and Day Care*, London: Age Concern England.

Cleaver, H., Unell, I. and Aldgate, J. (1999) *Children's Needs, Parenting Capacity: The Impact of Parental Mental Illness, Problem Alcohol and Drug Use and Domestic Violence on Children's Development*, London: The Stationery Office.

Cohen, P. (1994) 'Adding insult to injury', *Community Case* 6 October 037 14–5.

Cohen, S., Moran-Ellis, J. and Smaje, C. (1999) 'Children as Informal Interpreters in GP Consultations: Pragmatics and Ideology', *Sociology of Health and Illness*, 21: 163–86.

Comley, M. (1998) 'Counselling and Therapy with Older Refugees', *Journal of Social Work Practice*, 12: 181–7.

Compton, B. R., Galloway, B. and Cournoyer, B. R. (2005) *Social Work Processes* (7th edn), Pacific Grove ,Calif.: Brooks Cole.

Crawford, A. and Newburn, T. (2003) *Youth Offending and Restorative Justice*, Cullompton: Willan.

Cree, V. and Davis, A. (2007) *Social Work: Voices From the Inside*, Abingdon: Routledge.

Crisis (2003) *Mental Health and Social Exclusion: Crisis's Response to a Consultation Request from the Social Exclusion Unit*, London: Crisis UK.

Crown Prosecution Service (2007) 'Achieving Best Evidence in Criminal Proceedings: Guidance on Interviewing Victims and Witnesses, and Using Special Measures'. Available at: http://www.cps.gov.uk/publications/docs/Achieving_Best_Evidence_FINAL.pdf.

Daniel, B. (2000) 'Judgements about Parenting: What Do Social Workers Think They Are Doing?', *Child Abuse Review*, 9: 91–107.

Daniel, B. (2007) 'Assessment and Children' in J. Lishman (ed.) *Handbook for Practice Learning in Social work and Social Care: Knowledge and Theory*, London: Jessica Kingsley.

Darragh, E. and Taylor, B. (2009) 'Research and Reflective Practice' in Higham, P. (ed.) *Post-Qualifying Social Work Practice*, London: Sage.

Daycare Trust (1995) *Reaching First Base: Meeting the Needs of Refugee Children from the Horn Of Africa: Guidelines of Good Practice*, London : Daycare Trust.

De Jong, P. and Berg, I. K. (2008) *Interviewing for Solutions*, Pacific Grove, Calif.: Brooks/Cole.

Devore, W. (2001) 'Ethnic Sensitivity: A Theoretical Framework for Social Work Practice' in Dominelli, L., Lorenz, W. and Soydan, H. (eds) *Beyond Racist Divides: Ethnicities in Social Work Practice*, Aldershot: Ashgate.

DfES (Department for Education and Skills) (2003) *Every Child Matters: Change for Children* DfES/1090/2004, London: HMSO. Available at: www.everychildmatters.gov.uk.

DiClemente, C. C. and Velasquez, M. (2002) *Motivational Interviewing and the Stages of Change* in Miller, W. R. and Rollnick, S. (eds) *Motivational Interviewing: Preparing People for Change* (2nd edn), New York: Guilford.

Diggins, M. (2004) *Teaching and Learning Communication Skills in Social Work Education: Resource Guide,* London: SCIE.

Dingwall, R. (1986) 'The Jasmine Beckford Affair', *Modern Law Review* 49: 488–518.

Dogra, N., Parkin, A., Gale, F. and Frake, C. (2002) *A Multidisciplinary Handbook of Child and Adolescent Mental Health for Front-line Professionals*, London: Jessica Kingsley.

DoH (Department of Health) (1995) *Child Protection: Messages from Research*, London: HMSO.

DoH (Department of Health) (1996) *Focus on Teenagers: Research into Practice*, London: The Stationery Office.

DoH (Department of Health) (1998) *Modernising Social Services*, London: The Stationery Office.

DoH (Department of Health) (1999) *The National Services Framework for Mental Health: Modern Standards and Service Models,* London, The Stationery Office.

DoH (Department of Health) (2000a) *The Framework for Assessing Children in Need and their Families,* London, The Stationery Office.

DoH (Department of Health) (2000b) *No Secrets: Guidance on Developing and Implementing Multi-agency Policies and Procedures to Protect Vulnerable Adults from Abuse*, London: Department of Health.

DoH (Department of Health) (2001a) *National Service Framework for Older People*, London: HMSO.

DoH (Department of Health) (2001b) *Valuing People: A New Strategy for Learning Disability for the 21st Century*, London: The Stationery Office.

DoH (Department of Health) (2002) *Requirements for Social Work Training,* London: Department of Health.

DoH (Department of Health) (2004a) *The NHS Improvement Plan: Putting People at the Heart of Public Services,* London: The Stationery Office.

DoH (Department of Health) (2004b) *Choosing Health: Making Healthier Choices Easier,* London: Department of Health.

DoH (Department of Health) (2005) *Independence, Well-being and Choice: Our Vision for the Future of Social Care for Adults in England,* London: Department of Health.

DoH (Department of Health) (2006a) *Working Together to Safeguard Children: A Guide to Inter-agency Working to Safeguard and Promote the Welfare of Children,* London: The Stationery Office.

DoH (Department of Health) (2006b) *Our Health, Our Care, Our Say*, London: Department of Health.

DoH (Department of Health) (2006c) *Choosing Health: Supporting the Physical Health Needs of People with Severe Mental Illness*, London: Department of Health.

Dominelli, L. (1992) 'An Uncaring Profession? An Examination of Racism in Social Work' in Braham, P., Rattansi, A. and Skellington, R. (eds) *Racism and Anti-Racism*, London: Sage.

Doyle, C. and Kennedy, S. (2009) 'Children, Young People, Their Families and Carers' in Highham, P. (ed.) *Post-Qualifying Social Work Practice*, London: Sage.

Ebden, P., Bhatt, A., Carey, O. and Harrison, B. (1988) 'The Bilingual Consultation', *The Lancet* 331: 8581: 347.

Egan, G. (1990) *The Skilled Helper: A Systematic Approach to Effective Helping*, Pacific Grove, Calif.: Brooks/Cole.

Egan, G. (2007) *The Skilled Helper: A Problem-Management and Opportunity-Development Approach to Helping* (8th edn), Belmont, Calif.: Thomson Brooks/Cole.

Fanning, B. (2004) 'Asylum Seeker and Migrant Children in Ireland: Racism, Institutional Neglect and Social Work' in Hayes, D. and Humphries, B. (eds) *Social Work, Immigration and Asylum: Debates, Dilemmas and Ethical Issues for Social Work and Social Care Practice*, London: Jessica Kingsley.

Fell, P. (2004) 'And Now It Has Started to Rain: Support and Advocacy with Adult Asylum-Seekers in the Voluntary Sector' in Hayes, D. and Humphries, B. (eds) *Social Work, Immigration and Asylum: Debates, Dilemmas and Ethical Issues for Social Work and Social Care Practice*, London: Jessica Kingsley.

Ferard, M. L. and Hunnybun, N. K. (1962) *The Caseworker's Use of Relationships*, London: Tavistock.

Finkelstein, V. (1980) *Attitudes and Disabled People: Issues for Discussion*, New York: World Rehabilitation Fund.

Flores, G., Laws, M. B., Mayo, S. J., Zuckerman, B., Abreu, M., Medina, L. (2003) 'Errors in Medical Interpretation and Their Potential Clinical Consequences in Pediatric Encounters', *Pediatrics* 111: 6–14.

Fook, J. (2007) 'Reflective Practice and Critical Reflection' in Lishman, J. (ed.) *Handbook for Practice Learning in Social Work and Social Care*, London: Jessica Kingsley.

Forrester, D. and Harwin, J. (2004) 'Social Work and Parental Substance Misuse' in Phillips, R. (ed.) *Children Exposed to Parental Substance Misuse: Implications for Family Placement*, London: British Agencies for Adoption and Fostering.

Garrett, P. M. (2006) 'Protecting Children in a Globalized World: "Race" and "Place" in the Laming Report on the Death of Victoria Climbié', *Journal of Social Work* 6: 315–36.

Gilman, M. (2000) 'Social Exclusion and Drug Using Parents' in Harbin, F. and Murphy, M. (eds) *Substance Misuse and Child Care: How to Understand, Assist and Intervene When Drugs Affect Parenting*, Lyme Regis: Russell House.

Green, J., Free, C., Bhavnani, V. and Newman, T. (2005) 'Translators and Mediators: Bilingual Young People's Accounts of Their Interpreting Work in Health Care', *Social Science and Medicine* 60: 2097–110.

GSCC (General Social Care Council) (2005) *Specialist Standards and Requirements (Adult Services)*, London: GSCC.

Harbin, F. and Murphy, M. (2000) *Substance Misuse and Child Care: How to Understand, Assist and Intervene When Drugs Affect Parenting*, Lyme Regis: Russell House.

Hargie, O. D. W. (ed.) (1997) *The Handbook of Communication Skills* (2nd edn), London: Routledge.

Hargie, O. and Dickson, D. (2004) *Skilled Interpersonal Communication: Research, Theory and Practice*, London, Routledge.

Health Advisory Service (1995) *Together We Stand: The Commissioning, Role and Management of Child and Adolescent Mental Health Services*, London, HMSO.

Hildyard, K. and Wolfe, D. (2002) 'Child Neglect: Developmental Issues and Outcomes', *Child Abuse and Neglect*, 26: 679–95.

HMI Probation (2009) *Joint Inspection of Youth Offending Teams: End of Programme Report 2003–2008*, Manchester: HMI Probation.

Holland, S. (2000) 'The Assessment Relationship: Interactions between Social Workers and Parents in Child Protection Assessments', *British Journal of Social Work* 30: 149–63.

Hollis, F. (1964) *A Psycho-social Therapy*, New York: Random House.

House of Lords (2009) Judgments – *R* (on the application of G) (FC) (Appellant) v. *London Borough of Southwark* (Respondents). Available at: http://www.publications.parliament.uk/pa/ld200809/ldjudgmt/jd090520/appg-1.htm.

Houston, S., Magill, T., McCollum, M. and Spratt, T. (2001) 'Developing Creative Solutions to the Problems of Children and Their Families: Communicative Reason and the Use of Forum Theatre', *Child and Family Social Work* 6: 285–93.

Howe, D. (1998) 'Relationship-based Thinking and Practice in Social Work', *Journal of Social Work Practice* 12: 45–56.

Howe, D. (2005) *Child Abuse and Neglect: Attachment, Development and Intervention*, Basingstoke: Palgrave Macmillan.

Howe, D., Brandon, M., Hinings, D. and Schofield, G. (1999) *Attachment Theory, Child Maltreatment and Family Support: A Practice and Assessment Model*, London: Macmillan.

Howitt, D. (1992) *Child Abuse Errors: When Good Intentions Go Wrong*, Hemel Hempstead: Harvester.

Ivey, A. E. and Ivey, M. B. (2008) *Essentials of Intentional Interviewing: Counseling in a Multicultural World*, Belmont, Calif., Thomson Brooks/Cole.

Jack, G. (2001) 'Ecological Perspectives in Assessing Children and Families' in Horwath, J. (ed.) *The Child's World: Assessing Children in Need*, London: Jessica Kingsley.

Jack, J. and Gill, O. (2003) *The Missing Side of the Triangle*, Ilford: Barnardo's.

Jacobsen, T., Edelstein, W. and Hofmann, V. (1994) 'A Longitudinal Study of the Relationship between Representations of Attachment in Childhood and Cognitive Functioning in Childhood and Adolescence', *Developmental Psychology* 30: 112–24.

Jewett, C. (1984) *Helping Children Cope with Separation and Loss*, London: British Agencies for Adoption and Fostering.

Jones, P. H. (2003) *Communicating with Vulnerable Children*, London: The Royal College of Psychiatrists.

Kadushin, A. and Kadushin, G. (1997) *The Social Work Interview* (4th edn), New York: Columbia University Press.

Kaptani, E. and Yuval-Davis, N. (2008) 'Participatory Theatre as a Research Methodology: Identity, Performance and Social Action Among Refugees', *Sociological Research Online* 13(5). Available at: http://www.socresonline.org.uk/13/5/2.html.

Killick, J. and Allan, K. (2001) *Communication and the Care of People with Dementia*, Buckingham: Open University Press.

Kitwood, T. (1997) *Dementia Reconsidered: The Person Comes First (Rethinking Ageing)*, Buckingham: Open University Press.

Kohli, R. (2006) *Social Work with Unaccompanied Asylum Seeking Children*, Basingstoke: Palgrave Macmillan.

Koprowska, J. (2005) *Communication and Interpersonal Skills in Social Work*, Exeter: Learning Matters Ltd.

Koprowska, J. (2008) *Communication and Interpersonal Skills in Social Work* (2nd edn) Exeter: Learning Matters Ltd.

Kroll, B. (1995) 'Working with Children' in Kaganas, F., King, M. and Piper, C. (eds) *Legislating for Harmony: Partnership Under the Children Act 1989*, London, Jessica Kingsley.

Kroll, B. and Taylor, A. (2003) *Parental Substance Misuse and Child Welfare*, London: Jessica Kingsley.

Laird, S. E. (2008) *Anti-Oppressive Social Work: A Guide for Developing Cultural Competence*, London: Sage.

Laming, Lord (2003) *The Victoria Climbié Inquiry: Report of an Inquiry by Lord Laming*, London, The Stationery Office,. Available at: www.victoria-climbie-inquiry.org.uk.

Laming, Lord (2009) *The Protection of Children in England: A Progress Report*. Available at: www.everychildmatters.go.uk/laming.

Le Riche, P. and Tanner, K. (1998) *Observation and Its Application to Social Work: Rather Like Breathing*, London: Jessica Kingsley.

Lincoln, Y. S. and Guba, E. (1985) *Naturalistic Enquiry*. Beverly Hills, Calif.: Sage.

Lishman, J. (2009) *Communication in Social Work* (2nd edn) Basingstoke: Palgrave Macmillan.

Luckock, B., Lefevre, M. and Orr, D. *et al.* (2006) *Knowledge Review: Teaching Learning and Assessing Communication Skills with Children in Social Work Education*, London: SCIE (Social Care Institute for Excellence). Available at: http://www.scie.org.uk/publications/knowledgereviews/kr12.asp.

Lyons-Ruth, K., Alpern, L. and Repacholi, B. (1993) 'Disorganized Infant Attachment Classification and Maternal Psychosocial Problems as Predictors of Hostile – Aggressive Behaviour in the Pre-School Classroom', *Child Development* 64: 572–85.

Macer, J., Murphy, J. and Oliver, T. (2009) *Training Care Home Staff to Use Talking Mats® with People Who Have Dementia*, York: Joseph Rowntree Foundation. Available at: http://www.jrf.org.uk/sites/files/jrf/training-in-use-of-talking-mats-summary.pdf.

Marchant, R. and Page, M. (2003) 'Child Protection Practice with Disabled Children' in National Working Group on Child Protection and Disability (ed.) *It Doesn't Happen to Disabled Children*, London: NSPCC. Available at: http://www.nspcc.org.uk/inform/publications/downloads/itdoesnthappentodisabledchildren_wdf48044.pdf

Mattinson, J. and Sinclair, I. (1979) *Mate and Stalemate*, Oxford: Basil Blackwell.

McLeod, J. (1998) *An Introduction to Counselling*, Buckingham: Open University Press.

Mehrabian, A. (1972) *Nonverbal Communication*, Chicago, Ill.: Aldine-Atherton.

Mental Health Foundation (1997) *Knowing Our Own Minds*, London: Mental Health Foundation.

Mental Health Foundation (1999) *Bright Futures: Promoting Children and Young People's Mental Health*, London: Mental Health Foundation.

Mental Health Foundation (2000) *Strategies for Living: A Summary Report of User-led Research into People's Strategies for Living with Mental Distress*, London: Mental Health Foundation. Menzies, I. E. P. (1960) 'A Case Study in the Functioning of Social Systems as a Defence against Anxiety: A Report on a Study of the Nursing Service in a General Hospital', *Human Relations* 13: 95–121.

Miley, K. K., O'Melia, M. and DuBois, B. L. (1998) *Instructor's Manual and Test Bank for Generalist Social Work Practice – An Empowering Approach*, Boston, Mass.: Allyn & Bacon.

Miller, N. R. and Rollnick, S. (2002) *Motivational Interviewing: Preparing People to Change Addictive Behaviour*, London: Guilford Press.

Mitchell, W. and Glendinning, C. (2007) *A Review of the Research Evidence Surrounding Risk Perceptions, Risk Management Strategies and their Consequences in Adult Social Care for Different Groups of Service Users*, York: University of York Social PolicyResearch Unit.

Morales, A. and Sheafor, B. W. (2001) *Social Work: A Profession of Many Faces* (6th edn), Needham Heights, Mass.: Allyn & Bacon.

Morris, J. (2002) *A Lot to Say! A Guide for Social Workers, Personal Advisors and Others Working with Disabled Children and Young People with Communication Impairments*, London: Scope.

Morris, J. (2004) *Services for People with Physical Impairments and Mental Health Support Needs*, York: Joseph Rowntree Foundation.

National Assembly for Wales (2000) *In Safe Hands: Protection of Vulnerable Adults in Wales*, Cardiff: National Assembly for Wales.

National Assembly for Wales (2003) *Requirements for a Degree in Social Work*, Cardiff: National Assembly for Wales.

National Institute for Clinical Excellence (2002) *Schizophrenia: Core Interventions in the Treatment and Management of Schizophrenia in Primary and Secondary Care*, Clinical Guideline No. 1, London: NICE.

National Institute for Mental Health England (2005) *NIMHE Guiding Statement on Recovery*, London: Department of Health.

Nelson-Jones, R. (2005) *An Introduction to Counselling Skills*, London: Sage.

Nicolson, P. (1993) 'Motherhood and Women's Lives', in Richardson, D. and Robinson, V. (eds) *Introducing Women's Studies*, London: Macmillan.

Oliver, M. (1990) *The Politics of Disablement*, London: Macmillan.

Oliver, M. (1996) *Understanding Disability: From Theory to Practice*, London: Macmillan.

Oliver, M. and Sapey, B. (2006) *Social Work with Disabled People* (3rd edn), Basingstoke: Palgrave Macmillan.

Orford, J. (2001) *Excessive Appetites: A Psychological View of Addictions* (2nd edn), Chichester: John Wiley.

Osborn, D. P. J., King, M. B. and Nazareth, I. (2003) 'Participation in Cardiovascular Risk Screening by People with Schizophrenia or Similar Mental Illnesses. A Cross Sectional Study in General Practice', *British Medical Journal* 326: 1122–3.

Parr, S., Byng, S., Barnes, C. and Mercer, G. (2004) *Social Exclusion of People with Marked Communication Impairment Following Stroke*, York: Joseph Rowntree Foundation. Available at: http://www.jrf.org.uk/sites/files/jrf/814.pdf.

Parker, J. (2000) 'Social Work with Refugees and Asylum Seekers: A Rationale for Developing Practice', *Practice* 12: 61–76.

Parton, N. (1991) *Governing the Family: Child Care, Child Protection and the State*, London: Macmillan.

Parton, N. (2004) 'From Maria Colwell to Victoria Climbié: Reflections on a Generation of Public Inquiries into Child Abuse', *Child Abuse Review* 13: 80–94.

Parton, N., Thorpe, D. and Wattam, C. (1997) *Child Protection: Risk and the Moral Order*, London: Macmillan.

Pawson, R., Boaz, A., Grayson, L., Long, A. and Barnes, C. (2003) *Types and Quality of Knowledge in Social Care*, London: SCIE.

Paylor, I. (2008) 'Social Work and Drug Use' in Wilson, K., Ruch, G., Lymbery, M. and Cooper, A. (2008) *Social Work: An Introduction to Contemporary Practice*, Harlow: Pearson Education.

Perry, B. (2002) 'Childhood Experience and the Expression of Genetic Potential: What Childhood Neglect Tells Us about Nature and Nurture', *Brain and Mind* 3: 79–100.

Petit-Zeman, S., Sandamas, G. and Hogman, G. (2002) *Doesn't It Make You Sick?*, London: Rethink Publications.

Phelan, M., Stradins, L. and Morrison, S. (2001) 'Physical health of people with severe mental illness', *British Medical Journal* 322: 443–4.

Piaget, J. (1983) 'Piaget's Theory' in Mussen, P. H. (ed.) *Handbook of Child Psychology, Vol. 1: Theory and Methods*, New York: Wiley.

Pile, H. (2009) 'Social Worker Shortage after Baby P Puts Children at Risk', *Guardian*, 28 August. Available at: http://www.guardian.co.uk/society/joepublic/2009/aug/28/social-worker-shortage-baby-p.

Potter, C. and Whittaker, C. (2001) *Creating Enabling Communication Environments for Children with Autism and Minimal or No Speech*, York: Joseph Rowntree Foundation.

Prins, H. (1999) *Will They Do It Again?*, London: Routledge.

Prochaska, J. O. and DiClemente, C. C. (1983) 'Stages and Processes of Self-Change of Smoking: Toward an Integrated Model of Change', *Journal of Consulting and Clinical Psychology*, 51: 390–5.

Prochaska, J., DiClemente, C. and Norcross, J. (1992) 'In Search of How People Change', *American Psychologist* 47: 1107–14.

Proctor, G. (2001) 'Listening to Older Women with Dementia: Relationships, Voices and Power', *Disability and Society* 16: 361–76.

Quality Assurance Agency for Higher Education (QAA) (2000) *Social Policy and Administration and Social Work: Subject Benchmark Statements*, Gloucester: QAA.

Reder, P. and Lucey, C. (1995) *Assessment of Parenting: Psychiatric and Psychological Contributions*, London: Routledge.

Reder, P. and Duncan. S. (2001) 'Abusive Relationships, Care and Control Conflicts and Insecure Attachments', *Child Abuse Review* 10: 411– 27.

Reder, P. and Duncan, S. and Gray, M. (1993) *Beyond Blame: Child Abuse Tragedies Revisited*, London: Routledge.

Reid, D., Ryan, T. and Enderby, P. (2001) 'What Does It Mean to Listen to People with Dementia?', *Disability and Society* 16: 377–92.

Rhodes, P. and Nocon, A. (2003) 'A Problem of Communication? Diabetes Care among Bangladeshi People in Bradford', *Health and Social Care in the Community* 11: 45–54.

Richards, S., Ruch, G. and Trevithick, P. (2005) 'Communication Skills Training for Practice: The Ethical Dilemma for Social Work Education', *Social Work Education* 24: 409–22.

Richardson, D. (1993) *Women, Motherhood and Childrearing*, London: Macmillan.

Royal College of Psychiatrists, The (1998) *Changing Minds: Every Family in the Land. Recommendations for the Implementation of a Five Year Strategy*, London: Royal College of Psychiatrists.

Ruch, G. (2005a) 'Relationship-based and Reflective Practice in Contemporary Child Care Social Work', *Child and Family Social Work* 4: 111–24.

Ruch, G. (2005b) 'Relationship-based Practice and Reflective Practice: Holistic Approaches to Contemporary Child Care Work', *Child and Family Social Work* 10: 111–23.

Ruch, G. (2009) 'Identifying the Critical in a Relationship-Based Model of Reflection', *European Journal of Social Work* 12: 349–62.

Rustin, M. (2005) 'Conceptual Analysis of Critical Moments in Victoria Climbié's life', *Child and Family Social Work* 10: 11–19.

Rutter, J. (2003) *Working with Refugee Children*, York: Joseph Rowntree Foundation.

Rutter, M. (1985) 'Resilience in the Face of Adversity. Protective Factors and Resistance to Psychiatric disorder', *British Journal of Psychiatry*147: 598–611.

Salzberger-Wittenberg, I. (1970) *Psycho-analytical Insight and Relationships: A Kleinian Approach*, London: Routledge & Kegan Paul.

Sanford, F., Fox, J. and Murray, K. (1981) *Children Out of Court*, Edinburgh: Scottish Academic Press.

Sapey, B. (2009) 'Engaging with the Social Model of Disability' in Higham, P. (ed.) *Post-Qualifying Social Work Practice*, London: Sage.

Schofield, G. (1998) 'Inner and Outer Worlds: A Psychosocial Framework for Child and Family Social Work', *Child and Family Social Work* 3: 57–67.

Schön, D. (1983) *The Reflective Practitioner: How Professionals Think in Action*, London: Temple Smith.

Schore, A. N. (2001) 'Effects of a Secure Attachment Relationship on Right Brain Development, Affect Regulation, and Infant Mental Health', *Infant Mental Health Journal* 22: 7–66.

SCODA (Standing Conference on Drug Abuse) (1997) *Drug-related Early Intervention: Developing Services for Young People and Families*, London: SCODA.

SCOPE (2007) *Communication Aid Provision: Review of the Literature*, London: SCOPE.

Scottish Executive (2004) *Hidden Harm: Scottish Executive Response to the Report of the Inquiry by the Advisory Council on the Issue of Drugs*, Edinburgh: Scottish Executive.

Scottish Executive (2006a) *Social Work: A 21st Century Profession* Edinburgh: Scottish Executive.

Scottish Executive (2006b) *Changing Lives: Report of the 21st Century Review of Social Work*, Edinburgh: Scottish Executive.

Scottish Office (1999) *Aiming for Excellence – Modernising Social Work Services in Scotland*, Edinburgh: Scottish Office.

Seden, J. (2005) *Counselling Skills in Social Work Practice*, Maidenhead: Open University Press.

Shaw, D. S., Owens, E. B., Vondra, J. I., Keenan, K. and Winslow, E. B. (1996) 'Early Risk Factors and Pathways in the Development of Early Disruptive Behaviour Problems', *Development and Psychopathology* 8: 679–99.

Sheppard, M. (1998) 'Practice Validity, Reflexivity and Knowledge for Social Work', *British Journal of Social Work* 28: 763–81.

Sheppard, J. (2000) 'Learning from Personal Experience: Reflexions on Social Work Practice with Mothers in Child and Family Care', *Journal of Social Work Practice* 14: 38–50.

Sheppard, M. and Ryan, K. (2003) 'Practitioners as Rule Using Analysts: A Further development of process Knowledge in social work', *British Journal of Social Work:* 33: 157–176.

Sheppard, M. (2007) 'Assessment: From Reflexivity to Process Knowledge' in Lishman, J. (ed.) *Handbook for Practice Learning in Social Work and Social Care*, London: Jessica Kingsley.

Shulman, L. (1999) *The Skills of Helping Individuals, Families and Groups* (4th edn), Itasca, Ill., Peacock.

Shulman, L. (2009) *The Skills of Helping Individuals, Families, Groups and Communities* (6th edn), Belmont, Calif.: Wadsworth.

Skills for Care (formerly TOPSS) (2002) *National Occupational Standards for Social Work*, Leeds: TOPSS. Available at: http://www.skillsforcare.org.uk/developing_skills/National_Occupational_Standards/social_work_NOS.aspx.

Skills for Care and Development (2008) *Health and Social Care National Occupational Standards*, Leeds: Skills for Care and Development.

Smale, G. and Tuson, G., with Biehal, N. and Marsh, P. (1993) *Empowerment, Assessment, Care Management and the Skilled Worker*, London, HMSO.

Smart, C. (1996) 'Deconstructing Motherhood', in Bortolaia Silva, E. (ed.) *Good Enough Mothering: Feminist Perspectives on Lone Motherhood*, London and New York: Routledge.

Social Care Institute for Excellence (2004) *Teaching and Learning Communication Skills in Social Work Education*, London: SCIE.

Social Care Institute for Excellence (2009) *Dignity in Care Practice*, Guide No. 02, London: SCIE.

Social Services Directorate (2006) *Safeguarding Vulnerable Adults: Regional Adult Protection Policy and Guidance (Northern Ireland)*, Ballymena: Northern Health and Social Services Board.

Social Services Inspectorate (SSI) (2002) *Improving Older People's Services: Policy into Practice*, London: DoH Publications.

Social Services Inspectorate (2004) *Building a Better Future for Children: Key Messages from Inspections and Performance Assessment.* Available at: www.dh.gov.uk/publicationsandstatistics.

Speltz, M. L., Greenberg, M. T. and De Klyen, M. (1990) 'Attachment in Preschoolers with Disruptive Behaviour: A Comparison of Clinic-Referred and Nonproblem Children', *Development and Psychopathology* 2: 31–46.

Sroufe, L. A. (1983) 'Infant-caregiver Attachment and Patterns of Attachment in Pre-School: The Roots of Maladaptation and Competence', in Perlmutter, M. (ed.) *Minnesota Symposium in Child Psychology* 16: 41–81, Hillsdale, NJ: Erlbaum.

Stack, D. W., Hill, S. R. and Hickson, M. (1991) *An Introduction to Communication Theory*, Fort Worth, Tex.: Holt, Rinehart & Winston.

Stepney, P. (2006) 'Mission Impossible? Critical Practice in Social Work', *British Journal of Social Work*: 36: 1289–307.

Strauss, A. and Corbin J. (1990) *Basics of Qualitative Research: Grounded Theory Procedures and Techniques*, London: Sage.

Taylor, A. (1999) 'The Elephant in the Interview Room: Working with the Process of Denial with Chronic Drinkers', *Probation Journal* 46: 19–26.

Taylor, A. and Kroll, B. (2004) 'Working with Parental Substance Misuse. Dilemmas for Practice', *British Journal of Social Work*, 34: 1115–32.

Taylor, C. and White, S. (2000) *Practising Reflexivity in Health and Welfare: Making Knowledge. Buckingham: Open University Press.*

Taylor, H. (2008) 'Judgements of Solomon: Anxieties and Defences of Social Workers Involved in Care Proceedings', *Child and Family Social Work* 13: 23.

Thomas, C. (1999) *Female Forms: Experiencing and Understanding Disability*. Buckingham: Open University Press.

Thomas, C. (2007) *Sociologies of Disability and Illness: Contested Ideas in Disability Studies and Medical Sociology*, Basingstoke: Palgrave Macmillan.

Thompson, N. (1995) *Age and Dignity: Working with Older People*, Aldershot: Arena.

Tibbs, M. A. (2001) *Social Work and Dementia: Good Practice and Care Management*, London: Jessica Kingsley.

TOPSS (Training Occupational Standards for the Personal Social Services) (2002) *The National Occupational Standards for Social Work*, Leeds: TOPSS.

Trevithick, P. (2005) *Social Work Skills: A Practice Handbook*, Maidenhead: Open University Press.

Trevithick, P., Richards, S., Ruch, G. and Moss, B. (2004) *Teaching and Learning Communication Skills in Social Work Education: Knowledge Review 6*, London: SCIE.

Triangle (2002) *How It Is: An Image Vocabulary for Children About Feelings, Rights and Safety, Personal Care and Sexuality*. Available at: www.howitis.org.uk/ accessed 9 May 2010.

Turney, D. (2000) 'The Feminising of Neglect', *Child and Family Social Work* 5: 47–56.

UNISON (2009) *Still Slipping Through the Net? Front-line Staff Assess Children's Safeguarding Progress*. Available at: www.unison.org.uk/acrobat/B4416.pdf.

Velleman, R. (2001) *Counselling for Alcohol Problems* (2nd edn), London: Sage.

Warren, S. L., Huston, L., Egeland, B. and Sroufe, L. A. (1997) 'Child and Adolescent Anxiety Disorders and Early Attachment', *Journal of the American Academy of Child and Adolescent Psychiatry* 32: 165–78.

Welsh Assembly Government (2006) *National Service Framework for Older People*, Cardiff: WAG.

Williams, C. and Soydan, H. (2005) 'When and How Does Ethnicity Matter? A Cross-National Study of Social Work Responses to Ethnicity in Child Protection Cases', *British Journal of Social Work* 35: 901–20.

Wilson, J. C. and Powell, M. (2001) *A Guide to Interviewing Children: Essential Skills for Counsellors, Police, Lawyers and Social Workers*, London: Routledge.

Wilson, K. and Ryan, V. (2001) 'Helping Children by Working with Their Parents in Individual Child Therapy', *Child and Family Social Work* 6: 209–17.

Wilson, K., Ruch, G., Lymbery, M. and Cooper, A. (2008) *Social Work: An Introduction to Contemporary Practice*, Harlow: Pearson Education.

Woodcock, J. (2003) 'The Social Work Assessment of Parenting: An Exploration', *British Journal of Social Work* 33: 87–106.

Woodcock, J. and Sheppard, M. (2002) 'Double Trouble: Maternal Depression and Alcohol Dependence as Combined Factors in Child and Family Social Work', *Children and Society* 16: 232–45.

Woodcock, J. and Tregaskis, C. (2008) 'Understanding Structural and Communication Barriers to Ordinary Family Life for Families with Disabled Children: A Combined Social Work and Social Model of Disability Analysis', *British Journal of Social Work* 38: 55–71. BJSW Advance Access originally published online on 19 July 2006.

Woodcock, J. and Crow, C. (2010) 'Social Work Practice Strategies and Professional Identity within Private Fostering: A Critical Exploration', *Adoption and Fostering* 34(1) Spring: 41–51.

World Health Organization (2001) *World Health Day. Mental health: Stop Exclusion: Dare to Care*. Available at: www.who.int/world-health-day.

World Health Organization (2005) *Mental Health Action Plan for Europe. Facing the Challenges, Building Solutions*, Helsinki: WHO European Ministerial Conference on Mental Health. Available at: www.euro.who.int/mentalhealth/publications/20061124_1.

Zeanah, C. H., Boris, N. W. and Scheeringa, M. S. (1997) 'Psychopathology in Infancy', *Journal of Child Psychology and Psychiatry* 38: 81–99.

Index

Abuse and maltreatment, 43, 48, 55, 104, 135, 143
Accuracy, 43, 65
  assessing for truthfulness, 75
  non-leading questions, 57
  Statement Validity Analysis, 75
Achieving a shared purpose, 24, 26, 48, 68, 86, 99, 111, 114, 126, 138–43, 146, 158, 187
Active listening, *see* 'reflective listening'
Actively look for the channels of communication the service user is using, 138, 144, 149, 171, 177, 183
Addressing service user fears of stigmatisation, 115
Adult Support and Protection (Scotland) Act (2007), 135
Adversity, 22, 46
Ageism, 168
Agendas, 24–5, 92
Aggression (and hostility), 7, 14, 21, 24, 44, 83–5, 113, 122, 131, 154, 171, 175
Ambivalence, 7, 14, 24–5, 51, 83, 85
Assessing for remorse and willingness to reform, 77
ASSET, 61, 63, 64, 67
Asylum legal process, 152–3
Attachment styles, 10, 22, 44–5, 48, 83, 86, 111
Attitudinal obstacles, 14, 82–3, 91, 104, 109, 125, 135, 137, 145, 188, 190
Attuned, 11, 20, 30, 35–6, 55, 74, 132, 186
Augmentative communication, 43, 57
Authenticity, 23, 26, 136
Authority (legislative) role, 14, 25–6, 30, 48, 62, 92, 112, 152, 161, 187
Avoid exhortations to change, 116
Avoiding the how and why questions, 77

Basic communication skills, 6, 15, 18–38, 186
Being open to communication at all levels, 130–1
Beginning communication, 19
Body language, *see* non-verbal communication

Care Mapping Approach, 170
Challenging, 7, 122, 170
Change processes, 104, 117
Channel of communication, 130
Child in need, 74, 81
Children Act, The (1989), 1, 39, 74, 81, 105, 162
Children Act, The (2004), 40, 81, 105, 162
Children Act, The (Scotland) (1995), 105
Choice (giving choice), 67–8, 73, 167, 185
Clear about purpose, 14, 19, 29–30, 49
Clear on role, 26–9, 48–9, 67, 111, 161
Closed questions, 74, 99, 115, 149, 150, 162
Communicating consequences in a non-threatening manner, 69, 73
Communicating empathy for the experience of systemic barriers, 143, 144
Communication-enhancing environment, 43
Confidentiality, 122
Containing a child's feelings by being a safe place in which feelings can be explored, 46, 55

Containment, 12, 46, 55, 90, 96,130–2, 163, 176, 187, 190
Contracting, 25
Counter-transference, 10, 35, 46, 90, 97, 124, 178
Creative arts, 170
  see also pictures
Crime and Disorder Act, The (1998), 60
Cultural awareness, 153
Cultural background, 24, 32, 82
Cultural competence, 156
Cultural differences, 13, 32, 41, 82, 122, 156, 169
Cultural expectations, 12, 20, 40, 82, 154
Cultural relativism, 12–3, 82, 153, 162
Cultural sensitivity, 122, 153
Cultural stereotyping, 12–3, 20, 23, 35, 41, 82, 104, 110, 121, 125, 153

Decision-making capacity, 135
Defending the rights of the service user, 68
Dementia, stroke and other cognitive impairments, 124, 168–70, 175
Demonstrating cultural acceptance, 155–6
Demonstrating knowledge of the individual child, 97, 99
Developing early rapport, 63–5, 68
  phatic communication, 63
Development, 10, 22, 39–40, 44–5, 47, 81, 89, 91, 95, 97, 99, 104, 121
  developmental delay, 47, 77
  reflective function, 48
Developmental competence, 40, 47, 50, 56–7
  learning disabilities and learning difficulties, 61–2, 77–8
Dignity, 143, 145, 167, 171
Disability Discrimination Act, The (2005), 134
Disability Discrimination (Northern Ireland) Order, The (2006), 134
Distress, 22, 43–4, 46, 55, 122, 124, 149, 152, 163

Ecological approach, 9, 136
Emotional support, 121–4
  being (alongside), 55, 131
  emotionally available, 124
Emotional warmth, 21, 30, 32, 146, 153, 162
Empathy, 7, 19, 30–6, 46, 48, 64, 89, 111–2, 158, 161
  communicating empathy for the experience of systemic barriers, 143–4
Emphasising or exaggerating non-verbal communication without being patronising, 176, 183
Endings, 37, 57–8
Enter the world of substance-using families, 114–5
  genograms and ecomaps, 115
Establishing a vocabulary of feelings, 57
Every Child Matters (2003), 1, 40, 80–1
Experiencing the child's world, 43
Experiencing service user feelings (asylum seekers and refugees), 164
Experiential learning, 1, 2, 186
Expressing empathy and understanding without necessarily signifying agreement, 64, 76

Fear (and mistrust), 14, 30, 44, 45, 51, 55, 62, 64, 83, 85, 92, 95, 105, 112, 121, 124, 126, 153
Feelings as medium of communication, 11, 20, 30, 32, 34, 86
Focused communication, 7
Forum theatre, 2, 186–90, 192–3
Framework for the Assessment of Children in Need and their Families (2000), The, 9, 81, 91–2, 110
Frustration, 85, 89, 136, 149, 170, 181, 182

Gathering facts, 36–7, 74
Genograms and ecomaps, 115
Give time to process thoughts or feelings and respond, 131

Harm-reduction model, 110
Hidden Harm (2004), 105
High-order concepts, 77–8, 124, 162, 182
  short, simple sentences, 182
Hostility, *see* aggression

Identify coping and strengths, 84
Identify, discuss and empathise with systemic barriers, 92, 100
Identify, validate and use the child's medium of communication, 47, 77
Identifying a practical response of seeking to overcome the systemic barriers, 91
Identifying social workers' personal attitudes and preconceptions of parenting, 98, 99, 110
Illusion of work, 31, 99
Immediacy, 14, 30–32, 113
In Safe Hands (2000), 135
Independence, Well-being and Choice (2005), 134
Individual differences, 85–95, 124, 167, 190
Influence of self when managing uncertainty, 123
Informed consent, 54, 73
  communicating consequences in a non-threatening manner, 73

Interpreters, 153, 161
Isolation, 153, 164

Jasmine Beckford tragedy, 40
Judgmental attitudes, 7, 85
  non-judgmental, 73, 97, 104, 116–7

Listening for clues, 74
Loss, 22–3, 25, 37, 44, 46, 57–61, 84, 121

Maintain a non-threatening body position, 131
Managing aggressive situations, 54–5, 131–2
Marginalisation, 106, 110, 124, 153
Maria Colwill, 13
Media, 22–23, 47, 86
  packages, 138
Medical model of addiction, 109
Memory, 124
Mental Capacity Act, The (2005), 134–5, 168
Mental Health Act, The (2007), 120
Metaphors and images, 131
Mirroring, 130, 170, 174
Motivating service users to decide to make changes, 116–7
Motivational interviewing, 104, 116

No Secrets (2000), 135, 168
Non-verbal communication, 7, 32–4, 36, 52, 54–6, 72, 96, 135, 143–6, 157, 162, 164, 169, 171, 175
  maintain a non-threatening body position, 131
  managing aggressive situations, 54–5, 131–2

Observing, 32, 55–6, 130
Obstacle, 29, 177
  authority, 29, 34, 111
  intimacy, 126
  societal taboo, 182
ONSET, 62
Open questions, 34, 74, 89, 99, 115, 117, 129, 149, 162, 164

Paraphrasing, 33, 51, 113, 116, 129
Parent–child relationship, 44, 81–2, 91, 99
Parenting, 80–100
  normative expectations, 12, 82, 97–8, 154
  theoretical frameworks, 81–2
Parenting assessment (influence of self), 82–4, 97–100, 105
  attitudinal, cultural and societal templates, 83, 97, 105
  cultural relativism 82
  natural love, 83
  rule of optimism, 82
  surface-static, 83
Parents who use substances, 48, 62, 104–18
Parents with disabled children, 7, 13, 80–100
Partnership working, 19, 112
  of expertise, 135
Personalisation, 1, 14
Person-centred, 4, 8, 122, 124, 131, 134, 167–8
Peter Connolly tragedy, 40–1, 83, 86
Phatic communication, 63
Physical contact (touch), 169–70, 171, 176
Physical health symptoms, 123
Pictures, 47–50, 137, 157, 170
Positioning, 32–3
Positive communication, 136
Positive framing of development rather than using deficit notions, 97
Power differential, 24, 40, 48, 57
Private knowledge, 14, 85–6, 91–2, 144, 187–8
  private voice, 114, 165
Professional anxiety, 11, 15, 40–1, 76, 83, 97, 121, 123
Promises, 145–6
Promoting understanding of links between experiences and symptoms, 122
Provide affirmation, 116
Psychodynamic approach, 9–10, 42, 44, 124
Psychological defences, 1, 11, 12, 14, 21, 40, 78, 83–4, 175
Purpose (being clear), 14, 19, 29–30, 49
Putting feelings into words, 34, 64, 89, 116, 126, 143, 149, 161, 176, 182

Questioning, 7, 36–7
  open questions, 34, 74, 89, 99, 115, 117, 129, 149, 162, 164
  closed questions, 74, 99, 115, 149, 150, 162

Racism, 152–5
Reaching for feedback, 30, 48, 111
Reaching for feeling, 34, 116, 182
Recovery model, 122
Reflecting back (mirroring), 130
Reflective listening, 7, 32, 52, 55, 76, 89, 99, 113, 116, 129–30, 143, 146, 162
Reflexive processes, 11, 12, 14, 35, 125, 189
Reflexivity, 12, 14, 105
Relationship-based practice, 8–12, 20, 86
Relationship quality, 22, 44
Religious and spiritual beliefs, 122, 156
Reminiscence, 170

Resistance, 24, 83–4
Respect, 30, 50, 54, 104, 131, 185
Risk (assessing risk), 83, 123, 135
  risk of offending, 61

Safeguarding, 25, 29, 39, 41–3, 81–2, 99, 115, 135, 143, 149, 162, 168
Safeguarding Vulnerable Adults (Northern Ireland) (2006), 135
Safeguarding Vulnerable Groups Act, The (2006), 135, 168
Secrecy and denial, 103, 105, 113, 187
Shared agenda, 30, 92, 129, 177
Sharing social worker feelings, 35–6
Short, simple sentences, 182
  see also high-order concepts
Silences, 36, 52, 116, 131, 163
Single Assessment Process, 168
Social constructionist approach, 12
Social exclusion
  physical health, 123
  inequalities, 123
  isolation, 153, 164
  marginalisation, 106, 110, 124, 153
  stigmatisation, 103, 104, 115, 121, 125, 155
Social model of disability, 8, 13–4, 92, 135–136, 138, 187–8
Societal barrier, 157
Southwark ruling, 74
Stigmatisation, 103, 104, 115, 121, 125, 155
Strengths, *see* identify, coping and strengths
Stroke, dementia and other cognitive impairments, 123, 168–70, 175
Substance use, 61, 74–5, 102–18
Summarising, 34, 37, 96, 117
Systemic barriers, 13, 41, 84–9, 91–2, 105, 136–8, 143, 188, 190
Systemic perspective, 83–4, 99

Take time, 51, 148, 168, 177, 182
  give time to process thoughts or feelings and respond, 131
Third ear (objective distancing), 31, 131
Total communication, 136, 138, 149
Touch (physical contact), 169–70, 174, 176
Transference, 10, 12, 35, 89, 124, 164, 176–7, 187
  counter-transference, 10, 35, 46, 90, 97, 124, 177
Tuning-in, 19, 20, 43–8, 85, 109–11, 125, 138, 155, 157, 161, 170, 186
  to experience the child's world, 44
  to experience the individual experience of mental distress, 124
  to fear and uncertainty over citizenship, 155
  to social worker's personal attitudes and preconceptions of people who use substances, 110–11

Unconditional regard, 76
Use of self, 9, 11–12, 23–4, 35, 81–4, 99, 125, 164
Use of the 'third object', 54
Using a storyline, 48–50
Using humour, 68
Using the whole communication spectrum, 138, 144, 149, 158, 177, 183

Validation, 170, 171, 174, 176, 183
Valuing People (2001), 1, 134, 136
Victoria Climbie tragedy, 11, 40, 43, 86

Wishes and feelings of children, 39, 47, 56
Working Together to Safeguard Children (2000, 2006), 40, 81